On Matters Southern

On Matters Southern

Essays About Literature and Culture, 1964–2000

MARION MONTGOMERY

Edited by Michael M. Jordan
Foreword by Eugene D. Genovese

McFarland & Company, Inc., Publishers
Jefferson, North Carolina, and London

ALSO BY MARION MONTGOMERY
AND FROM MCFARLAND

*Eudora Welty and Walker Percy: The Concept
of Home in Their Lives and Literature* (2003)

*John Crowe Ransom and Allen Tate: At Odds about
the Ends of History and the Mystery of Nature* (2003)

LIBRARY OF CONGRESS CATALOGUING-IN-PUBLICATION DATA

Montgomery, Marion.
    On matters southern : essays about literature and culture,
1964–2000 / Marion Montgomery ; edited by Michael M. Jordan ;
foreword by Eugene O. Genovese.
    p.   cm.
    Includes bibliographical references and index.

    ISBN-13: 978-0-7864-2224-1
    softcover : 50# alkaline paper ∞

    1. American literature — Southern States — History and
criticism. 2. Southern States — Intellectual life.
3. Southern States — In literature. 4. Southern States —
Civilization. I. Jordan, Michael M. II. Title.
PS261.M655   2005
810.9'975 — dc22   2005013992

British Library cataloguing data are available

©2005 Marion Montgomery. All rights reserved

*No part of this book may be reproduced or transmitted in any form
or by any means, electronic or mechanical, including photocopying
or recording, or by any information storage and retrieval system,
without permission in writing from the publisher.*

Cover photograph: Marion Montgomery by Mark Morrow, from
Images of the Southern Writer (University of Georgia Press) ©1985
by the University of Georgia Press

Manufactured in the United States of America

McFarland & Company, Inc., Publishers
  Box 611, Jefferson, North Carolina 28640
    www.mcfarlandpub.com

Acknowledgments

I am grateful to the Earhart Foundation for its generous support in preparing this work for publication, especially to David B. Kennedy, former president, who encouraged me to collect these southern writings of Marion Montgomery. I am also grateful to Marion Montgomery himself, who worked with me on this as well as on other literary endeavors. He is one of the men I have chosen as father.

The brief introduction to "Bells for John Stewart's Burden" contains an excerpt from one of Donald Davidson's letters to Allen Tate. The letter is among the Allen Tate Papers, Manuscripts Division, Department of Rare Books and Special Collections at Princeton University Library. It is published with permission of the Princeton University Library.

— Michael M. Jordan

The purpose of the study of philosophy is not to learn what others have thought, but to learn how the truth of things stands.
— St. Thomas Aquinas

The truth of things, which must be our concern always, is revealed through words rightly used and rightly taken. That revelation is the art of all liberal arts.
— Marion Montgomery, *Liberal Arts and Community*

Table of Contents

Acknowledgments   v
Foreword by Eugene D. Genovese   1
Preface by Michael M. Jordan   13

Part I
The Author at Work and at Home

1. The Country, Here   19
2. Of Mulls and Memories   24

Part II
On Place and Region

3. Georgia as a Place for Writers   31
4. Is Regional Writing Dead?   37
5. Ceremony and the Regional Spirit   41
6. The Sense of Violation: Notes Toward a Definition of "Southern" Fiction   47
7. Southern Letters in the Twentieth Century: The Articulation of a Tradition   57

Part III
On Fugitives, Agrarians, and New Critics

8. Bells for John Stewart's Burden   79
9. The Agrarians: Here and Now   114
10. Misunderstanding Criticism   120

Part IV
On Individual Authors

11. For Andrew, in Celebration — 129
12. How to Get Here From There: A Tribute to Madison Jones on Our Passage through Gehenna — 133
13. Remembering Who M.E. Bradford Is — 142
14. Walker Percy and the Christian Scandal — 167

Part V
On Books and Schooling

15. Books, Books, Books: Difficult Choices in Time of Intellectual Stress — 183
16. To My Son, Going Away to School — 195

Books by Marion Montgomery — 199

Index — 201

Foreword
Eugene D. Genovese

This volume of extraordinary essays and reviews comes when the need is sorest. They were written over some 40 years, the earliest during the 1960s—that ghastly decade of "cultural revolution" during which the long festering moral and political crisis of Western civilization took a decisive turn. Marion Montgomery, in far-ranging writings on literature, philosophy, and social thought, has applied his enviable intellectual gifts to a searching examination of the roots of our current miseries. A student and worthy heir of the Agrarians, he teaches us, as for years he taught students at the University of Georgia, the importance of time, place, and tradition for those who would engage the deepest problems of a world that is steadily being shrunk by an economic and technological revolution of unprecedented power and scope. Hence, he always pays close attention to the South, where he was born and reared and continues to live, and he unabashedly views the world through southern eyes.

Publication of these essays and reviews in one convenient volume comes when sorely needed since a particularly insidious feature of recent trends on our campuses has been the reduction of southern history and culture, when taught at all, to a story of slavery, racial segregation, and all-round bigotry and irrationality. Montgomery meets this reductionist challenge, much as the Agrarians and such successors as Richard Weaver and M.E. Bradford met it, but he brings a fresh eye and a clear appraisal of its dangerously new content and forms. A counterattack against the cultural revolution of nihilism requires attention to the long struggle waged by the South from the earliest days of the Republic. It requires, too, an understanding of that struggle as part of a worldwide resistance to assorted forms of anti-Christian totalitarianism. Montgomery's contributions to this resistance could hardly be overestimated.

Laying out a principal theme of these essays and reviews, Montgomery writes that whether one is a small farmer in Georgia or a maker-and-shaker in Washington politics, "The gesture toward order and growth is inevitably a gesture beyond the Self and toward the cause of order." Picking up the relay from Allen Tate, Montgomery rejects the gambit that dismissively labels, with little argumentation and even less evidence, the South, its culture and intellectuals "provincial." He provides his own evaluation of provincialism from the standpoint of what he calls "regionalism"—a rootedness in time and place that provides a firm opening to the universally attractive in world culture. Universally great literature—indeed, all good fiction and poetry—necessarily has been "regional" from the time of Homer. Montgomery asks: What determines whether a poet turns out to be provincial or regional? Montgomery answers: "the *discriminating reverence* with which the poet takes and uses the local." He adds, "It is the mode of his ceremonial awareness of time and place." It is possible, he maintains, to abstract oneself from place through an act of will, but only at the price of denying one's own being. Montgomery's southerner transcends time and place from within his immediate community: "The importance of place lies in his immediate community's consent to both the virtues and the limits of any person's existence and of the existence of all that is other than himself." The frequent attempts by supercilious critics to isolate the Agrarians geographically arouse his ire, and he exposes them as especially devious maneuvers to discredit the larger purpose of *I'll Take My Stand* as a broad defense of Western civilization and its essentially Christian roots and character. Montgomery knows whereof he speaks. If, as a citizen in Georgia who spent the first half of his life in New York City, I may have my two-cents' worth: Nowhere in America will you find more ignorant and bigoted provincials, replete with breathtaking personal nastiness, than among Manhattan's vaunted literati.

Homer, Aristotle, and a few other dead, white males taught that the family is the cradle of the state, and Montgomery enters the lists in defense of both family and state: "At the heart of the decay is the destruction of the institution most basic to Agrarian tenets, as it has been basic to the civilization of the West since Homer: the family as a stabilizing element of society." He looks to the family "for whatever stability is possible to us in this great wave of Western history now ebbing." I doubt that Montgomery has missed the irony: It has been feminist consciousness-raising that has enshrined the insight in the places of detention that pass for colleges and universities these days. With a small difference: In feminist and radical left-wing interpretation, the contribution to social stability, for which Montgomery praises the family, brands it as the ultimate source of the oppression of women, children, blacks, and homosexuals—the cradle of the naturally oppressive state.

The radicals' proclaimed intention to destroy both family and state proved politically inefficacious once extended beyond the campuses to sensible people. In a quick reversal of strategy, they backed off from a program barely removed from anarchism and announced that they, too, loved families. They sought only to liberate them from hierarchical and heterosexual constraints; to extend "rights" to children, including the right to divorce their parents; to establish a woman's absolute right to do as she wishes with her body; to facilitate "gay marriage"; and, more generally, to compel recognition of the equal rights of all "five genders." Notwithstanding Montgomery's good temper and southern manners, he barely hides his outrage at the nihilist atrocities we are living through, and, more to the point, in these pages he offers a running critique that is as devastating as it is elegant.

Montgomery quotes Andrew Lytle: "Not to know the difference between the public thing, the *res publica*, and the intimate is to surrender that delicate balance of order which alone makes the state a servant and not the people the servant of the state." Montgomery offers his own excellent insights on the tension between "order and growth" and "the problem of evil," so horribly manifested in Nazism and Stalinism. Without applying labels or taking cheap shots, he uncovers their principal successor in the radical ideologies that emphatically deny the difference between "public thing" and "the intimate." Feminism arose with the claim, "The personal is political." Well, not quite everything personal is political. It seems a woman's "right" to kill the baby she is carrying in her womb is a strictly private matter of no legitimate concern to the state or community — nor to the church, for that matter. (For those who wish an able defense of the wretched theory of the personal as political, I recommend Italian Fascism's official *Dottrina*, penned by Benito Mussolini and the philosopher Giovanni Gentile. To the best of my knowledge, no feminist theorist — or "theoretician," as they prefer — has come close to providing anything as coherent.)

The stability and health of families begin with piety — with faith in God. Montgomery tells us that the southern writer is likely to look on his immediate world with "wonder and curiosity," delighting in "his immediate neighbor's multitudinous engagements of that world, both for his neighbor's and his art's sake." The southern writer, that is, does not confuse himself with God the Creator. In this respect, as in others, Montgomery implicitly distinguishes between "southern writers" and writers who come from the South, much as M.E. Bradford explicitly distinguished "southern conservatives" from conservatives who were born or lived in the South. These distinctions rest, above all, on piety — and beyond piety, on firm Christian doctrine. Flannery O'Connor, explaining the difference between twentieth-century northerners and southerners in *The Habit of Being*, suggested that a great many more southerners than northerners still believe in original sin. Montgomery transforms her observation: "We are all born into the provincialism of the self—which some of us call the state of original sin." He summons Adolph Eichmann and Jim Jones: "We are astounded by the seeming disparity between the destruction and the insignificant, obscure agent." We are astounded "because we have been willingly led to forget the complexity of human nature spoken to by the concept of original sin, a doctrine many southern writers are loath to abandon." Montgomery analyzes the deplorable plunge from a Christian concern with individual salvation to a Gnostic dream of unfettering the individual by uprooting the unjust social systems that oppress him—a dream that promises nothing less than the transformation of men into new beings entirely. It is a plunge, he demonstrates, that ends with the destruction of the individual who is ostensibly being liberated.

In Montgomery's reading, Hannah Arendt suggested that Adolf Eichmann is innocent of wickedness because a mere instrument of forces beyond his understanding and control. I am not sure that Montgomery is reading Dr. Arendt as she intended. But if we put aside his specific charge against her and focus on his central point, we can readily appreciate the strength—and urgency—of his position: "The supposition that wickedness is not necessarily a condition for evil-doing is scarcely new; it is a doctrine progressively advanced these past two hundred years till it has in fact become the new orthodoxy. But tolerance of evil as a social principle out of philosophical determinism has had little support in the American South." He indicts the "soft sciences"—sociology, psychology—for advancing these tendencies, and as a historian, I regret to have to chide him for not mentioning the historical profession, which has sunk to an unprecedented low level, intellectually as well as morally. Montgomery cites Walter Burns' insistence that we recognize those who commit evil deeds as inviting us to respect their humanity by punishing them—that we thereby acknowledge their autonomy in commission of their crimes. I know that Montgomery does not approve of Hegel, and for good reason. But fair is fair: In *Philosophy of Right*, Hegel made a powerful case against what he called "superficial psychologizing." Come to think of it, that famous Hegelian-of-sorts Karl Marx would have roared with laughter at the notion that criminals should be spared because their personal or social circumstances determined their criminality. And after laughing, he would have recommended their execution. If you doubt it, turn to his scathing denunciations of the *Lumpenproletariat* in *The Eighteenth Brumaire of Louis*

Bonaparte, among other works. At issue here is the long way down the Left has traveled from the days of its greatest thinker to the petulant sentimentality that has reigned since the 1960s. Montgomery, in any case, takes up these questions in the forms that intrude upon us today, and he resolutely repels specious arguments that obfuscate our personal responsibility for what we do in this world.

As a literary critic no less than as a social and political critic, Montgomery displays his impatience with, not to say justifiable contempt for, the resort to theories of environmental determinism to reduce the sense of personal responsibility. He traces the fascination that southern fiction has for southerners and non-southerners alike to "that informing sense one finds at its heart, a sense of man's awful responsibility." He dissects the "mood writing" of John Dos Passos, Ernest Hemingway, Carson McCullers, and others as "a substitute for a sense of the outraged reaction to violation," which requires a character with a strong sense not only of violation but of its consequences. In the southern fiction he most admires, "The violation is taken personally and the violence is personal. If you kill a man, you at least know his name and why he in particular is the victim."

Denigration of the South, Montgomery recognizes, has been a favorite tactic in the strategy of the barbarians who are determined to pursue to the end the logic of their "cultural revolution"—to get rid of "the old crap," as Marx contemptuously called religion, tradition, and every other obstacle to the making of a secular New Man and a New World. Combating the mounting effort to eradicate all memories of the South other than Manichean distortions of slavery and racism, Montgomery compels a reassessment of the cultural life of the Old South, making acute observations in a war waged on several fronts. He eschews nostalgia and myth-making but insists on proper recognition of the finer qualities of the Old South. To begin with, he repels the denigration of its classical culture: "I am not interested in such concerns as whether the study of Greek and Latin in the Old South is the source of an influence but only in the obvious presence of such a kinship." In a review of a dreadful book on the Agrarians by John Stewart, Montgomery takes Stewart to task for his ignorant assertion that classical studies in the Old South were superficial, a mere gloss of Greek and Latin quotations and idle references, and for the even utterly preposterous assertion that the literary culture of the southern planter came "from conversation, not from reading."

Montgomery scorches Stewart with William Byrd, John Randolph, and Thomas Jefferson, and he might have piled up evidence from countless lesser lights, including yeomen as well as ordinary planters. Here in Georgia, where Montgomery and I live, Moses Waddel, a justly famous teacher of classical studies before he became president of Franklin College (later, the University of Georgia), taught the flower of the southeastern political, social, clerical, and intellectual elite at Willington Academy in South Carolina. Probably no other academy matched Willington, but every southern state had its share of superior academies. How do we know? Well, for one thing, the folks at Harvard, Yale, and Princeton left their comments on the quality of the training their southern students arrived with. Montgomery is on solid ground when he refers to the popularity not only of Virgil but of Dante in the Old South; he might have added a long list of Greek and Roman writers, not to mention later gems as Tasso and Ariosto, Cervantes and Camoes. When the Reverend E.T. Winkler described *Divine Comedy* as "the grandest, sweetest, and most tender epic that ever poured its passion into human speech," he was not being more effusive than were the leaders of southern education and intellectual life, among them, Thomas Roderick Dew, Hugh Legare, Joseph B. Cobb, William Holcombe, and the Reverends Richard Furman, George Howe, and Robert Lewis Dabney. Thomas a Kempis' *Imitation of Christ* and Boethius' *Consolation of Philosophy* were also widely read, perhaps especially by women, among them, Mary Chesnut and Mrs. Henry Rowe Schoolcraft, Catherine Edmonston, Margaret Junkin Preston, and Augusta Jane Evans. When Montgomery writes of the Fugitives and Agrarians that they were "far less isolated from the larger world of complicated time and place" than superficial critics think, he knows he is speaking of the intellectuals of the Old South as well.

Yet Montgomery may implicitly concede too much to the judgment of Allen Tate and others that the Old South was obsessed with politics, to the detriment not only of its art but of its broader intellectual life: "The masculine energies of the mid-nineteenth century were occupied by the political and military destinies of the South — leaving, as it must, its art to the feminine mind, such a mind as Henry Timrod's or Edgar Allan Poe's." (I confess that the attribution of a feminine mind to the author of "Ethnogenesis" jars me, but so much for my own prejudices.) What must not be obscured is that in political and social theory and political economy the South produced figures at least as formidable as any the North had to offer. Perhaps more to the point, the South at least held its own in theology and moral philosophy. For one thing, the intellectuals of the Old South displayed considerable philosophical literacy, as they waged war on both materialism and idealism, especially subjective idealism. In his powerful running attack on the "arrogant subjectivism" of current thought, Montgomery has in fact proceeded in the spirit of the antebellum southern theologians and secular theorists.

Montgomery is even rougher than Tate on "the general Protestant evangelicalism" of the South for encouraging a kind of materialism akin to that of the pernicious influence of Puritanism in New England. Here, as elsewhere, he mounts a formidable critique of bourgeois society and its marketplace mentality. But the leading theologians and preachers of the southern churches had few equals anywhere in America in subjecting bourgeois society to devastating assault. To recall a few: the Presbyterians James Henley Thornwell, Robert Dabney, and George Armstrong; the Baptists Thornton Stringfellow, Iveson Brookes, and Basil Manly; the Methodists George Foster Pierce, William Smith, and R.H. Rivers. And they were joined by some outstanding secular intellectuals, including George Frederick Holmes and William Gilmore Simms. Montgomery is right to find the roots of the South's tragic complicity in America's cultural degradation in antebellum days, but I would suggest that those roots were unable to produce their bitter harvest until the postwar decomposition of a southern Protestantism that had gallantly upheld Christian orthodoxy while the North was plunging into doctrinal liberalism — as heresy and apostasy are called in polite circles.

Although Montgomery does not directly plunge into politics, much less recommend a particular course of political action, his discussions of diverse subjects, most notably literary, compel engagement on political terrain. Thus, he attacks both Left and Right for their attempts to foster culture through government agencies, mentioning the experience of M.E. Bradford when President Reagan nominated him to be chairman of the National Endowment of the Humanities. A savage barrage, much of it from the Right, compelled Bradford to withdraw. It seems that no one critical of Abraham Lincoln was fit to hold the post. (We can only suppose that the politicians and ideologues who shot down Bradford's nomination would have done the same to Edmund Wilson, although we may doubt it.) Now, as Montgomery makes clear, Bradford ranked among the most principled of men, and no one of his generation held higher the banner of southern conservatism. Yet he was willing to accept the position, and no one who knew him could believe for a moment that he was motivated by personal considerations or anything except his sense of the public good.

Repeatedly, Montgomery returns, explicitly or implicitly, to the cultural and moral disintegration threatened by the worldwide technological and economic revolution known as globalization. He never shields his eyes from the ominous homogenization of world culture. More than once he invokes the dictum, "Intelligence is international; stupidity is national; art is local." Recalling "stupidity is national," he confesses to "a rather dark view of the possibilities of our survival as a nation." He writes, "That stillness some of us call 'regionalism'—a way of looking out such a window as mine, past such a garden, on to such secret creatures as grass and stray bear in the streets of 'Advancing Athens,' so that we may understand St. Paul and St. Augustine, who in peace and with assurance say we have here no abiding city." But, like the prophets of old, he offers us, "It is written ... but I say unto you." He notes that our world, while in the throes of decay, is giving birth to "a new paganism such as the world has never before imagined." And those words, as I understand them, call for political action.

Walker Percy opened a window on the political confusion we are living through, and Montgomery's discussion offers a model of hard criticism of the work of an artist he admires. Percy spoke of his sympathy for such ostensibly liberal causes as the welfare of minorities and the poor and his abhorrence of abortion and euthanasia. Percy here seems to me to have been trying to follow the social teachings of the Catholic Church, as exemplified in that great Encyclical, *Rerum Novarum*. Montgomery, taking his own tack, asks whether Percy's juxtaposition presents a paradox or a contradiction and—"a more troubling question"—whether liberals embrace good causes along with bad within an ideology that cannot readily distinguish between the two. As he sees it, the liberals' simultaneous embrace of wretched as well as good causes is, therefore, neither paradoxical nor contradictory: "In other words, it is possible that one may deport oneself, even to good causes, without one's heart being 'in the right place'." His critique of liberal sentimentality—its separation "from its source in Christ" and ominous social consequences—is unanswerable.

Percy, reflecting on the economic and social transformation of the South during the last half century, suggested that his grandchildren are pretty much like children in Iowa—in effect, that North and South have, for better or worse, converged culturally. Montgomery's response in "Walker Percy and the Christian Scandal" deserves extensive quotation:

> The importance of encounter of person with immediate existence, the accommodation to *this* place and *this* time, which is so heavy a theme in recent literature of the American South, is exactly the issue, though reduced in its implications whenever frozen in our accounting for it by a reduction to mere history or geography. That is, the concern requires a metaphysical perspective beyond the account of history or naturalistic geography.
>
> The liberal response of tenderness, then, which makes the Louisiana child and the Iowa child hardly distinguishable in their manifestation in time and place, begins with a denial of personhood in its fundamental

actuality. Put briefly, sentimentality is a distortion of proper sentiment as oriented by the realities of time and place and thus a distortion of significant creation. It begins with a dislocated emphasis on egalitarianism, a shifting of perspective from the essence of personhood to the accidents of personhood in a reductionism of discrete entities to identities of each other in the name of "equality." It is accomplished through a nominalism in service to pragmatic attempts to restructure the accidents of existence, under the mistaken supposition that accident is substance. Thus the dislocation of sign from reality by nominalism makes ready the manipulations of gnostic intellect.

I confess to having some difficulty with Montgomery's several references to "accidents" but shall let it pass with a cautionary word from that renowned modern philosopher, Don Vito Corleone: "Accidents don't happen to people who take accidents personally."

Montgomery maintains firmly that the spirit of his favorite modern prophets—Richard Weaver, Eric Voegelin, and Alexander Solzhenitsyn— "does not echo despondency" and the nostalgia that "so easily atrophies into an appetite for the fanciful and sentimental." On this matter, Montgomery, in effect, elaborates the argument he has made elsewhere. Notably in "On Reading Tolstoy's *What Is Art?*" in his recent book, *Romancing Reality*, he bares the social and political consequences of the reduction of the intelligence to sentimentality, noting that it fell to Lenin to decree and enforce what is implicit in Tolstoy—"materialistic limit to man's nature."

Of central importance to Montgomery's analyses of modern and postmodern decadence is his well-taken indictment of the egalitarian swindle, promoted not only by the Left but by influential segments of the Right, most notably those for whom a free market in everything is the closest thing possible to the Second Coming. He is not in the least entranced by the pseudo conservatism of the suburbanites once deliciously described in *National Review* as the right-wing enthusiasts for low taxes and low morals. Montgomery quotes Dorothy Sayers on our callings: "It is the work that serves the community; the business of that worker is to serve that work." He thereupon reflects, "Not comfortable words to us, who are taught from the cradle to the grave that we can 'be whatever we want to be' regardless of the limits of gift." It is appropriate that Montgomery should fire some of his more thunderous volleys in his essay, "Remembering Who M.E. Bradford Is," for Bradford parodied Marx by declaring equality the opiate of the intellectuals. Montgomery aptly refers to "our careless and sometimes studied abuses of distinction" and to hierarchy as "a most heinous devil term in the 1990s."

These incisive essays and reviews invite debate at every turn. To

Montgomery's everlasting credit, he compels us to confront the ills that John Randolph of Roanoke and John C. Calhoun, among numerous nineteenth-century southerners, identified and warned must not be allowed to fester. Especially valuable are the remarks he makes in several essays—"How to Get from Here to There," "Remembering Who M.E. Bradford Is," "Walker Percy and the Christian Scandal"—on Cartesianism as an invitation to self-isolation. But especially important among the problems that Montgomery reopens is the vexing problem of the mischief wrought by nominalism. Like Richard Weaver and Marshall McLuhan in his "southern" days, Montgomery, here and in his other work, makes rejection of nominalism a major theme. For one thing, he observes that liberal bourgeois and radical socialists have shared a Gnostic ideology—"a common strategy to control learned from nominalism." This reaction, like so much else, recalls the quarrels among the more impressive intellectuals of the Old South.

South Carolina's great Presbyterian Reverend Dr. James Henley Thornwell, "the Calhoun of the Church," as he was called, hated medieval Realism and applauded the nominalism he associated with Baconian induction. Thornwell, supported by the Reverend John Girardeau—another South Carolinian who does not deserve the obscurity into which he has fallen—associated Realism, if problematically, with the idea that the individual is nothing and humanity everything—a doctrine he attributed to the socialists. It did not much matter that Thornwell was opposed by the theologically liberal Episcopalian James Warley Miles of Charleston; it did matter that he was also opposed by such staunchly orthodox Presbyterian theologians as his friends Benjamin Morgan Palmer, T.E. Peck, and Robert L. Dabney, who perceived tension in his effort to square a conservative social corporatism with a quasibourgeois Protestant ethos. During the War for southern Independence, Palmer declared, "We must renounce the shallow nominalism which would make such a word as 'nation' a dead abstraction, signifying only the aggregation of individuals. It is an incorporated society, and possesses a unity of life resembling the individuality of a single being." Thornwell notwithstanding, conservative and orthodox Christian southerners have waged a running battle against nominalism, seeing in it the philosophical foundation of our modern ills. I do wonder, however, who will bell the cat of a philosophical development that arguably laid the foundations for modern science. Nominalism, I must admit, makes me nervous, and I share Montgomery's distaste for William of Occam, but I am not sure just where a blanket rejection leaves us.

There is another, more immediately dangerous cat to be belled. Montgomery reminds us of the Christian roots of our society, asking that we recapture its spirit and build on its legacy. In this respect he, like the Fugitives and Agrarians, departs from his Old South ancestors, who insisted that the South had social foundations unlike those of the North and of post French Revolution Western Europe, and that the outcome of the worldwide struggle to uphold Christianity and, with it, the traditional family and the centrality of community life would depend upon the maintenance of a social system based on organic, rather than marketplace, social relations. Slavery was such a system. For that reason, southerners took high ground in defending it and by no means merely defended the property rights in man they claimed for themselves and the incomes derived there from.

The Agrarians tried but failed to finesse the slavery question. More often than not, they sounded like shamefaced Yankees when they touched it. The best they could propose as a social basis for a healthy society was a strengthening of the rural property and small-town life that could still be found in the Midwest as well as the South. That will-o'-the wisp led nowhere, and the problem remains—for Montgomery and for all of us. Recall the war against philosophical idealism waged by the intellectual leaders of the Old South — a war Montgomery continues to wage effectively in his literary and social criticism of the manifest forms of egocentric subjectivity. He has not offered us a solution to the paramount question of how to establish social relations capable of sustaining a wholesome culture, but, then, neither has anyone else. What he has done — continues to do in ever-fresh ways— is to remove the countless obfuscations that threaten to paralyze even our most admirable intellectuals.

These essays and reviews open many more doors than they close, inviting us to revisit the old questions and attitudes so that we may better grapple with new questions and attitudes, or what seem, often deceptively, to be new. Since the death of M.E. Bradford no one has spoken for southern conservatism as has Montgomery: with a voice so strong, clear, and simultaneously, cool and passionate—cool in its frank statement of premises and its appeal to reason and good sense; passionate in its indignation against injustice and nihilism and its commitment to common decency.

Among the features that make reading Montgomery a delight, he has a way of speaking volumes in one or two sentences. Thus, Andrew Lytle took "genuine pleasure in our presence as only those comfortable with life can manage." Thus, M.E. Bradford, that quintessential southern gentleman and epitome of the civilized human being, "was a truly generous spirit, a disposition not always recognized by those who took his manners as simply an exaggeration of a residual 'southernism'." Thus, "Significant action is necessarily accompanied by spectacle," and "Spectacle mistaken for substance is the death of understanding." And in the wonderful essay "Ceremony and the Regional Spirit," he writes, "Ceremony is the acting out of form whereby we move out of our natural provincialism: manners devoutly and awfully taken. ...Ceremony is absolutely necessary to [our] sanity and health. ... At its most basic, ceremony is *orderly awareness*."

Montgomery's loving but critical evaluations of the Fugitives, Agrarians, and such successors as Richard Weaver, Flannery O'Connor, and M.E. Bradford alone should make this book required reading for everyone who seeks to understand the cultural crisis of Western civilization. Those familiar with Montgomery's books and articles will not be surprised to find here penetrating appraisals of T.S. Eliot's life's work and of the "masculine" art of William Faulkner and Flannery O'Connor. Among other insights, he explores the difference between the Fugitives, who had firm roots in time and place, and kindred spirits like Eliot and Ezra Pound, who had to try "to choose their origins by an act of the will, through essay and art." Prepare to enjoy, along with other gems, an appreciation of the achievements of the New Criticism, spiced with a forceful retort to its superficial critics—an appreciation presented in combination with a stern reply to the New Criticism's subjectivist tendency to confine attention to the text alone and "to isolate criticism from the larger arena proper to intellect." That tendency Montgomery never succumbs to. Rest assured, as you turn to his essays, he practices what he preaches.

Preface
Michael M. Jordan

Long an admirer and advocate of Donald Davidson and the southern Agrarians, I was delighted to receive a request from an editor to promote Davidson's pivotal role as a man of letters. In October 2001 Gary Mitchem of McFarland & Company wrote to me asking if I had an interest in collecting and editing Donald Davidson's letters or the correspondence of Davidson and John Gould Fletcher. Mark Winchell, author of the excellent biography *Where No Flag Flies: Donald Davidson and the Southern Resistance* and a much better Davidson scholar than I, had recommended me. Winchell himself was too busy to undertake the task. I discussed the prospect of editing the Davidson-Fletcher letters with Louise Cowan, who knew Davidson and wrote about him and others in his circle in *The Fugitive Group: A Literary History* and in *The Southern Critics*. I also discussed prospects with Marion Montgomery, a second-generation southern Agrarian who has written on Davidson and his Fugitive, southern Agrarian, and New Critic associates. Both Cowan and Montgomery noted that collecting and editing Davidson's letters (his letters alone or with Fletcher's) was a major undertaking that would involve a good bit of travel and a great deal of time. They also said it was a worthy undertaking. Anyone familiar with Davidson's correspondence (such as his letters in *The Literary Correspondence of Donald Davidson and Allen Tate*, edited by Fain and Young) knows how valuable his letters are in revealing the literary, social, and political currents in the American South (indeed, in America in general) from the 1920s until the 1960s. One also thinks of other valuable collections of the correspondence of Agrarian men of letters: Young's and Sarcone's *The Lytle-Tate Letters*, Vinh's *Cleanth Brooks and Allen Tate*, Grimshaw's *Cleanth Brooks and Robert Penn Warren*, and Dunway's *Fugitives and Exiles* (the letters of Jacques and Raissa Maritain, Allen Tate, and Caroline Gordon).

A new collection of Davidson's letters would be valuable, but, like

Mark Winchell, I was much too busy to take on such a large literary undertaking. McFarland was, however, interested in other literary projects involving the Fugitives and southern Agrarians, and wondered if I might discuss some of the possibilities. Since my own sparse and sketchy work on the Vanderbilt group (a dissertation, several articles and book reviews) did not qualify me, I didn't have anything of my own to suggest or to offer. However, I did know of a manuscript and an author that fit the bill. I wrote McFarland that Marion Montgomery had a "little book" (about 200 pages) "juxtaposing [John Crowe] Ransom as Kantian to [Allen] Tate as incipient Thomist." My recommendation proved fruitful: in 2003 the publisher brought out Montgomery's *John Crowe Ransom and Allen Tate: At Odds About the Ends of History and the Mystery of Nature.* A meeting and correspondence between Mitchem and Montgomery led to the publication of a second volume: *Eudora Welty and Walter Percy: The Concept of Home in Their Lives and Literature* (2003). A third Montgomery volume on yet another Southern literary luminary will soon be published by McFarland: *Hillbilly Thomist: Flannery O'Connor, St. Thomas and the Limits of Art.* If one cannot himself have the baby, he can still be a midwife, and I am glad to have played one of the midwife roles in bringing these three volumes into print.

This present collection is also the fruit of those early discussions about possible studies of the Fugitive-Agrarian writers. In mentioning Montgomery's manuscript on Tate and Ransom, I mentioned as well another possibility: a collection of Montgomery's writings on the Fugitives, the Agrarians, and the New Critics— on Davidson, Tate, Ransom, Warren, Lytle and Brooks— participants in varying degrees in all three remarkable "movements." Editing these writings would not require a great deal of travel and time on my part, and it would bring again to light some of Montgomery's best writing on southern themes and men of letters.

As Marion and I discussed the possible contents of the collection, we broadened the scope to include Marion's work on southern letters in general, not merely his thinking on the writings and influence of the Fugitives, Agrarians, and New Critics. And we limited the scope as well, deciding not to include writings that had been collected in other volumes or published as unified book-length studies. Thus we did not take anything from *Possum and Other Receipts for the Recovery of "Southern" Being* (which treats in detail Fugitive-Agrarians writers and writings), from *The Men I Have Chosen for Fathers,* which contains focused essays on noteworthy southern writers Flannery O'Connor, Cleanth Brooks, and Richard Weaver and which claims "Solzhenitsyn as Southerner." We have included writings with focused discussions of the Vanderbilt group and its legacy (in Part III, "On Fugitives, Agrarians, and New Critics," and in the long essay on M.E. Bradford, in Part IV), and a number of other pieces engage them as well, in Montgomery's discursive way. Flannery O'Connor, perhaps our greatest short story writer, is treated in these essays, but there is not much on Richard Weaver or Eudora Welty. This is to say that the collection does not have in it everything Montgomery has said on "Matters Southern," for that would make many books, so prolific a writer is he.

These essays on Matters Southern are a good introduction to Montgomery's larger corpus (see the list of his books at the back of the present work). Some of his major works are formidable, because of length but also because of Montgomery's philosophical habit of mind and his wide-ranging discussion of ancient and modern theology, philosophy, literature, and history and of modern politics, science, technology, higher education, and even popular culture. His trilogy *The Prophetic Poet and the Spirit of the Age*, with the provocative individual titles—*Why Flannery O'Connor Stayed Home, Why Poe Drank Liquor*, and *Why Hawthorne Was Melancholy*—will tax a strong reader's abilities. Something similar might be said of his shorter works: *Liberal Arts and Community, Romantic Confusions of the Good*, and *Possum* ("a roller-coaster ride through the trilogy," according to a friend of mine)—shorter though they are, they are demanding reading. Readers who want a more approachable general introduction to Montgomery's thinking, and especially an introduction to this thinking on Matters Southern, will find it here.

In the longer, unified studies and in these essays on Matters Southern, Montgomery writes as family man, as citizen, as teacher, and as poet and philosopher. A family man (husband and father), Montgomery offers glimpses of a family in community held together by ceremony, by love, and by memory. A citizen, he is concerned with the relationship of language (whether in fiction, verse, journalism, political rhetoric, or academic treatise) to the person living in community. He insistently puts the writer's flights of individual imagination in the contest of a corporate reality, a corporate reality that goes back to Faulkner, to St. Thomas, to Augustine, to Homer—indeed, back to Adam and Eve. A teacher, Montgomery reminds us of the significance of great writers in the Western tradition, and of our responsibility to be good stewards in our reading, that we might "pursue a rescue of tradition in the light of the truth of things." As poet, he is no alienated artist, but enjoys and shares humanity with his neighborhood and community—as do many other southern artists. Montgomery speaks in the voices of vatic poet and philosopher—now using metaphor for illustration, now using definition for clarification. Refusing to accept arbitrary divisions between academic disciplines, or between the world of mind and the world of life, he addresses his concerns with an associated sensibility, with head and heart, with faith and reason, in concert.

He tells us in these pages what is wrong with the world: modern man has divorced himself from creation, from tradition, and from transcendence; the autonomous individual will not countenance the claims of the past or the limits to his nature imposed by a Creator and Lawgiver. Happily, Montgomery notes, the southern writer is more likely than his northern cousin to recognize the claims of the past and to accept a transcendent Cause. In short, differences between northern and southern fiction often stem from theological differences. As an antidote to the acid and disorder of modernity. Montgomery recommends piety — intelligent piety, or prudential humility, or a reverential awareness of what is given: the physical creation, moral and spiritual realities, individual gifts such as reason and imagination, and values and customs inherited from the past. Time and place, consciousness and conscience, memories and tradition — these are givens, and they should be approached with a *"discriminating reverence,"* to use a term Montgomery attaches to the good regional poet.

Both reason and faith should cast light on old traditions and modern circumstances. Marion Montgomery therefore calls upon both intellect and orthodoxy in his essays on Matters Southern. He is calling us, too: calling us back to known but forgotten truths.

Part I

The Author at Work and at Home

1

The Country, Here

In this evocative essay, Marion Montgomery introduces himself to us, but what is more, he introduces us to the artist at work, and to the proper work of the artist. Montgomery distinguishes between regionalism and local color. Both types of writing use the local scene: the one to engage the universal, the other merely to paint a local or provincial scene. Focusing on a particular place (his old office in Crawford, Georgia, and the history of this place) and using the details that bring fiction and poetry to life (particular plants: cockscomb and morning glory; particular sounds: buzzing fly or "curled, brown elm leaves" scudding and scrapping along the pavement), Montgomery illustrates how the artist can save place from the ravages of time by sensing earlier presences and by pointing to what T.S. Eliot called "the still point": eternity in time. Echoing St. Paul and Augustine, Montgomery reminds us we have no abiding place on this earth (our final home is eternity). Nevertheless, if we are attentive to the place we live in, that concrete place may evince the universal; that place in time may point to the eternal.*

I sit here above Hurt's Sundries in Crawford, Georgia, where I write when I may. Outside it is clear, cool September, with fall in the look and feel of it. I drove the quarter mile from home, though I usually walk, and heard in the car with me a fly trying to get out through the windshield. Or thought I heard a fly. With the back window open, I was hearing curled, brown elm leaves the car fanned on the asphalt. I parked near a cockscomb growing from a crack where cement meets the brick building I am in. It is a strangely symmetrical plant, given the pressures on it, though it has to slant outward for its form. The fading cones of blossom rise out of leaves that are turning, like a planted garden of false evergreens. I remark it since Boots Hurt and I looked at it and talked about it this morning, he leaning on his awkward crutches. He is recovering from an accident with a horse.

---

*This essay first appeared in *Southern Humanities Review* 2.4 (Fall 1968): 402–407.

Up the dark stairs, to my office, which was until I came several years ago a storage room. Before that it was a doctor's office, when Oglethorpe County had eight or ten doctors, where there is now but one.

There is my fireplace, almost needed today. And board shelves on bricks, with books and papers and boxes with notes. A filing cabinet that once belonged to a friend who sang Elizabethan songs on Shakespeare's birthday. He is long dead now, though not his singing. A rocking chair there by one window.

My desk is a piece of plywood, rescued after our explosion five years ago that wrecked much of the town. The board replaced broken window glass downstairs until glaziers came. It rests now one end on a window sill, the other over a card table, on it my typewriter. I have written three or four books here, occasionally looking out the window in front of me or letting in more air or stirring the fire.

And knowing where I am now, somewhat, I consider where I have been. Most recently deep in Ezra Pound, learning much from him, as all of us who value words have or must. One thing learned in particular I think of. Not the marvels of the English verse line, though that is a rich gift from him. Rather, a negative thing. Somewhere he repeats an adage: *art is local, stupidity national, intelligence international.* An adage that cost him much to learn thoroughly, though out of that learning fine song from time to time. Some of it my dead friend could have sung. Pound's search for the metropolis of art carried him wandering from Idaho east, through Europe to Rapallo. That journey seems now to me an expense of spirit that might have been better spent or conserved — much of it. Eliot learned the adage sooner, settling in London, less haunted by the search for place, knowing a deeper adage: *here have we no abiding city.* Not even through art.

I look out my window. Below me, in what was once a filling station, is a beauty shop. Before that small building, with its steep blue roof there was another building, larger. A store. Near it the town well, whose waters are remembered by more of my neighbors than can remember quite where it was. This morning, Emory (Boots) Hurt marked the precise spot on cement, a few steps from the cockscomb, with his crutch. Then he marked out the lines of the older building, showing me a cement corner of it overgrown with grass.

I look beyond, to the flower garden Emory Hurt kept weeded and growing till his accident, from which the seed of the cockscomb blew. The garden itself is not so beautiful this year. Grass, candy wrappers, a bottle. Beyond it is the railroad. A train comes mornings, bringing pulpwood cars, quarry cars, assorted others. In the afternoon or evening it returns, but does not stop. At the station, now a warehouse, Alexander Stephens used to stretch his legs while the train gave up mail and passengers and took on others. On his way home from Washington or Atlanta. That is in the memory of a man in whose father it was a living memory, now in mine. On that platform too another man's father had words with a conductor, maintaining he had *bought* the pillow he rested on all the way from Atlanta, the conductor insisting he'd only rented it and could not take it home.

Inside the stone station, abandoned, are old records. Among which Reese Stevens, who runs Crawford Grocery and Hardware and is Railway Express Agent, discovered that Crawford was once called Russell, a name our history books don't remember. He discovered it when he received a shipment of hounds from Arkansas, addressed to Russell, and having delivered them, looked in the records out of curiosity.

The railroad, now so little used, once brought several trains a day, before the highway took its work with trucks and buses and cars, leaving it to freight granite and pine logs. But before that, and before Crawford was Russell, Georgia, it was Lexington Station, two miles from the County seat. So placed because those capital citizens feared diseases and other invaders if the railroad came too close. That was before steam engines, when cars were drawn to Augusta on the rails by mules and horse.

The old separation of Lexington and Crawford, its initial causes generally lost among us, as we have generally lost the exact spot of the town well, is nevertheless still with us. Lexington looks down its nose a bit because of its governors, though William H. Crawford, secretary of state, almost president instead of Adams, lived in our limits. Also, Crawford is the larger now, with better water system. We have a good volunteer fire department which on occasion responds to fires in Lexington, which does not. Our advantage of late lies somewhat in that we are two miles nearer Athens, the city fourteen miles off. Athens now calls itself "Advancing Athens," celebrating what Lexington would take to be vulgarity should Crawford so presume. Still, much of Lexington (as of Crawford) drives those miles to Athens in the morning and back late in the afternoon. Chicken-slaughter houses and the State University alike call us. That is beyond the railroad, on past the post office, where old men wait morning and afternoon for mail delivery, star route service. For whatever pensions and with

> talk of the Argonne, Belleau Wood, scoffing Viet Nam
> and the mailman not in yet.

Lexington is two miles behind me. Behind me, and closer — two doors from the stairs I climb to this office — are the foundations left when Crawford exploded that November morning five years ago, with mysteries and coincidences. Two buildings leveled, damage a mile away. The chicken hatchery, rented by strangers, was under investigation by state and federal men beforehand. The renters had come to Crawford out of Memphis, by way of Atlanta, then Athens, maintaining a post office box in Lexington, two miles farther on the line of their flight.

But no one injured at 7 A.M. A law-abiding Lexington lady can't explain why at that moment she chose to run our only traffic light on her way to Athens, the light by the exploded building. The impact came just as she crossed the railroad. A stranger, passing in the other direction, stopped at the railroad to check his tires. Got out. Looked. Just enough time to have been at the building for the explosion. Half a score like incidents, some more puzzling, to think about here at my typewriter. Who will remember the damaged walls of the Chevrolet agency across the street, or that now a dry cleaning plant and insurance office rest on foundations that held a chicken hatchery, where outsiders with great secrecy hatched so few chickens, working at night, until incubators became bombs, their fans drawing into the pilot light butane gas from a small space heater?

There is much for me to dwell on, some of which I know looking out this window this September afternoon, past the lost well, the neglected garden, the slow tracks, on toward Athens, which prides itself in slogan as being "on the go." There I know, for I have seen it, grass out of pavement. If one will be still long enough to look. And no doubt some flower, if no cockscomb. This morning's paper from Athens tells an odd story headlined "Creature May Be Bear, Wildlife Experts Conclude." With a picture of the experts examining tracks, along with a citizen who has seen it — large and black. Several dogs are dead by it, and chickens. One woman, with a rifle, rescued her dog. Citizens are asked to cover any tracks with tub or pan till they can be examined. Looking from my window toward Athens, I remember how once in another golden age wolves came down from the Apennines into the suburbs. In a way more fundamental than nature or art our strange creature, so easily explained when caught, engages me.

For myself, I know something of what feeds the plant by the wall downstairs. There are presences more than the ladies who are having their hair done this afternoon. And along the railroad and in the post office, and beyond in Athens. And here in this room where I write as well.

Not simply presences out of this September and the past. Sometimes one, if he is still and looks and listens, glimpses the future. That stillness — that pause in place so that place may gather to it ways of seeing and hearing — that stillness some of us call "regionalism." We do not mean, as poor poets and polemicists engaging that term from either side sometimes mean,

1. The Country, Here

"local color" or "detail of image or character" or any such mere arresting of a particular into dead time. We mean a way of looking out such a window as mine, past such a garden, on to such secret creatures as grass and stray bear in the streets of "Advancing Athens," so that we may understand St. Paul and St. Augustine, who in peace and with assurance say we have here no abiding city.

It is a way of seeing the relation of Boots Hurt's garden, this year neglected, to cockscomb blooming out of cement, to his marking out with his crutch the spot of cement beneath which the well that always held sweet, cool water in his telling.

It is provincialism, not regionalism, that allows one only sweet water or only immediate presences walking into the beauty shop. Whether in Lexington or Crawford or Athens or Atlanta, and beyond them New York, London, Paris, Rapallo. From a still center, as Eliot came to say, the defeat of *time*, the old enemy.

Not *place* the enemy. Art is regional. Presences abide in place, as they have appeared or do or will appear. As one puts words on paper, from the still point that place allows, those words harbor presences more than the writer's self on this September afternoon in Crawford, Georgia, over Hurt's Sundries. If he is gifted (no credit to him) and diligently still (some credit to him), those words save place from time, make place itself more concrete than the literal accident of Crawford or beyond.

To use words well is to make a window through which one looks as from a still point we may call place. Beneath vagrant cockscomb to secret waters, bitter-sweet. Beyond Athens on to Rome, and beyond it that other Athens.

That is how one hears the imagined fly at the window, becoming the sound of dry elm leaves riding home in the September afternoon. Why both become larger than either in man's peculiar gift, awareness.

The wind moves the curled leaves now, swirling them. But it is not the speed of my passing, on the go. My driveway, near which Johnsongrass, an old enemy, bends with closed morning glory blossoms. Who should wish to stop the wind, or keep random marks of time, morning glory or cockscomb, from wasting or falling? Long thoughts are not reserved to youth or age, but to the still point. Out a window. Crawford, Georgia, and only perhaps September 13, 1967.

2

Of Mulls and Memories

> *Using a soup recipe as his metaphor for family, Montgomery fondly introduces us to his own family living in the small village of Crawford, Georgia, and their friends and neighbors (the ingredients of any healthy community). A family crisis, service on the local volunteer fire department (which grows from a one truck fleet — it was a pickup — to the more respectable two engine fleet), neighborhood adventures, family stories (old and new, always kept alive in memory by the telling) — these things related in the essay give us a sense of both family and community. In this age of family destruction and community decay, it is good to be reminded that the basis of the community is the family, and that the family is kept alive by love and memory.**

My recipe is concerned with mulls and stews, though better cooks than I must supply local ingredients. I do know how to begin: first, catch a turtle (or go rabbit hunting with Allen Huff). But in these lean times, with few turtles or rabbits, we may have to substitute chicken — white meat, both breast and thigh, approved as Grade A by the USDA. Such, all of our first steps, start on the ground where we are. Some of our family and I have learned this, and are still learning it, since moving to Crawford in June of 1961, into this house, then known as the Old Blanchard House, before which it was the Anse Little House. After us, it may, for a little while, be remembered as the Old Montgomery House.

We moved in, a younger couple then than now, with our four small children, the oldest a first grader. Within days, a newer disaster. In a sudden thunderstorm (unrelated to La Niña or El Niña back then), lightning ran along the power line, into the basement, and started a fire in the new wiring. No 911 to call, and whether Crawford even had a fire department, we didn't know. The storm suddenly seemed larger, especially to

---

*This recipe for family was published in *A Taste of Heaven: Oglethorpe Cooks with Family and Friends*, edited by Kate Finch and the Oglethorpe County Middle School, 2000.

2. Of Mulls and Memories

our children. For they were latched on the front porch to give me room to fight the fire while their mother tried to summon help by phone. The two older were charged with calming the two younger, as a way of calming themselves. (The storm was by then moving away.) It is remembered in the family now as a high, heroic, family moment, since we escaped with little serious damage out of initial panic. In a few minutes (it seemed longer at the time), a pickup truck with an old reel of hose showed up. John Brooks and Johnnie Faust were in it. That was the Crawford Fire Department at that time.

The children were rescued from exile on the front porch: Priscilla and Deana (Lola Dean), oldest and, by accidents of birth (to hear them tell it back then), wisest over the younger. And Marion, at four, already considerably confused by this new country, was hardly confident that his mother and I had been wise in fleeing Athens for the wilds of Oglethorpe. Not that such words were his, but that knowing was. "Marion," I'd said a few days earlier, "go bring me the hammer. It's on the hearth in the living room." How baffling — a "living" room, and an "upstairs." And there were hearths and mantelpieces and fireplaces never seen before. In a moment of nostalgic frustration, in an experience with memory when only four years old, he asked, "What ever happened to the carport?"

And Heli, then the youngest at almost two, and the boldest of the lot, was quick as a rabbit in escaping, so that in the first weeks in the neighborhood, there were repeated alarms. "Alert! Heli has escaped!" And the neighbors (Katherine Howard and Doc Stokely in particular) said under their breaths no doubt, "Again!" In calmer moments, there might be the flapping sound of loose wallpaper, with the attic fan on, most variously affecting small children charged to go to sleep upstairs. There was the plumbing to be redone, and the dead coal furnace to dismount and haul off. Slowly. Slowly.

As slowly, there grew the evolving Volunteer Fire Department, with regular training nights — led by foreign instructors, the professionals from Athens; though one of them turned out to have been born in Oglethorpe, with family still here. A used fire truck was purchased surplus. And along that slow way, on occasion, a turtle or rabbit mull was found at the firehouse, with memories stirred as someone stirred the pot. There was talk of "grabbling" with hands under the banks of Oglethorpe streams, of catching sometimes a fabulous turtle (because so big), on Buffalo or Long Creek, on Clouds Creek, reminding me of boyhood rambles, of my own grabbling for catfish under rocks in Flint River shoals and so feeling more at home in Oglethorpe, and even beginning to like the mull of the moment.

There was the climbing of ladders, set up (*straight* up) between the

Commercial Bank and Brooks Chevrolet, held in place only by fellow volunteers. My professional instruction: up to the top and over and back down on the other side. See, the professional instructor would say, you can depend on your buddies when you work together. There were late night fires—houses and chicken houses, some outside Crawford. After which discussions were held with Mayor George Brooks about the legality of our going as far as Devil's Pond, since insurance companies gave a rating on the understanding that the protection was for *inside* the city limits. But, "it was old _____'s chicken house!" And so we would go anyway, though I don't remember any talk about insurance for climbing ladders in the middle of North Street.

Now Crawford has *two* first-class fire trucks, and younger and better-trained men to answer the call. And recently, the Woman's Club did a fine feed for them in community appreciation. In the interval, we had another child, and by now, many grandchildren. Our last child, Ellyn, is the only one born to this house, in the Old Little-Blanchard House. And that makes it legitimately the Old Montgomery House now, though yet to be referred to as such. Houses become homes nevertheless when loved ones are born in them, or when loved ones die in them.

Now, 40 years later, we, as a family, know and understand this better; understand how each person in a family makes a most unusual addition to the recipe for family, though one family is very like, as well as unlike, other families in the neighborhood. We come to better understand how families as families become necessary ingredients to any mull of families, to any desirable community—to Crawford and Lexington and Arnoldsville and Stephens and Maxeys. But that is the sort of thing we come to know most certainly from inside this family and its relation to others. We come to know it from the kitchen, as it were, and from gathering at evening meals, in relation to community gatherings for whatever feast—festival or funeral.

With some time, and memories from old times then, we come to value salt in relation to sugar, vinegar in relation to syrup, in the recipes of family and community, requiring a tolerance of manners that is more important than taste. We know at least possibilities of family and community, differing though families always do from Crawford to Goose Pond or to Philomath, and beyond. We know this, waiting for a phone call perhaps while stirring the family mull: a call perhaps from the youngest and hers in Vermont; from the oldest and hers in the shadows of Washington, D.C., and closer to home, from Heli and hers in Stephens; Marion and his here in Crawford on Park Avenue; from Deana and hers on what is called, under new 911 name, the "Athens Road," across from Allen Huff. We keep, as best

2. Of Mulls and Memories

we can, a weather eye out in this season of storms so destructive of families and communities— stirring whatever pot as best we may, relishing the rich if ghostly steam rising from it. In 40 years, if memory serves me still, we caught a good many turtles and rabbits, and even a possum or two, since moving into the Old Little-Blanchard House in Crawford, Georgia.

Part II

On Place and Region

3

Georgia as a Place for Writers

Though he occasionally lectured and read his creative work in other places, Marion Montgomery stayed home as a writer and teacher. His birthplace was Thomaston, Georgia (in Upson County, about 100 miles south of Atlanta — the "exploding provincial city" in this essay). Receiving his bachelor's and master's degrees from the University of Georgia, and spending two years in the creative writing program at Iowa, he finally settled in Crawford, a small village in Oglethorpe County about 15 miles from Athens. He taught at the University of Georgia for 34 years — and followed the muse as well, writing four novels and hundreds of poems, along with over a dozen works of criticism. Asked by a journalist what sort of place Georgia was for the writer, Montgomery offered the following humorous, colloquial essay. He mentions southern writers who migrated elsewhere — and some who stayed home. His essay reveals that he enjoys a shared humanity with his neighbors, hunting coons and rabbits, fishing for horney-heads and catfish, fighting fires as a member of the volunteer fire department, gratefully receiving produce from various gardens. This sharing of humanity with a local, rural people, Montgomery suggests, has something to do with the abundance of good literature produced in the South in the twentieth century.*

Mr. Frank Daniel
Atlanta *Journal*

Dear Frank:

You ask me about Georgia as a home for writers. It has been a thing to do among writers (some of them) to get away from home to look at it — see it clearly from Paris or Majorca or Oregon. So that is what I'm doing

---

*This essay originally appeared in the September 1964 issue of a short-lived magazine, *North Georgia Life*. In *Eudora Welty & Walker Percy: The Concept of Home in Their Lives and Literature* (McFarland, 2004), Montgomery discusses at length the significance of place (Jackson, Mississippi, and Covington, Louisiana) for two famous southern writers.

this time, being up here in South Carolina for a few weeks. What of Georgia as a home for writers? And specifically, what of Oglethorpe County for me?

First of all, as I see it there are two dangers for the writer if he stays home. One is (setting aside the great world beyond home that more or less concerns him, depending upon who he is) that his own people will ignore him. The other is that they won't. For a while Byron Herbert Reece was ignored, as you know. I remember him as a shy, lean man out of the North Georgia hills, reading his poems before writers and pretend writers, his shyness making one not realize at first the strong center that was in him, threatening him more immediately than the little gathering listening to his poems. Of course, all that was necessary to a recognition was to look into those poems he was reading. There it was: a firm but troubled way of looking at a dark world that reminds one of Thomas Hardy or of Job. But there is often more fascination to an audience in that exotic creature called *poet* than in that mythical creature's work, which when he is the poet always reveals him as mythical in an older, legitimate sense of the term *mythical*; the term is now trivialized to mean *fictional* or *illusional*. The truly mythical poet witnesses to reality beyond sentimental reductionism, which, alas was Reece's value among his own. He became, locally at least, fashionable even in the precincts of Atlanta. And if he became less shy, he never became comfortable among his home state admirers who would advance him against the world as a genuine Georgia poet. Little wonder that some among them were not only shocked and puzzled by his tragic death, but felt some of the anguish of betrayal as well. Such are the fruits of not being ignored.

The danger of neglect? There was a bookstore lady — guardian and purveyor of our golden letters in your fair city — who resented the inconvenience attendant upon an autograph tea for Reece, especially I suspect since he was an out-of-town writer. (The bookstore is in our progressive city, in which one of the most subtle forms of provincialism is so often to be discovered: the fear of being thought provincial.) Reece had come all the way from the remote mountains, where now many of those nonprovincials spend frantic weekends. "I could have beautiful thoughts too, " allowed the lady, "if all I had to do all day long was look at the rear end of a mule."

There speaks one who — the gods being just — should be fitting ladies prefabricated foundations or selling chewing gum. So between the dangers of adulation and of hostile indifference, what chance has one of being at home in Georgia, either in the mountains or in our exploding provincial city?

And what if there is another kind of hostility, sprung not from local soul deadness but from an honest (if perhaps mistaken) resentment of, say, the notoriety of *Tobacco Road*? To California, then? (And I'm remembering Reece here.) Or perhaps to a shining city in the East, where there are those who know what literature is *really* about and how to appreciate true virtue in one's writing? One begins to wonder, though, as does Donald Davidson, when a reviewer from way off up there complains of a southern novel's being "heavy with the scent of camellias." That reviewer is very likely cousin, if distant, to the bookstore lady. What profit in reminding such minds that camellias have no scent? Indeed, one wonders whether such minds may be at all trusted to bear witness with valid immediacy to the experience of provincial cities, north, west, or south.

Some leave home in anger, hurt. And some leave in the bloom of success. But some do not leave at all, choosing to adjust to the neglect or notoriety, trying to come to terms with bookstore ladies, wounded citizens, the applause of those who sometime intend to read their books. Better to be at home among suffocating kindred than alone and sick for home amid some alien camellias. For in that far country also lies danger for the writer. Is there not a something very like the "scent of camellias" that intrudes itself almost inevitably into the ex-southerner's writing — into Carson McCullers' *Clock Without Hands*?

Of course some leave home not as an escape of home. Sidney Lanier had pursuing dragons other than Georgians. And some stay home because it is home — not because they are writers trying to get a purchase upon home for the sake of their writing. Augustus Baldwin Longstreet, perhaps? And at a higher level of gift, in our own day, Flannery O'Connor, who is so unlike Mrs. McCullers in this respect as in so many others. Also, some return home, as Conrad Aiken lately did. Occasionally we even have with us a brave stranger to discover old kinships, like a wandering Aeneas. There is your own Maggie Davis, and that most remarkable recovered "southerner," Eudora Welty.

Certainly I intend to return home, in July. To Crawford. Writer friends have asked me your question, out of their different places: how is it with you in Georgia? How do your neighbors take you? Don't they think writers a bit mad or subversive? My neighbors think some people, perhaps most, mad and subversive. Rather, some of them do. Some of them don't even think about the writer and some don't think about people. A curious circumstance that some of my writer friends from the great world out there (which means from some other local place) don't seem to realize is that Georgians are people too. My neighbors are gifted with those universal human inclinations that we diagnose as virtues and vices. They are capable of concluding on observing any of their fellows, there but by the grace of God go I. Which is to say, they are capable of concluding that others are mad, subversive, treacherous—maybe even evil. And in the lot thus set aside, writers or preachers or school bus drivers may as easily abound as any other. But those neighbors are also capable of concluding that, mad or not, a writer shares in humanity. If not celebrated, then tolerated. And perhaps even supported within the body of humanity.

My next-door neighbor brings me spring onions and, a little later, tomatoes. Another called me a few weeks ago and said, "Let's go catch some horney-heads on Long Creek." I hadn't caught that little fish since Upson County days—days spent in another country which is in this latter day revealed to me increasingly as the country we always inhabit when we truly experience what Hopkins calls the "instress" of existence—whether in relation to a mule's rear end or to a shy mountain poet in a big city bookstore awkwardly signing copies of the strange and foreign creature he holds in his hand—his first book.

Another neighbor has a good pack of beagles that we both love to hear run. And every once in awhile, the fire siren goes off and I'm with them, there before most of them — putting out a grass fire that threatens a chicken house, or putting out a kitchen fire. Two years ago we fought fire together all one morning after an explosion wrecked half the town. They didn't seem to hold it either against me or for me that I am a writer, letting me wrestle the hose with the best of them, expecting me to take my night patrol shift to save the remnants from the curious or the scavengers who migrated to the scene, drawn by the spectacle of such large destruction of our small orderly town. They may even approve of my being a writer, some of them. None may tomorrow.

But they are a particular kind of people it seems to me, with some long memory of humanity which is not always a conscious memory that they may articulate. That they lack that gift makes them at once wary of the writer, but inclines them as well to value him gingerly. Some of them will still bring me spring onions and tomatoes, and I'll still go rabbit hunting or coon hunting with some of them. And there in Georgia woods I shall be safer in many ways—even when three rabbits are up and running—than I should be in that shining city of the East or the West, or even in Atlanta. They even put some of my books in our library, with some pride. And if I get a call to teach over in South Carolina, or perhaps even get called down to your big city about my books, one of them will sell me a bus ticket, a round trip one if I want it.

But perhaps I can draw my answer to your question together with personal experiences, those precursors of poems and novels critics look for as "biographical." Not long ago, a year or so, I was invited to a city in our state to read my poems, invited into a very sophisticated circle devoted to the arts. The prospect was exciting, so that I got myself a round trip ticket. On the appointed morning I rose from my flu-bed before dawn, rode on into the morning, misery contending with excitement. Hours later I was greeted at the bus station, my hostess a little surprised at my coming on the bus. Then and there I entered a Henry James world of the internationally sophisticated — me with my country verses. An elaborate formal dinner. A reading to respectful applause. Next day a tour of the historic city. And then time for my turning home. My hostess, who the evening before had been full of enticing conversation about her pending trip abroad in the spring, about the delight of a summer excursion in amateur archeological pursuits at classical sites, called me aside to ask what my expenses had been. I gave her a round figure, something like "about seven dollars." "No, no," she said. "I need the exact figure for my records." With a slight flush of anger, I gave her one: "Seven dollars and forty-three cents." With no change of demeanor from her high seriousness, she wrote out the check and handed it to me. But when I got back home, I had a message waiting for me from our filling-station bus man. He had given me the round trip ticket alright, but had charged me only the one-way fare. It was with relief that I settled home again, gladly suffering the difference. I never corrected the matter with my hostess, since irony would have gone unappreciated.

And now, just as your question comes, I have news here in South Carolina from my wife at home in Crawford. A banister rail got knocked out by one of the children, and since there might have been some danger to the youngest, she'd asked our gardening neighbor to please nail it back, explaining that I was away as a "visiting professor" over in South Carolina. He did the repair. But he remarked to his own wife when he went home that he didn't quite understand me, off visiting some professor in South Carolina instead of taking care of my proper duties. Such is local fame.

In all of this, then, is something that makes Georgia for the writer, and the South for the writer, quite special to me. I suspect that the texture of life would be different in California, judging from your newspaper. Just what is the difference is difficult to say, though I could supply a considerable bibliography of attempts at saying it: why the South, *even* Georgia (given the benighted view of us by other locals) has produced so many good writers in this century. I'm going back to Oglethorpe County in the middle of July, and go catfishing — and perhaps write some poems. Come fall, when my neighbor turns his garden under for the winter (except for the collards), we'll go bird hunting. I'll write some stories perhaps, and get started on another novel.

If collards somehow help me to make a good story, fine. And if it takes looking at the rear end of a mule to have beautiful thoughts, what miraculous economy to borrow or steal a mule and plow my garden. I may even buy one, if my books start selling. Beautiful thoughts are rare, not only in Atlanta, as your long experience there will have shown you, but even in Oglethorpe County.

4

Is Regional Writing Dead?

> *Montgomery is answering an editor's question regarding the status of regional writing. His theme is a constant in his writing on regionalism and literature: "the viable particular in art must always have regional anchor," and one gains a "vision of the transcendent and the timeless — through the local." This we see in "Shakespeare, that sixteenth century London regionalist," as well as in other worthies such as Homer, Aeschylus, and Dante. In short, while modern provincialism (not limited in space but limited in time since divorced from the past — in Allen Tate's formulation) is the death of art, a healthy regionalism is the lifeblood and hallmark of great literature.*

An adequate response to your question about the state of southern regional writing would take many pages, but if I may answer briefly: Good fiction or poetry is always "regional" in a sense crucial to its art, whether one look at the tap root and feeders of community as detected in the *Iliad* and *Odyssey* or explore the immediacy of fifth century Athens to Aeschylus's tragedies. For the viable particular in art must always have regional anchor. Even when the poet himself is restless gnostic, discomforted by his regional anchor and struggling within himself between the pull of his own will to determine reality and his deeper inclination to give consent to a reality independent of his will. I'm thinking here more locally than of Homer or Aeschylus: of Joyce and his quarrel with Dublin, through which quarrel he recognizes affinities to those older poets. Joyce is tempted to a dissociation from "sow Ireland" no less than his Stephen. But Ireland as anchor to the tensional war in Joyce gives a body, a very local presence, to his best work.

To revert to the ancients: Vergil's concern for "the tears of things" in the *Aeneid* gives that work an existential resonance — an anchor in *esse*

---

*This brief essay appeared in *The Student* (a Wake Forest University publication) and was published in the spring of 1980.

through the necessarily local *ens*, particularly anchored in the ground of being. Thus Vergil's concern rescues his epic beyond polemic or program. The *Aeneid* is no less "regional" than the *Georgics* when one's sensibilities (themselves necessarily anchored in the local) are ordinately grounded in one's own and the community's existence within the created world. (The point is worth considering, perhaps, in reflecting on Vergil's popularity in the "old" South.) For though we travel in this world, we travel from local to local, sometimes gaining brief vision of the transcendent and the timeless—*through* the local.

What a strong sense of the local there is in *The Divine Comedy*, giving that great work its body within which spirit pulses alive. And how immediately at home in place are Plutarch's creatures when given local habitation by Shakespeare, that 16th century London regionalist. E.A. Robinson is right when he has his Ben Jonson remark with a mixture of awe and irritation that Shakespeare, "out of his / Miraculous inviolable increase / Fills Ilion, Rome, or any town you like / Of olden time with timeless Englishmen." The relation of the "timeless," the universal, to the regional is an intimate one, as any artist recognizes in his most lucid reflective moments.

As I suggest above, Joyce's Dublin is not so fanciful but that it echoes the stones and speech of that certain town upon our immediate, most local senses. Indeed, when I reflect on our 2,500 years of great regional art, I must wonder just what is the larger context of Walker Percy's remark that "The day of southern regional writing is all gone." Even his work, at its best, belies the remark. I recall an old saw of Ezra Pound's, with which I become more and more comfortable: "Intelligence is international; stupidity is national; art is local." Pound is no "local colorist"—no artist as provincial—though he is always devoted to the "local gods," as he affirms and reaffirms. This is by way of urging the young writer to be most cautious in digesting such remarks as the one isolated from Walker Percy. He might with greater profit reflect on the difference Allen Tate makes between the regional and the provincial in "The New Provincialism." Tate's is a distinction pursued at length and depth by a various mind—poet, critic, philosopher. And increasingly so of late as we more and more sense that we have come to crisis through a rampant provincialism that parades as enlightenment. I have in mind such prophets as Richard Weaver, Eric Voegelin, Alexander Solzhenitsyn, though the list might be extended considerably.

Tate remarks a profound difference between the terms, worth my quoting:

> Regionalism is limited in space but not in time. The provincial attitude is limited in time but not in space; provincialism is that state of mind in

which regional men lose their origin in the past and its continuity into the present, and begin every day as if there had been no yesterday.... It is a difference between two worlds: the provincial world of the present, which sees in material welfare and legal justice the whole solution to the human problem; and the classical-Christian world, based upon regional consciousness, which held that honor, truth, imagination, human dignity, and limited acquisitiveness, could alone justify a social order however rich and efficient it may be.

Tate speaks here of that regional consciousness as if it were more nearly doomed than besieged. He is writing at the end of World War II, at a point where Faulkner is known only sparsely in our nation, though known well on the continent. At a point before Flannery O'Connor has begun to write. "From now on," Tate adds, "we are committed to seeing *with*, not *through* the eye: we, as provincials who do not live anywhere." His remark seems reflected by the Percy quote above; but then, Percy had not himself begun to write at that time. Solzhenitsyn's arresting Harvard commencement speech very much echoes Tate's distinction, though grown out of a quite different regional soil. It is in a spirit more spectacularly buffeted, more so than the regional consciousness so often remarked in southern writing. But it does not echo despondency. Solzhenitsyn's address is to your questions, with an affirmation of the distinction between the regional and provincial consciousness. He is concerned that the regional consciousness be rescued because it is necessary to the health of both community and art. But his cry of concern affirms the abiding, which will be maintained by some saving remnant, whatever region of creation bounds that remnant's habitation.

To return to your question, then: the day of *regional* writing is never over, whether the term be limited from time to time by calling it "southern" or "Irish" or "Russian." But when the particular writer succumbs to the provincialism which is everywhere rampant in our "national spirit," he will cease to be regionalist and increasingly become a provincial writer, with all the weaknesses that provincialism intrudes upon art. His state of mind will be reflected in his art, and his art in turn will become increasingly the historian's province of interest rather than the aesthetician's. The writer himself will probably be revealed by the historian as secular gnostic (in Eric Voegelin's sense) or as secular Manichaean (in Flannery O'Connor's). For his provincial consciousness will have superimposed distortions upon the reality of being that is the prime source of art's life. Whatever the limits of the vision that is his gift, it too will suffer the inevitable glaucoma of gnosticism. While the tensions between what he sees and what he would see are growing, he may write the sort of arresting fiction that Joyce does in *Dubliners, Portrait, Ulysses.* Incidentally, this tensional Joycean struggle I find in Walker Percy's own novels. I seem to sense a struggle in Percy himself lest vision be distorted by will, so that I view his remark on southern regional writing with some alarm for what it may portend to his art out of that struggle. For if the gnostic vision triumphs, one may create only such a display of the regional paralyzed as *Finnegans Wake*, which speaks life increasingly disjoined from art.

5

Ceremony and the Regional Spirit

> "It is the regional deportment which ... achieves a transcendence of the local," and this achievement comes when the regional poet has piety, or a "discriminating reverence," for the times and places he writes about—so Montgomery argues in this essay. The regional poet's piety distinguishes him from the provincial poet, and so does his loving embrace of the local. Both regional and provincial poet will invoke the ceremonial, but the regional poet will do so in a self-effacing way, showing that he is moved by love. These literary concerns lead Montgomery to a consideration of the decay of public discourse and the loss of orderly ceremony in the family. He calls for the restoration of the ceremonial nature of language in public life and of "ceremonies of innocence" in the family. Concluding his essay, Montgomery reminds us of America's national decadence, but he also hopefully points to the one institution that has a chance to arrest the decline: "It is to the restoration of ceremony in the family that I look for whatever stability is possible to us" in this age of public and private disorder.*

> We come into the sun out of the mystery of silence and move toward the dark wisdom of silence; we manage to make an amazing deal of noise by the way.

I should like to begin by citing two texts as background for a brief commentary on my approach to poetry. The first is an epigraph which Ezra Pound cites approvingly:

Intelligence is international; stupidity is national; art is local. The second is from an essay by Allen Tate, in which he expresses alarm over our civilization's general decay from the local through the international

---

*This essay originally appeared in *Southern Humanities Review* 5.1 (Winter 1971): 25–29. A version of the essay also appears in Montgomery's *The Men I Have Chosen for Fathers*.

levels. His essay is called "The New Provincialism." And a segment of it says:

> Regionalism is ... limited in space but not in time. The provincial attitude is limited in time but not in space.... [P]rovincialism is that state of mind in which regional men lose their origin in the past and its continuity into the present, and begin every day as if there had been no yesterday.

With Pound, then, I take poetry to be local. It uses the world immediately adjacent to the poet's mind and senses, whatever coloring that mind give it. It uses the language the poet hears, or thinks he hears, however he may adapt that language to his sense of form. Time and place are always aspects of poetry, like man's body, at once defining its spirit as they threaten to overcome that spirit. The world to the poet, as to any man, is a tyrannical host. [Two senses to each word: *tyrannical* as we speak it of Pisistratus or of Stalin; *host* as we speak it of Chaucer's Franklyn or the oak's relation to mistletoe.]

The local — the adjacent world as it is revealed to the poet's mind — is the relevant concern of the poet insofar as he hopes for a transcendence of time and place by his poetry. And the greatest of our poets knew this; in consequence of which, time and place is a point we turn to in our attempt to understand the effect of great poetry upon us. After the effect of *Oedipus the King* we look to fifth-century Athens. So on down the line — you supply the poems and poets of thirteenth-century Florence; fourteenth- and sixteenth-century London; nineteenth-century Paris; twentieth-century Nashville.

The problem a poet has in achieving transcendence — in moving, his poetry beyond the limits of time and place — lies not in his struggle with time and place so that he may escape them, though this has been the poet's general inclination in my lifetime. As if one might, by going to New York or London or Paris, thereby throw off all iron weights upon the wings of song. The problem I take to lie rather in the poet's *address* to his time and place. If all poetry is in some sense local, still it may be said that some poetry is provincial, in Tate's sense of the term, while other poetry is regional. It is the regional deportment which, finally I believe, achieves a transcendence of the local. Dante's election of vulgar Italian is evidence of that regional spirit in operation against a provincial attitude toward Latin as the necessary instrument of high poetry. Shakespeare's address to Plutarch might exasperate a Ben Jonson, but it leads to that regionalizing of history which, as E.A. Robinson puts it, allows Shakespeare to fill

5. Ceremony and the Regional Spirit

>...out of his
>Miraculous inviolable increase
>...Ilion, Rome, or any town you like
>Of olden time with timeless Englishmen.

Whether a poet turn out to be provincial or regional in his deportment in the presence of the local is determined by his piety. Piety, I would have it, is the *discriminating reverence* with which the poet takes and uses the local. It is the mode of his ceremonial awareness of time and place.

The poet *must* use the local: that which is immediate to his mind and senses. But he *may* use the local in a provincial or regional way. A difference is revealed by his deportment in relation to his origins and materials. We might note on this point that the terms *academic* and *beat*, as applied to our poetry, have been about equally terms of derision. When either term is used in derogation, it is intended to describe a provincialism in the poet. *Academic* poetry means poetry which takes form to be a mechanical relating of metrics to metaphor by wit, the whole operation divorced from the poet's commitment to what he is saying. *Beat* poetry means those ceremonies of naïve innocence, "full of passionate intensity," whose origins the beat poet takes to be at least no more remote than that last great "Happening" for his benefit: World War II.

But whether regionally or provincially academic or beat, one aspect all poetry has in common — some degree of the ceremonial. From Homer's invocation of the muse to Allen Ginsberg's mad incantation through a catalogue of epithets. It is through the ceremonial that I think one may recover that regional state of mind which I believe to be desirable. Indeed, *regional* as I mean it is that state of mind in which one is most acutely aware of the necessity of those ceremonies of innocence that Yeats announced our age as having lost. You remember these desperate lines from his "Second Coming":

>Turning and turning in the widening gyre
>The falcon cannot hear the falconer;
>Things fall apart; the center cannot hold;
>Mere anarchy is loosed upon the world,
>The blood-dimmed tide is loosed, and everywhere
>The ceremony of innocence is drowned;
>The best lack all conviction, while the worst
>Are full of passionate intensity.

Maturity, which I assume as desirable, is a growth in which the blood-dimmed tide of the self is reduced from anarchy by ceremonies of innocence. Maturity is a growth from that provincialism in which we each initially find ourselves, toward a regionalism which requires of us, for instance, that "brotherly deference" Confucius speaks of or that "charity" which St. Paul extols.

I came along when some of the ceremonies of innocence were still practiced more generally than now, though they were in obvious decay for reasons that my provincialism prevented me from understanding. (You should remember that we are all born into the provincialism of the self—which some of us call the state of original sin.) I recall now that my grandfather held a position in his family, whether blessing the family meal or presiding at the fall hog-killing, that few of my contemporaries hold as fathers or will as grandfathers. His was a position maintained through forms of ceremony more ancient than he, through which he acknowledged nature's seasons and his own responsibilities, however imperfect his acknowledgement.

Ceremony is the acting out of form whereby we move out of our natural provincialism: manners devoutly and awfully taken. The forms whereby we discover ourselves at least a little higher than mere vegetable or animal; the forms whereby we acknowledge with generosity the existence of that which is separate from the self. Ceremony is absolutely necessary to that sanity and health whereby we can say that we are at home in the world, or at a higher level, whereby we may say we are acceptable guests of nature. At its most basic, ceremony is *orderly awareness*. Its most immediate instrument at man's disposal is of course language. Language implies the imperative nature of ceremony, whether one look to the grammar of a sentence or to the meter, rhyme, logic of a sonnet. The major poets of our century—Yeats, Eliot, Pound, the Nashville Fugitives—have felt that at certain points of our history there was a more general respect for the ceremonial nature of language than in our own age; of course they recognized in history as well periods very like our own in which ceremony decayed. I cite but one indication of such ancient decay: Thucydides says, in the *Peloponnesian Wars* (III, 82- 84) in discussing that growth of a provincialism which destroyed the Greek states:

> The meaning of words had no longer the same relation to things. ...The seal of good faith was ... fellowship in crime. An attitude of perfidious antagonism everywhere prevailed; for there was no word binding enough nor oath terrible enough to reconcile enemies .

Ours then is not the only age plagued by a "credibility gap." Our Thucydides, Ezra Pound, has for 45 years warned us to look to our language, lest we find ourselves overcome by disorderly un-awareness. To little avail, for the vestigial manifestations of ceremony have become for us

5. Ceremony and the Regional Spirit

so routine and mechanical as to allow us to virtually abandon intelligence: the government forms filled out in quadruplicate, to be filed alphabetically and thrown in the trash can; the traffic rituals involved in getting home through the evening rush hour; the envelope-mailing to the Community Chest at the end of the month when we pay the light bill. Discrimination abandoned, it is little wonder that one take any piece of music or art or any poem to be as good as any other — so long as none of them break too disturbingly into our awareness. We have become accustomed to, and prefer, only a foggy throbbing of the heart.

I repeat, ceremony is an imperative wherever and whenever there is a legitimate necessity of addressing oneself to something or someone other than the self. Impious ceremony is the mechanical, self-conscious conduct of the self in nature and society. As a poet, I am disturbed that impious ceremony predominates in our lives: the order of precedence in our traffic rituals, whether in freeway competition or doorway competition; whether in the presence of stranger to stranger, teacher to pupil, father to son. We have manner still; but we have lost manners. Consider the ceremonial aspects of this common experience: we each of us on occasion, and many of us as matter of course, stop at some Burger Haven for a hamburger, french fries, milkshake. In a building vaguely reminiscent of the temple we encounter a hierarchy of servers, each related by rank to his fellows. They wear robes of office, inscribed shirt and cap; they perform a service through the discipline of rituals. The immediate priest at the window performs a final act. From the beginning of the operation we have gestures of communion, but they are gestures from which the significance of "give us this day our daily bread" has been rather carefully removed. Any spilled orange juice — or in our new ceremonial language "O J" — is hardly a libation. When I compare my awareness of myself in this world of the Burger Temple to my recollections of my grandfather's table, it seems to me that the Burger Temple hardly feeds the body what is required, however fresh the beef or vitamin-added the O J. It is measurably efficient: if we don't get a flat tire or don't have an ulcer, we can keep going, and millions of us do. But toward what?

I have a rather dark view of the possibilities of our survival as a nation, having too regularly borne in upon me the evidence that "stupidity is national." At least it will seem a dark view to many. I do see cause for hope, the same cause that there has always been for recovery from any decline of an epoch. You will notice that I am repeatedly concerned in my work with an institution in which the ceremonies of innocence have been traditionally exalted, from Homer's day to our own, though it is an institution in rapid decay in our time, as it was at Athens in Thucydides' day and at Rome when Petronius wrote his black humor novel, the *Satyricon* (first century A.D. under Nero). I mean the institution of the family. It is to the restoration of ceremony in the family that I look for whatever stability is possible to us in this third great wave of Western history now ebbing. Through ceremony, one learns that piety which I think necessary, a piety which binds father to son as Odysseus and Telemachus were bound. Out of ceremony — the discipline of body and mind in respect to itself as the self relates to all that is not the self — out of ceremony eventually comes a manner of being larger than that naturally provincial being of a child before he finds his place in the family. The reverence of family leads to reverence of families, and to the possibilities of civilization. It is to the family then that I look. Lest I be misled by a sentimentally attractive Utopia I remember at once St. Paul's statement to the Hebrews: "Here we have no continuing city." But also I remember T.S. Eliot's imperative words against despair to those of us who accept the decline as inevitable:

> if the Temple is to be cast down
> We must first build the Temple.

But always we build the Temple of stones from the rubble.

6

The Sense of Violation: Notes Toward a Definition of "Southern" Fiction

A review of Carson McCullers' Clock Without Hands in Time Magazine is the point of departure for this essay on violence and violation in southern fiction. Montgomery begins by pointing out that violence is not the exclusive domain of southern writing, though taken to be so by thoughtless critics. A sense of violation, however, is a distinguishing characteristic of southern fiction when compared with northern. In a series of comparisons, Montgomery likens southern fiction to the writings of Homer and Aeschylus: in southern and ancient Greek literature, the protagonists (Huck Finn, Francis Marion Tarwater, Odysseus, Agamemnon) will take risks and are personally responsible for taking risks. Furthermore, Montgomery sees contrasts between Homer's Odysseus and Crane's newspaper reporter (in "The Open Boat"), between Faulkner's Thomas Sutpen (Absalom, Absalom!) and Dos Passos' J. Ward Morehouse (U.S.A.) or Dreiser's Clyde Griffiths (An American Tragedy). Likewise, distinctions can and should be made between southern writers (Faulkner and O'Connor, for example) and southern writers with "northern" sensibilities (McCullers, Capote, Tennessee Williams). Ultimately, the differences noted are due to theological considerations. The southern writer has a sense of violation and earned retribution, "a sense of man's awful responsibility." Thus Montgomery finds "a fascinating healthiness in southern writing, whose power comes finally not from its local materials but from the writer's sense that, good or bad, we are members one of another and violate each other and must pay for the violation (usually through violence) because of the wrathful love of whatever gods we believe in." This sense of violation is obviously connected to what Flannery O'Connor called "the Christ-

*This essay originally appeared in The Georgia Review 19.2 (Fall 1965): 278–287.

haunted south," a place in which men are "very much afraid that [they] may have been formed in the image and likeness of God." After reviewing a manuscript copy of this essay, O'Connor wrote to Montgomery (October 17, 1962): "I sure do like this and wish I could write me one as good. We ought to be on the same program and reinforce each other's views sometime."*

The seminar game of what makes contemporary and recent southern fiction so fascinating to the world outside the South continues, and the voice of the explainer promises to be heard pretty long throughout the land. *Time Magazine,* as one might expect, has the golden key. In its review of Carson McCullers' *Clock Without Hands,* it says: "Violence colors the surface of southern writing, but its core is a sense of violation." True, so true. But the statement itself, as *Time* puts it in its review, seems to reflect a surface understanding, as might also be expected. The evaluations that come to us from beyond the paper curtain, not only from such popular commentators as *Time* but also from such literary critics as Alfred Kazin, repeatedly comment on southern fiction as if violence and grotesqueness were its unique characteristics — as if one doesn't find violence and grotesqueness in Algren or Hemingway or Dreiser or Dos Passos. It is as if southern fiction were some strange and exotic plant which does not grow on native grounds. Violence, surely, is the sine qua non of fiction, whether it be a general slaughter of wooers or the sagging character presented through the fluoroscope stream of consciousness, that magic lantern that throws the nerves in patterns on a screen — whether it be violence as handled by Homer and Faulkner or Euripides and Joyce. Violence, then, doesn't set "southern" fiction off from "northern" fiction, though *violation* does suggest the key to what I believe its distinguishing characteristic. To speak of the typical is dangerous but necessary, and so I shall say that the difference between good southern fiction (in which term I do not include all fiction that uses the South) and good eastern or midwestern fiction (which I shall hereafter label "northern" fiction) is the different sense of man's part in the violation peculiar to each fiction.

A "southern" writer, such as Faulkner, is more nearly kin to Homer and Aeschylus than is a "northern" writer like Stephen Crane. Odysseus risks outraging Poseidon because the principle of hospitality is grossly violated by Polyphemus. And it is with violence that he summons the god's wrath, by blinding his son Polyphemus. The consequences he expects, and he struggles against the ocean, battered by the reef, not purely to survive (though life is sweet to him as to Crane's hero in "The Open Boat") but because there is in him a strong sense of his own rightness in blinding Polyphemus, a feeling that the more remote god, Zeus, and his laws take

6. The Sense of Violation

precedence over the immediate, though threatening, god of the sea. Unlike Crane's introspective newspaper reporter, Odysseus knows very well what temple there is to throw rocks at, and his struggle to survive is the manner in which he throws his rocks. The virtue of Odysseus over Crane's hero doesn't have to do with whether there is, in fact, a Poseidon as opposed to no god at all, but that Odysseus possesses, in addition to his sense of rightness, the courage of self-responsibility. This is an extremely important difference so far as my concern for the fascination of the southern hero goes, because whatever the psychological explanations, the human mind responds quite differently to Odysseus as he struggles up the beach than to Crane's newspaper reporter. Odysseus stands straighter for his experience, one feels— after his night's sleep. Crane's characters sag.

Or consider (instead of Homer's comedy), as a measure of definition of southern writing, Aeschylus' tragedy, where the consequences of personal violation make a better parallel to the consequences of merely happening to be in the world by accident as in Crane's tragedy. In that Abraham-Isaac situation at Aulis, an act of violation by Agamemnon is inescapable; either he must slay his daughter upon the altar or bring distress to his companions in arms. Which? Damnation lies either way. Agamemnon attempts to act in the direction of the lesser evil, but he must (because he is a man and not a woman) act. The inability to act, we might remember, is considered in Homer and Aeschylus to be a womanish trait. Agamemnon must act, and, as Aeschylus is quick always to remind us, man is less than the gods and doomed therefore to self-delusion. Agamemnon knows as much, but he takes upon himself the terrible possibilities of his act. That "frenzied counselor" delusion, says Aeschylus, leads him to boldness. Agamemnon himself by his decision seeks the knife that waits him after his triumph at Troy; he is aware that the flaw in the universe is at least partly in himself.

How does "southern" writing compare to Aeschylus and Homer? I am not interested in such concerns as whether the study of Greek and Latin in the Old South is the source of an influence but only in the obvious presence of such a kinship. Though it may seem absurd at first sight, compare the hero of the first great "southern" novel, Huck Finn, in the midst of his journey to Agamemnon at Aulis as presented by Aeschylus. When Huck Finn says with such finality, "All right then, I'll go to hell," siding with Jim, we are moved more than amused. It is the high point of the novel we feel. Not, however, because Huck is on the right side of the slavery question, as we have been conditioned to applaud, for Twain's book, almost in spite of Twain, is something greater than a revised version of *Uncle Tom's Cabin*. Huck is firmly of the belief that he may very likely go to hell for his act, and if we smile at his innocent seriousness, it is largely our way of applauding courage. Similarly, Odysseus. All right then, says Odysseus, I'll risk Poseidon's wrath — and thereupon he blinds Polyphemus. This is not the place to attempt in detail the relating of frontier humor to the Greekness of southern fiction except through figurative suggestions (though one should consider whether Homer's humor is not in fact frontier humor): it is as if, in southern fiction such as *Adventures of Huckleberry Finn, The Hamlet, The Violent Bear It Away,* one has a combination of Homer and Aeschylus. And it is important to remember that, just as in Homer, the humor in these novels is a serious humor. Look at the straight faces of Faulkner's actors (as opposed to his story teller) in *The Hamlet.* The actions seem preposterous to an outsider (but then so is Agamemnon's slaying of his daughter to appease Artemis); those involved with spotted horses are led to a serious boldness by that "frenzied counselor" delusion, though the effect is comic.

On a level where there is less concern for man's outrageously comic relationship to the world, let us look at the serious, straight-faced, humorless southern fiction — though one seldom finds all humor removed. Compare William Faulkner's version of the dynasty builder, Thomas Sutpen, to the northern version of John Dos Passos' J. Ward Morehouse. The sense of violation and earned retribution hovers over *Absalom, Absalom!* as it does not over *U.S.A.* Sutpen is a self-doomed man, and he knows it, and the sign of his knowledge is his restless drive to escape the furies angered by his violations. Morehouse, on the other hand, is a Model A, not a man, with gas enough to get him a certain distance before the new model with its higher octane fuel overtakes him. Sutpen is man caught alive and kicking in permanent art; Morehouse is inevitably destined for waxwork display in some Smithsonian Institute of literary history. Or take Dreiser's version of Sutpen, Clyde Griffiths in *An American Tragedy,* where the self-responsibility is largely explained by environmental determinism. Griffiths is a case study of the sagging character that I take as typical of the northern grotesque, of the man so cut off from the ennobling possibilities of violation (whether divinely right or satanically wrong) that he cannot move his hand to take a life or to save one. He is depressingly pathetic. It is as if Dreiser's main purpose is to comment that something is missing in the northern view of man, whether that man "succeeds" as Dos Passos' hero does for the moment or fails miserably as does Clyde Griffiths.

But consider a Clyde Griffiths by a southern writer. Who cannot see something more noble than Griffiths in Flannery O'Connor's Francis Marion Tarwater, who comes to an inescapable moment of life so much like Clyde Griffiths'? Like Clyde's, Francis Marion's final temptation occurs on a boat in a lake, and with the alterative of saving or taking a life — of baptizing or drowning God's or the Devil's (he wonders which) implacable

6. The Sense of Violation

accuser, the moron child whose love seems unbearable. Tarwater knows, as Miss O'Connor puts it in her title to the novel's first chapter when it appeared in *New World Writing*, that "You Can't Be Any Poorer than Dead." It is his life he risks, not at man's hands, but at God's. His is Agamemnon's dilemma, and Huck's, put squarely in Christian terms: to baptize the child is to be enslaved to his great Uncle and the terrible Christ that haunts him for Adam's sin; to drown the child is to become enslaved to his immediate uncle, an environmental determinist, and to that more terrible Devil whose name is Nada who art in Nada, as a famous northern writer has put it. Tarwater's act of drowning the child in those terrible moments becomes, paradoxically, an act of baptism also, and he — less prideful — rises to the new life of self-responsibility, terrified by the inevitable loving wrath of God. For in spite of his will to be free, he has come to an uneasy understanding of that idea which in Christian terms (but also terms familiar to Aeschylus) says that one gives up his will to God, whose service is the only perfect freedom. It is an understanding to be earned through violation. Tarwater, like Huck and Agamemnon, has said, "All right then, I'll go to hell. It is my act," the first step toward any redemption of a free man as opposed to a machine man. Unless Christ be willingly slain, he cannot harrow hell and rise triumphant; unless God be offended there can be no merciful salvation. What an inevitably telling title then: *The Violent Bear It Away*. Not just from the days of John the Baptist, for ever since the days of Homer and Aeschylus, at least, the kingdom of Heaven has been given to the violent, and the violent bear it away. Grotesque? Aeschylus would not have thought so, who says:

> to us, though against our very will,
> even in our own despite,
> comes wisdom
> by the awful grace of God.

It is even probable that the father of Greek tragedy, who was concerned with the actor's masks and costuming so that his figure might loom large before his audience, might well have considered J. Ward Morehouse and Clyde Griffiths far more grotesque than Francis Marion Tarwater or Sutpen. Prometheus with the vulture at his liver, as huge as he is, is not so grotesque a figure of man as is Mickey Mouse.

This, then, rather than the surface materials of southern fiction, in large part explains the fascination that southern fiction has for readers in and out of the South: that informing sense one finds at its heart, a sense of man's awful responsibility. When Mencken was attacking the poverty of the South's contribution to art, ridiculing the Bible Belt morality, he did not appreciate that the immediate pressures of the South's history made it impossible for the South to meet a magazine's or newspaper's deadline for submission of art. For the South's has been a history which until recently required its masculine energies toward more immediate ends. Odysseus does not sing of Troy until Troy's fall and his own safe landing in the land of the Phaeacians. While waiting to sing, the South was holding firmly to an older view of man's relation to the world than the new sciences and philosophies of the North would allow. The masculine energies of the mid-nineteenth century South were occupied by the political and military destinies of the South—leaving, as it must, its art to the feminine mind, such a mind as Henry Timrod's or Edgar Allan Poe's. After 1865, there was the problem of sheer survival, and again art was left to the feminine mind, to Sidney Lanier and Thomas Nelson Page, while the masculine mind conjured for itself Agamemnon's waiting knife, in one way or another, in a southern or northern way.

The southern: consider Wade Hampton, a fabulous general as wily as Odysseus in the war, as full of blind rage for justice as a Greek hero. When Hampton sees his son fall mortally wounded before him, he kisses him a farewell that Odysseus and Hector would be moved by, and turns back to the battle which he controls, as full of righteous anger as ever Achilles knew. He fought until the end, until Appomattox was already history, and in the end returned to South Carolina to rebuild the burned state, the hero of his people who sent him to the Senate, until the demagogue Ben Tillman—the liberal, shouting "nigger"—unseated him. If he would appear in the state legislature as it came to a vote on the senatorship, his friends urged, the legislature could not but honor him. But in such a supplication there could be no honor, and he refused: "The Senatorship is a place to be bestowed and not to be sought or begged for."

The northern way, the way a southern mind metamorphoses to a northern: consider John B. Gordon of Georgia. A brilliant general, and a courageous one in the war. At Appomattox with his tattered troops receiving and returning the salute of the Federal troops with such dignity that the pain on both sides was almost unbearable, only to ride away from Appomattox with a northern congressman with railroad interests, and to a concern for railroads and power, using his war glory in later years as Ben Tillman used "nigger" to expand and hold his power. A southern and a northern way: Wade Hampton and John B. Gordon: John Sartoris and J. Ward Morehouse. Which is by way of saying that southern writing is very much aware of the Civil War, but that the war is only part of the background. Wade Hampton and Lee are important figures in our myth, not only for their having lost their Troy, but also for the manner of their homecoming. Wade

Hampton comes home to be slain by his Clytemnestra, South Carolina; John B. Gordon comes home to slay his, Georgia. To understand this distinction is to understand Colonel Sartoris in Faulkner and why he commits suicide, in effect, though Redmond is the instrument: Sartoris dies for fear he will murder his own.

The South, then, during and after the return of whatever tragic Agamemnons or wily Odysseuses, held tightly to its most basic unifying heritage, not one that grew so simply out of the Old South of the slave plantation, the moonlight and magnolia tradition of Thomas Nelson Page, as the North is romantically fond of thinking. The violation at the heart of southern fiction may sometimes be presented symbolically through the race question, but that slavery and a sense of guilt in the southern mind concerning the Negro is the gospel truth is only the northern version of moonlight and magnolias. If one reads that cycle of powerful stories by Faulkner, *Go Down, Moses,* with the idea I have tried to develop, he may begin to feel that here is another Homer, singing of a crime against some god of the land instead of god of the sea, requiring expiation that may be a comic one, as in "Was," or more nearly tragic as in "The Bear." Faulkner does not take his southern pen on shoulder and go to New York to write for strangers who do not recognize it as southern pen, as Robert Penn Warren of late, we hope unwittingly, has done. For in his recent book, *The Legacy of the Civil War,* Warren, like *Time,* finds an easy key to the South—the sense of guilt. Mr. Warren should remember that the prophecy requires Odysseus to return to Ithaca to find a peaceful death. Mr. Faulkner has taken his southern oar to Stockholm, and has now come home holding still firmly his and our and man's one principle of humanity which makes survival either possible or desirable—that terrible sense of personal responsibility which holds that man violates the world and the gods at least as much as the world and gods (or history, in Mr. Warren's terms) violate him.

It is this basic principle that such diverse southerners as the violent Protestant preachers of Flannery O'Connor's novels and the Catholic writer herself share, just as it was once the basic principle that Willie Stark and Robert Penn Warren shared, though they seem to have become estranged I think, since *Brother to Dragons.* Appreciating this principle, one can see that the hard cold light Miss O'Connor casts on the southern characters in her fiction is not Miss O'Connor's open invitation to the reader to ridicule them, as her strong sense of humor leads some readers to suppose. There is as much praise as condemnation—not praise of the folly and wrong-headedness that is as inevitable to a southerner as to a northerner, but praise of the courage of willing self-responsibility for the delusion that led toward folly and wrong-headedness. If her characters are blind, which is another way of saying they are human (as we learn from Sophocles' Oedipus), the ones she admires are those obviously willing to bear the consequences of their blindness—Bible salesman or Misfit. Hers is the hard cold light of love, the salient quality of which I would call masculine. One might, in fact, point out that those characters of her fiction with whom she is least sympathetic are precisely those who have lost their sense of "southernness," who have been changed by Gordon's railroad, Henry Grady's industry, and the immediate products thereof—including television. Consider her sociologist-characters, or the people her Misfit slaughters in "A Good Man Is Hard to Find." Except for their speech patterns, they are initially more northern than southern.

Which brings me to a final comment on the difference between "northern" and "southern" fiction. When I call Faulkner's and Flannery O'Connor's fiction masculine, I imply that the northern fiction I've talked about is feminine. The difference concerns the backbone the hero is left with when his actions are over, whether he sags into our pity or stands resolutely before our pity. It is the difference between Sutpen and Francis Marion Tarwater on the one hand and Clyde Griffiths and J. Ward Morehouse on the other. But it needs to be said that there is a special subspecies of northern fiction which is confused with what I have meant by southern. I will call it northern writing which uses southern materials. People who would not dream of calling Hemingway a Spanish writer because of some of his Spanish stories nevertheless call Truman Capote or Tennessee Williams southern writers because of their southern stories and plays. It is quite common, in fact, to find Faulkner, Flannery O'Connor, Capote, Carson McCullers all yoked together as southern fiction writers of the same stamp. The temptation with McCullers and O'Connor is well nigh irresistible, since both are Georgians. But surely Capote and McCullers are feminine writers in my terms—"northern" writers. When *Time Magazine* complains of southern writing as depending more on mood than craftsmanship, citing Mrs. McCullers as the particular example, the comment is wide of any telling mark. (In some of his work Faulkner is not unworthy of comparison to Joyce as craftsman, and *Time's* writer must have a very peculiar definition of craftsmanship if he misses Miss O'Connor's skill in her recent novel or Eudora Welty's careful pen.) The criticism does bear some relevance when applied, not to southern writing but to northern, when applied to McCullers and Capote and Hemingway and Dos Passos and Dreiser. For mood writing itself is a substitute for a sense of the outraged reaction to violation. Without a character with a strong sense of violation and of its consequences, a writer is almost forced to a dependence upon mood in action's stead. The loneliness that *Time* finds at the heart of Miss McCuller's fiction is related to this very characteristic of her technique, for the loneliness grows from a basic conception of man's relationship to the world quite unlike that of Faulkner or O'Connor. Nor does the self-responsibility in Miss O'Connor's characters mean an isolation of the character: it means quite the contrary, since the character's self-responsibility defines for him his relationship to the world. In the South of southern fiction (as opposed to fiction *about* the South) the violation is taken personally and the violence is personal: If you kill a man, you at least know his name and why he in particular is the victim, and that is something quite different from the accidental slaughter by auto on a turnpike or the knifing of a stranger in Central Park. It is a more human violence than that in a story by Capote where the violence lacks the burden of responsibility, especially on the victim's part. I think that just such a distinction as this may explain that rather puzzling incident in Miss O'Connor's *The Violent Bear It Away*, in which Tarwater, after murdering the child, is impersonally seduced by the citified homosexual, a leather-jacket boy in a convertible. Here is the old enemy again, not an excuse or explanation, the old enemy innocent of responsibility, and therefore more innocent and dangerous than Tarwater, though the surface worldly knowledge of each makes it appear the other way round. No wonder Tarwater tries to bring judgment day, set the world on fire.

Carson McCullers' and Truman Capote's world is a dream world through which characters float in search of an awakening. Their characters have a grotesqueness which defines them as separate from mankind, while Faulkner's and O'Connor's characters have their grotesqueness as a definition of their relationship. Consequently, McCullers' and Capote's fiction bear about the same relation to the "southern" fiction I have been defining as a bale of cotton in the Atlanta Airport Terminal bears to the South. The isolation from or relation to mankind is, as it must be, always primarily in the author. If loneliness is his understanding, he can write a kind of autobiography from a character's insides—his own—or he can describe a character from the outside, using lyric mood to disguise his detachment. That is the way Joyce, in some of his stories, convinces one of sympathetic irony. But there is always a detachment, which I think reflects a sickness of "northern" writing. This is not to say that Capote or McCullers or Joyce are incapable of "good" writing; it is merely a way of saying that there is a fascinating healthiness in southern writing, whose power comes finally not from its local materials but from the writer's sense that, good or bad, we are members one of another and violate each other and must pay for the violation (usually through violence) because of the wrathful love of whatever gods we believe in. Ultimately a writer with this sense of violation and its consequences will leave the longest scar on the world. (For art itself is a species of violence.)

There are, of course, southern and northern readers, and a northern reader, who has been lost from the old tradition of man's responsibility to the gods and the world, usually experiences an uncomfortable shock of recognition when confronted by southern fiction; he is puzzled because he is at once alien to the land he has entered and at home in it. He has intimations of immortality from that older childhood of his race which he had explained away so that he might forget it. He becomes fascinated, even sometimes revolted, not knowing whether to believe the character a mirror or wish it a mirage. If he is patient, I believe, he will come to realize that "southern" fiction is not finally about the South at all, but about that human heart Faulkner talks of in his famous Nobel Prize speech, that speech being Faulkner's act of driving an oar in foreign ground before turning home. It is not southern writing, but writing about the human heart at war with itself and the gods, capable of terrible violations, but capable also of the terrible consequences of violation through which alone, as Aeschylus says, its awful wisdom comes.

7

Southern Letters in the Twentieth Century: The Articulation of a Tradition

This essay expands upon the previous essay, "The Sense of Violation: Notes Toward a Definition of 'southern' Fiction," emphasizing the "spiritual regionalism" of southern writers as well as other cultural and literary traditions and attributes evident in southern writing: a conviction that art is mimetic, that literature can reflect the real world; an awareness of the mystery of evil; a belief in original sin; a reverence for place; a humble acceptance of the multitudinous differences evident in persons, places, and things; and recognition that existence is a gift, a grace, which points to a gracious Giver. Montgomery uses the word "southern" in two ways: as a geographical designation (thus his analysis of Faulkner's and O'Connor's fiction) and as a spiritual condition, which permits him to claim Alexander Solzhenitsyn as a southerner. His theme is that for the "southern" writer, "the slant of the sun upon a particular person in a particular place is more deeply significant of the large mystery of creation than is allowed by any conception of existence as a continuous accident or dead mechanism with which man is forced to struggle for an order of his own devising." Once again, we see Montgomery's concern with the theological assumptions underlying the Christ-centered southern writer (such as O'Connor) and the God-haunted southern writer (such as Faulkner). His point is that when the southern writer touches the world, when he treats of persons and places and things, he finds himself reaching toward the Cause of the world. Many of the texts and themes examined here are treated at greater length in Montgomery's Trilogy, The Prophetic Poet and the Spirit of the Age, *especially in volume I,* Why Flannery O'Connor Stayed Home *(Sherwood Sugden, 1981).**

*This essay originally appeared in *Modern Age* 24.2 (Spring 1980): 121–133.

I

Southern literature, like the South itself, is such a various creature that one is ill-advised to pronounce dogmatically upon it, though that is a temptation difficult to resist — caught up as we have been by that impressive flowering of letters in this century known as the "southern Renaissance." At risk of some presumption, then, I should like to limit attention to a particular kind of southern literature — or rather to a particular kind of southern writer who may be distinguished from a variety of his brothers, in and out of the South. I feel a special affinity to this writer, and for that reason let me here give warning that my testimony is partisan, though I believe it will support sound generalizations.

The writer I want to single out from his fellows is, however, an illusive creature, sometimes even to himself — self-knowledge being the treacherous knowledge it is. Besides which, our writer is not likely to practice his art from a position he has established firmly by dogma or ideology, though he may come to such a pass by the long labor of art. He is more likely intent upon looking at his immediate world with wonder and curiosity; he takes a delight in his immediate neighbor's multitudinous engagements of that world, both for his neighbor's and his art's sake. He grows from within that world, rather than choosing to stand outside it as separate from or superior to it. Certainly he does not suppose himself its creator when he is pleased by its reflection in the work he makes with words. One of his habits is that, though he may wander from his neighborhood, he is apt to return and settle down in it. That is, he does not long believe that in order to make artful use of his world he must live in New York City or on the continent. He does not feel driven, as James Joyce's young artist Stephen does, into "silence, exile, and cunning." Another sign of his peculiarity may be that he survives in his native, or even adopted, land in part through his sense of humor — without which he might well be left with only the resources of wit and irony to reach an accommodation with the mystery of existence. For wit and irony, unmoderated by some humor, become modes of dissociation from existence. The point is difficult to refine briefly, but I am attempting to point to a humor in the writer himself which reflects his acceptance of the limits of his power to shape or create existence, an acceptance of his own humanity, which is more difficult to the writer sometimes because he so easily confuses himself as maker of *a* world with God, the Maker of *the* world.

Compare the general attitude of two great writers toward the country and countrymen who feed their fiction, James Joyce and William Faulkner. There are many likenesses between them, particularly the strong attraction they share to the immediate and local, to a history that is in their blood and memory, at every point adjacent to their senses in an immediate way. Still, I at least sense in Joyce's fiction a feeling of discomfort with the ordinary Dubliner, almost at times an embarrassment in his presence, which seems to require the poet's distancing himself through irony and wit, but not for his art's sake alone. Not just Stephen Dedalus, but Joyce himself must fight against sounding like that agonizing Quinton Compson at Harvard who insists at the top of his voice that he *doesn't* hate the South. I'm suggesting that the distance between Faulkner and his Quinton is more marked than that between Joyce and his Stephen. In Faulkner one senses an amused acceptance of the ordinary Mississippian, an openness to the foibles of the simple, an attitude that sometimes rises to lyrical paeans or becomes entangled in a comedy of the ridiculous given an epic sweep, as in "Spotted Horses."

Incidentally, I am not suggesting that our southern writer inevitably creates masterpieces—that such a fellow by his loving acceptance of limitations, the humility that evidences itself often as humor, is the superior of Joyce. In fact, irony and wit may afford such control of one's art that the writer protects himself against that excess sentiment which so easily turns into sentimentality. The fear that sentiment may turn treacherous to his art haunts Joyce, I think, but I think one must search hard to find instances of just plain bad writing in the body of his work; the task is easier in Faulkner's. Our southern writer is not always the consummate craftsman, though he is often so. For craft has to do more immediately with the mystery of a writer's particular gifts and with his industry in the service of that limited gift. These more personal characteristics will always set him apart as discrete from any category like southern or Irish or Russian.

We must not confuse our writer with the southerner who may be said to write "about" the South, anymore than we would confuse any writer using Irish matter with a Joyce or a Yeats. We certainly don't want to confuse him with those who intend to please a tourist curiosity—those who cater to an amorphous, deracinated audience whose number in this world is legion, whether they be titillated by "Too-allure-a-lure-a" or "Way down upon the Sewanee River." Frank Yerby or Margaret Mitchell may serve as example here of the writer who cultivates an audience's residual interest in the historical—our vague nostalgia for origins which so easily atrophies into an appetite for the fanciful and sentimental—the last sad state into which our ontological hunger may fall. Our writer to the contrary is intense in his concern for concrete reality as it may give body to his art, incorporate his word world. But that interest includes his concern for the hard complexities of history. He knows that our history, anchored in place, has both a threatening and a loving immediacy which our indulgent fancy violates at hazard to artist or audience. That is, he knows in words I adapt from T.S. Eliot that "A people without history / Is not redeemed from time, for history is a pattern / Of timeless moments" which bear inexorably upon this very moment, in this very place. Those moments may not be denied without fatal distortions of the present which, in a favorite Faulknerean word, "bequeath" deformations of reality to the future — a sort of congenital spiritual distortion of community, if I may be allowed a metaphysical trope.

Our writer, we are saying, has a strong sense of place and person in a relationship which is nucleus to the growing body of a community in time; community always bears deep down both the past and future. He does not suppose that the particulars of either setting or character in his fiction are created *ex nihilo* by the artist, though he may and should enjoy those special freedoms Aristotle distinguishes in art as opposed to history, the freedoms of the possible or probable. He knows through his very breathing that in the world he inhabits as man, the seasons of being are affected at a depth more profound than any empirical measure of time or place allow. Thus, although he is likely to focus upon a single house and family, a small town, a county, he does so — not to lament social poverty or psychological isolation, as temporal uses of the world might be content to do — but to reveal a largeness hidden in the limited. Nor does he use the local — the "southern" — to dramatize what turns out to be only a private, isolated version of the fabulous Self lost among the accidental stars. That sort of writer may write of any place or no place, since place is neither congenial to nor particularly relevant to his concern; he is a displaced person by preference. If he were to put the point, he might preach it as a Haze Motes does in Flannery O'Connor's *Wise Blood:*

> I preach there are all kinds or truth, your truth and somebody else's, but behind all of them, there's only one truth and that is that there's no truth.... Where you come from is gone, where you thought you were going to never was there, and where you are is no good unless you can get away from it. Where is there a place for you to be? No place. Nothing outside you can give you any place.

The placeless writer may use the same material world as a Flannery O'Connor, but it will not be used in the same way, for what Miss O'Connor sees and what our Motes-like writer sees are quite different, though they look at the same object.

Our southern writer does not see himself as merely the creator of a textual world, a cage of words such as Haze's, which he builds to serve as

7. Southern Letters in the Twentieth Century 61

an arena for the antics of that aberrant modern god, the Self, which has lost its belief in any reality separate from its own marooned awareness. And if he does not believe that his own consciousness occupies such a closed world, neither will he see art as so divorced from his fellows that each lonely mind is forever trapped within its symbolic posturings—its symbols having no extrinsic referents and its order internally willed but irrelevant to any meaning, even to the trapped Self. That is the current fad in much of our criticism and philosophy and art, but he sees it as a fad, perhaps not unrelated to such mass isolationism as disco dancing.

Put in a positive, older, and intellectually more viable way: our southern writer is mimetic. He believes that art, however else it may differ from the other modes of the mind's hymns to existence—the modes of science or philosophy or theology—also bears an appreciable relation to reality beyond itself. His position on art and its ends is a corollary to his belief that the individual Self has real and not illusional relations with other Selves in communities wherever two or three are gathered together. That is, he believes we are bound in a mystery larger than his mastery of art, without which binding one's art or science or philosophy becomes only a form of magic. Such a binding is larger and more inclusive than any particular calling to us within the world—to be a doctor or lawyer or writer. And our writer will very likely begin to suspect that we are bound not only in time but beyond time, in a calling which speaks to him through the one given which underlies all the structures of his awareness, all the symbols through which he may attempt to touch reality. That one given is *existence itself*.

That larger binding, he at least senses, is within an ordering of all being which should satisfy our desire for beginning and end; without the limits of beginning and end, particularity itself ceases to have any meaning. Those are deep hungers in us for a completeness of the Self, hungers buried essentially in the soul. For *ontology* and *teleology* are not merely technical names of categories of thought created by the rational mind for its entertainment, though often so used. If the philosopher, scientist, theologian wrestle in their several ways with these seemingly abstract terms, our writer attempts as poet to incarnate a reality that feeds the hunger, to give local habitation and a name to our desire—whether he presents his hero as struggling to return to some Ithaca, or as a pilgrim with momentary vision of a multifoliate rose embraced by an inexpressible light beyond all our purgatorial struggles with dark and light, or a possessed creature trying to subdue a hundred square miles of Mississippi wilderness to his own bent desire. The end we reach toward may be a false one; our struggles for origins within the middleness of reality may be quite misguided.

But our beginnings within the complexity of reality stir a valid desire for large ends. Caught in the muddling middle, we begin where all drama of the spirit must begin, in that middle. As Flannery O'Connor says of us, recognizing our shared experience of this confusing *metaxy*, this "in-between-ness" that threatens us: "There is something in us as storytellers and as listeners to stories, that demands that what falls at least be offered the chance to be restored."

For our writer, man's being — man's Self — cannot be an absolute agent without originating cause or proper end, not an accident of accidents and thus always and only the meaningless victim of a meaningless middle. For he senses or believes or knows that even accidental existence must happen within some inclusive reference if the concept of the *accidental* is to have any meaning at all. And he cannot believe that his own mind is a sufficient inclusive reference. For him, the hunger for a "chance to be restored" will become foil in his drama of fallen man's several dreams of progress, spawned by gnostic presumptions against being that are as ancient as that first fall in the garden, the old presumptions of the Self as dominant power in this infinite, swampy middle. Thus pride or hubris — however low and common or high and royal his agents may be — becomes the high theme of his storytelling.

Now the modern reader hungers for the redemptive act, in spite of his being inhabitant of a world which tries to deny redemption except as it may be used metaphorically to describe some psychological or sociological recovery that implies man the ultimate god of the meaningless middle. And I contend that such a hunger is a sign of the possibility of his return to health. One hungers because there is such a creature as food, St. Thomas says. One is ill because there is such a state as health. One founders or fails or falls only as measured against some high calling to a graceful dance. Such modern hunger speaks ancient origins. But, as Miss O'Connor adds in the passage just quoted, our writer's audience has largely forgotten the cost of restoration, for our "sense of evil is diluted or lacking altogether." From her own position, the cost of evil to the individual is an absolute beyond all worldly inflations, all relative scales, being the absolute loss of the Self. Her Tarwater, in *The Violent Bear It Away*, discovers that the cost exceeds the Self's solvency. He is consumed almost to extinction, but also discovers some restoration in the terror of an absolute mercy which beyond all reason buys him out of self-centered bankruptcy.

Our southern writer may not, of course, be so resolutely convinced by faith and reason of a transcendent God. Flannery O'Connor is; William Faulkner is not. But it is in the light of such argument as she makes, I think, that one begins to recognize the considerable difference between the visions radiated by the God-haunted writer like Faulkner and those versions of existence made by Man-haunted writers like Flaubert, James, Hemingway, Fitzgerald. Or, nearer home, the difference becomes conspicuous between Flannery O'Connor, Andrew Lytle, Madison Jones as southern writers and Carson McCullers, Shirley Ann Grau, Truman Capote as southern writers.

To borrow from our writer's Yankee cousin, Nathaniel Hawthorne, we may say that he is reluctant to stray too far from the town pump or the well on the old family place precisely because, despite the reflections of the local in such waters, he knows they are deeper than time and more healing than any words the Self may speak of and to itself alone. Still, this inclination to the local is easily misunderstood by those who would believe the homeplace well polluted by provincialism. As I have already hinted, there is misunderstanding not only by the postmodernist anarchist mind that would drink out of any muddy puddle and smack in delight to outrage the supposedly innocent among us, denying the existence of thirst even as he does so. I say supposedly innocent, remembering the Bible salesman in "Good Country People," who shatters Hulga, the existentialist with a Ph.D.: "You ain't so smart. I been believing in nothing ever since I was born."

In another direction, our southern writer is misunderstood by that postnaturalist mind which is so heavily at home in the academy, particularly by those who see literature as a sector of our intellectual estate to be seized by the pseudo-sciences of sociology and psychology and turned to social and political ends. The anarchist of whom we spoke first sees mimesis as an illusion; for him, in Gerald Graff's words, there is "no such thing as a real object outside language, no 'nature' or 'real life' outside the literary text, no real text beyond the critical interpretation, and no real persons or institutions behind the multiplicity of messages human beings produce. Everything is swallowed up in an infinite regress of textuality."[1] Such anarchy, while destructive of the fabric of society, is not so conspicuously destructive as the alliance of sociology and psychology when turned upon the social fabric. One is tempted to remark then with the irony Chaucer uses about his Doctour of Phisyk and apothecaries: " ech of hem made other for to winne." The sociopsychologist or psychosociologist takes our writer's work as a local naturalism which may be made to yield evidence suited to his own gnostic ideology.

Yet his denial of nature or life is only partial in contrast to the anarchistic structuralist's. He must admit the existence of some reality — the social world for the sociologist, the psychic world for the psychologist. Still, he sees it existing for the sake of being shaped, being restructured to suit some primarily human dream. It is no accident that sociology and psychology have become dominant forces in the civil state since World War II, subordinating even Harvard economists to janitorial status in the halls of Congress and in the White House. For since the days of Auguste Comte the state has been gradually transformed into the gnostic son of the world, the substitute Emmanuel, and the Holy Spirit of social humanity has been increasingly called into a presence as lord and giver of life to individual man, filling the embarrassing gap between human knowledge and human power in the ideological struggles to subjugate existence to human will. A humanistic priesthood has emerged, through which one is required to worship an abstraction — humanity — as the official state religion under the threat of exile for both heresy and treason. Its principal established college of priests is called H.E.W., pronounced *hew*, as you know, and its energy and our substance are spent largely in hewing individual persons to fit its vague dream of an ideal citizen.

II

We must observe carefully, then, how our southern writer differs in his address to reality, not only from the anarchist mind, but from the gnostic directors of social and psychic being also. No matter how particular nor how local his material, however deeply colored by literal social and psychological aspects of man's being, he is not so much acting as reporter or statistician of particularity as he is bearing witness to depths in reality beyond all facts or photographs. For he knows, again to summon Flannery O'Connor, that a "view taken in the light of the absolute will include a good deal more than one taken merely in the light provided by a house-to-house survey." One is not likely at this late date, despite those large forces that distort reality, to miss this point in Faulkner's postage stamp county, unless one's intellect and sensibilities have been fatally atrophied. To cite once more that very articulate spokesman for our southern writer, Miss O'Connor, "the longer you look at an object, the more of the world you see in it; and it's well to remember that the serious fiction writer always writes about the whole world, no matter how limited his particular scene." That is why the dedicated, unblinking naturalist will always write more largely than the academic definition of *naturalism* — assuming in him a talent and industry in support of his courage in the presence of creation.

To misunderstand this point, as many critics have done in attempting to come to terms with the complexity of the southern Renaissance, is to see this southern phenomenon only at its social and psychological level, the point at which our southern writer himself begins. That is why I keep underlining my theme: for our writer, the slant of the sun upon a particular person in a particular place is more deeply significant of the large mystery of creation than is allowed by any conception of existence as a continuous accident or dead mechanism with which man is forced to struggle for an order of his own devising. He sees both the postmodernist anarchist and the gnostic disciple of old Enlightenment thought attempting to reorder creation under their Banner of Progress, when he is seeking the dance. We turn towards an immanence that denies transcendence with the coming of nominalism, of Machiavelli, the Philosophes, and their disciples. It is a turning Chesterton capsules in remarking the difference between Chaucer's world and ours: up to a certain point in the West life is understood as a dance, after which we decide it is a race.

The southerner of whom we are speaking is going to be suspicious of any appeal to progress as substitute for a profound teleological object. He remembers something of the grace of the dance. He will know, in his heart if not his head — by *intellectus* if not by *ratio* as the medieval man of letters might put it — that the anarchist or the Sons of the Enlightenment dedicated to power operate out of the same false ground. For both of them the In-between they wish to manage is an accident which has inexorably thrown them up on the shores of a dead world. Our writer, to the contrary, sees both being itself and the conditions of man's particular being as givens. And the given implies a giver, however confounding the approach to the giver through the agency of those gifts. Therefore, our writer by his art opposes those violations of the world that proceed from any premise of existence as either random chaos or ordered but spiritless mechanism.

A reading of his work at what criticism has called the naturalistic level, as a ground for exercising social or psychic manipulations of complex existence, will overlook the spiritual dimension of that work, particularly its reverence of person and place and thing. For our writer, whether he presents us a version of community on so small a scale as one of Miss O'Connor's decimated families or so large as Faulkner's rich Yoknapatawpha County, reflects the community as a spiritual organism, though fallen from fullness. Nor need one be the Thomist Miss O'Connor is to realize that in man's limited estate he necessarily approaches the spiritual in the concrete, created world that is always just at hand. To touch that world is already to reach toward its cause, even if one realize that act as a spiritual one only feebly or not at all. The gnostic manipulator is himself subject to such a shock of recognition, as occasional conversions suggest. Man has believed for a very long time that the first intellectual step along the spiritual road is made within the country of naturalism, through one's body;

it is a step made within a context of our sensual response to some reality separate from the self. The belief is in Homer and Aristotle, in Dante and St. Thomas.

So the southern writer we speak of observes that the increasing power claimed by a denatured naturalism these past hundred years or more — *denatured*, since nature divorced from its cause by gnostic will can be seen only as unnatural — that growing power has strangled the spiritual dimension of creation itself. Or rather, it has estranged us from that spiritual dimension, for such gnostic reconstructions of reality are fundamentally illusions. Our writer understands such a power to be a retrogression into a provincialism, into a primitivism, more limited than that we encounter in Homer or find revealed by the highly sophisticated exploration of scholars like Mircea Eliade. It is a provincialism exposed to us by Richard Weaver, Gerhart Niemeyer, Eric Voegelin — such scholars whom our writer may or may not have read. Our writer sees the distortions of reality, but he knows also that it is still at the level of nature that he must work. That is where the artist begins, and particularly at the level of human nature with its spectacles of the psychological and sociological and historical upon which he depends heavily for his incarnational act as artist. Each person, he says along with John Donne, is a little world made cunningly of elements and an angelic sprite. And through representations of that little world — which he places in the larger context of family and community in nature — a much larger world is revealed by his practice of similitude and dissimilitude. The more fully he reveals that little world, the more largely he speaks outward to a world beyond the boundaries of any literal time or place.

He recognizes, in words I adapt from Stark Young's contribution to *I'll Take My Stand*, that he is called to witness certain principles intrinsic to creation, not because those principles belong to him, but because he belongs to those principles. To put the point as Allen Tate might do, he is a spiritual regionalist,[2] not an intellectual provincial, that secular gnostic of whom Eric Voegelin has written so revealingly. In Voegelin's sense of the term, which we have used repeatedly here, our writer finds himself deeply engaged by the "In-between," the only immediate source for the material of his made world.[3] But he does so with an openness of mind and spirit toward the complication of existence, in consequence of which he finds himself inevitably anti-gnostic. Thus he celebrates the rich complexity of existence, although to celebrate that complexity does not mean to present it with an artificial sweetness and light. We may see this point everywhere in William Faulkner's work. In *Absalom, Absalom!* Thomas Sutpen attempts to limit existence to an arena of a hundred square miles by sheer dominance over the land and the creatures bounded by that artificial measure of nature; his attempt to manipulate man and nature is tragically shadowed. And in *Go Down, Moses* Ike McCaslin attempts to reject any binding by place or history, abandoning his inherited land and sacrificing persons dear to him beyond his romantic imaginings, as he comes at last to realize. For Faulkner distinguishes between the responsibility of a man's stewardship within the grounds of being and man's old temptation to control being itself, the gnostic principle which Christian orthodoxy sees in our first parents' violation of creation in the Garden. There is a very complex dramatization of this distinction in *Go Down, Moses*, which I may only touch upon here to make my point a little clearer, though the rich texture of Ike's place in nature and history warrants a longer devotion.[4]

In those stories we witness two gnostic forces in conflict. There is the obvious active destruction by the invading timber companies that ravage the Big Woods, but it is an encroachment upon a world Ike McCaslin has already abandoned through the illusion of his sacrificial act. Ike McCaslin may be described as a passive gnostic; in an ultimately destructive way he abandons his responsibility as steward of place in time. Caught between these two forces, trying to rediscover and redefine man's ordinate responsibility in nature is McCaslin Edmonds, who must even bear Ike's name more heavily in consequence of Ike's refusal. For he is an Edmonds and not so directly descended as Ike. Ike supposes that by relinquishing his title to Old Corothers McCaslin's land, he may separate himself from tainted history by repudiating it and in some degree "anneal" the wrongs of his forefathers. He intends a sacrificial act, but he presumes to rescue the world he inherits, to redeem time as it were, as if he could command grace. As he comes to realize at last in the story "Delta Autumn," man may be a waster of the world through the ravenous appetites so general in community, but man may also mistake himself as sufficient agent of grace, whether grace will or not. That is, Ike presumes a role which orthodox tradition allows only to Christ.

If we call this kind of southern writing mimetic, we acknowledge that its limits are determined by the order of creation. Its limits must also be distinguished from those of science or philosophy or theology. The possible or probable are displayed as dramatic speculation upon the complexity of existence in a way quite separate from those explorations made by biochemist or historian or metaphysician, as the artist slowly learns, sometimes with great difficulty. He may nevertheless present our nature in such a way that it becomes increasingly difficult for the sensitive mind to deny a spiritual dimension to reality, most particularly that spiritual dimension in man that is man's by virtue of the elemental gift of his existence. For it is out of this gift that scientist or philosopher or historian or poet fashions his responses to creation. Whether one clear and plant a few acres or exercise civil authority in Washington, D.C., the gesture toward order and growth is inevitably a gesture beyond the Self and toward the cause of order, however willful or blind one is to the root cause of his gesture. It is the gift of being that makes gesture possible, and within this gift we are inexorably bound one to another.

For this reason we must not overlook, in our brief sketch of the southern writer, his appearance in places other than the American South, as if we supposed him to be found only below the Potomac River and east of the Mississippi. So then one may well put "southern" in quotation marks. I have, for instance, called attention to a close kinship between those Soviet dissidents who published a collection of essays called *From Under the Rubble* in 1974 and those southerners who published *I'll Take My Stand* in 1930. (See my essays on Solzhenitsyn in *The Men I Have Chosen for Fathers*.) And Allen Tate's essay of the 1940's called "The New Provincialism" has passages strikingly interchangeable with Solzhenitsyn's essay "The Smatterers," particularly as they express a mutual reverence for place and a concern for man's stewardship in place as that commitment to the created world relates to man's spiritual nature. Solzhenitsyn, like our southern writer, recognizes in the aberrant refusal to serve, or in the rapacious pursuit of self-service, the shadow of an evil inclination in man's will that neither anarchy nor gnostic reconstructions of reality have succeeded in explaining away.

It is to this problem of evil in man that we might turn in detail, given world enough and time, to suggest why the southern writer's very conspicuous concern for willful violence reflects a failure in man not peculiar to the South nor to recent history, though modern responses to violence are so confused as to make it appear that we here encounter a new problem. It is a sign of hope in a dark time that this literature speaks resonantly to the world in general. It is a prophetic literature, prophetic in the sense that it recalls us to the once known but now largely forgotten gifts of being. And it is this aspect of our writer's work, as well as his superb craftsmanship, that attracts attention outside the South. Man's deliberate and random evil, in the face of his obligation to pursue good, speaks to the large confusions all about us— wherever man touches the created world. But wherever man touches the world, somewhere among his number will be found this creature we have been pursuing, the so-called "southern" writer. He does not turn away from the problem of evil, not attempt to explain evil away in such a manner that we may be left comfortably irresponsible, the self-made victim of appetites we tend to elevate to the role of spiritual callings of the Self to the pathetic Self.

III

I begin with a quotation from Richard Weaver's *Ideas Have Consequences*, that very large little book which traces the intellectual decline of the West back to William of Occam. But let us recall here that Weaver's small book was written after his intense study under Cleanth Brooks and Robert Penn Warren, published posthumously as *The Southern Tradition at Bay*. The intrusion of Occam's nominalism into that larger realism which held creation in relation to its transcendent cause, Weaver argues, is an intrusion whose consequences divided man against himself. Early on in *Ideas Have Consequences*, Weaver says that we moderns find ourselves trapped between sentimentality and brutality: "sentimentality, with its emotion lavished upon the trivial and absurd ... brutality, which can make no distinctions in the application of violence." "Those who [base] their lives on the unintelligence of sentimentality fight to save themselves with the unintelligence of brutality." Thus our senseless affections and hatreds, rising out of the "unintelligence of sentimentality," lead to the large destructions of recent history with which we are so familiar, effects out of our struggle for self-justification. In our time — that is, from the time of Adolf Eichmann and Auschwitz down to the Reverend Jim Jones of Jonestown, Guyana — the gnostic's detachment from being seems increasingly to assault our residual sensibilities in terrible tableaux. It disturbs us particularly when the effects reach a level of sensational action whose spectacle no longer allows out inattention. The horror at Auschwitz or Jonestown seems a personal assault because we have forgotten the evil that is potential in each man's power over nature but are reminded by events beyond our understanding that we are nevertheless members one of another, even in such dark displays of community as mass murder. The gnostic manipulators of being, Voegelin's "directors" of the reconstructions of reality to fit millennial dreams of an infinite variety, find it expedient to obscure that potential evil common to all men, for in order to distill power from the ferment of the "popular spirit of the age" it is important that they not disturb that volatile source. Otherwise their reductions of being in the name of humanity make the power highly unstable. Not only must the dreamed end be persuasively presented as a common good, but the source of that power to be directed to the good end must be assumed uncontaminated, lest the hint of spiritual pollution at the source of power affect the consent of our will that the power be used to construct the dream. Little wonder then that "original sin" in that source — individual man — as either metaphorical or literal must be removed from our reflection as a species of Neanderthal theology. But when an Eichmann or a Jones at last stands before us as agent of murder on a statistically grand scale, we are astounded by the seeming disparity between the destruction and the insignificant, obscure agent. Our easy dreams become disturbed. And the popular spirit stirs in a threatening way. The death penalty might even be reinstated.

We are shocked, I suggest, because we have been willingly led to forget the complexity of human nature spoken to by the concept of original sin, a doctrine many southern writers are loath to abandon. For if the hero need not be an Oedipus or a Count Roland or a King Richard I, neither must the villain be so conspicuous a figure on the stage of our awareness as Iago or Count Ganelon, a point Faulkner makes with disturbing effect through his unfolding of Flem Snopes and Popeye. We tend to come to terms with a Sutpen, or with a Stalin or Hitler, our anger and bafflement assuaged as our understanding is flattered by submerged Hegelean thought. These agents are instances of a coincidence of power in dynamic if terrifying figures, when seen in that reduction of reality into the myth of our age, historicism. Through such figures move the great contending forces of an age. They become "archetypal" like Attila or Robespierre or Napoleon. Their great acts of destruction underline climaxes in the flux of history, seeming to give history a god-like direction in the flow of time when measured by our post-Hegelean mind. But then comes such a functionary as Eichmann, a high school dropout, the failed son of a tram company accountant, who becomes an efficiency expert in transporting millions beyond time in a "final solution." He becomes an absolutist of ordered fact beyond his father's fondest dreams. And what of such a peripheral figure as the Reverend Jim Jones, who scatters the random lees of our progressivist social world on a jungle floor to be displayed in unliving color on the cover of *Time*? What of such an inconspicuous West Virginia child as that small boy buying candy at the corner store in West Virginia who suddenly blooms darkly in our evening paper out of California under the name of Charles Manson?

Anonymous, hidden evil breaks out, rises to the level of a name no longer inconspicuous, for the name itself gains a magnitude by the enormity of effect wrought by the obscure agent of history bearing that name. *Adolf Eichmann* is to be forever a substitute for the millions of nameless common and uncommon people he helped destroy in the name of the apocalyptic "final solution." Hannah Arendt, having attended the Eichmann trial in Jerusalem, is arrested by a new idea, "the banality of evil."

The apparent contradiction between her new concept of evil and what she calls "our tradition of thought" which sees evil as "something demonic" led her to a two-volume reconsideration of the problem, *The Life of the Mind*, in which she examines the nature of thinking, willing, judging. Whether she would have held to her new concept is problematic, since she did not live to complete the section of the work on judging. But in setting out she says of Eichmann: "I was struck by a manifest shallowness in the doer that made it impossible to trace the uncontestable evil of his deeds to any deeper level of roots or motives. The deed was monstrous, but the doer ... was quite ordinary, commonplace, and neither demonic nor monstrous." The "only notable characteristic one could detect in his past behavior as well as in his behavior during the trial ... was something entirely negative, it was not stupidity but *thoughtlessness*." And reflecting on the "macabre comedy" resulting from Eichamnn's helplessness, caught as he was in his "cliché-ridden language," she adds: "Clichés, stock phrases, adherence to conventional, standardized codes of expression and conduct have the socially recognized function of protecting us against reality," lest we exhaust ourselves by the necessity of a constant intellectual engagement of the events and facts always pressing upon us. The consequence of such a withdrawal from reality is the disjunction of thought and action, leading to such macabre comedy as that in Eichmann as he stands before the Israeli court.

That staged spectacle leads Miss Arendt to the questions she is to pursue in her two volumes: "Is evil-doing (the sins of omission, as well as the sins of commission) possible in default of not just 'base motives' (as the law calls them) but of any motives whatever, of any particular prompting of interest or volition? Is wickedness, however we may define it, this being 'determined to prove a villain,' *not* a necessary condition for evil-doing? Might the problem of good and evil, our faculty for telling right from wrong, be connected with our faculty of though?" If the answer to these questions is *yes*, as Miss Arendt implies, then we are left with an enormous problem in attempting to deal with an Eichmann. For we must conclude in this line of thought that he is innocent of wickedness, that his participation in the slaughter of other innocents is an accident of forces which have not yet yielded to the science of thought, an accident of forces loosed by history but not yet subjected to the control of gnosis. Even the ground of our outrage at brutalities is eroded, since outrage is itself presumably susceptible to the control of knowledge.

Now the supposition that wickedness is not necessarily a condition for evil-doing is scarcely new; it is a doctrine progressively advanced these past two hundred years till it has in fact become the new orthodoxy. But tolerance of evil as a social principle out of philosophical determinism has had little support in the American South, at least up to the present. Indeed, the fierceness with which the South has resisted such a principle has intensified some judgments of the South as evilly and sinfully inclined, in a blatant violation of its own principle on the part of the principle's most rabid partisans. The murderer, an old argument said, is no more guilty of his so-called "crime" than is his knife, an argument still generally rejected as nonsense by most southerners— and specifically rejected by some advocates of that principle when it is the South to be judged.

What brings Miss Arendt's question into arresting focus is not that it is a new doctrine, but the enormity of its effects upon our world in our recent history. And what is called into question most particularly is our growing tolerance toward evil, a tolerance established as one of the conditions of millennial progress from the days of Machiavelli into our own recent machinations of human rights as a political instrument in foreign policy. It is one of history's little ironies that we witness a president from the South operating within this new tradition, though professing the opposite. (Richard Weaver's warning of the relation between sentimentality and brutality ought to be heeded, particularly by a certain presidential hopeful from Massachusetts.)

When the Machiavellian figure is discovered operating in the large movements of history, our judgment is tempered by questions of net gain. Evil effects, in pursuit of progress, are a consequence of high motives. But when a figure who in his effects looms large and Machiavellian is discovered among the ordinary everyday members of humanity, rather than in the pantheon of the gods of progress, we are likely to reexamine our intellectual tolerance of evil. An Eichmann, a Jones, a Manson may be sleeping in the room upstairs or sitting down with us at our last supper. We might even encounter him on a deserted dirt road in Georgia, as Flannery O'Connor's grandmother does in her story "A Good Man Is Hard to Find."

The argument that wickedness is not the necessary ground in the individual out of which evil deeds grow is the line of thought which has, of course, been overwhelmingly advanced by those new sciences, sociology and its handmaiden psychology; the arguments of those disciplines have generally narrowed the possibilities of individual freedom and responsibility until, in the cliché language of Miss O'Connor's Rayber Tarwater in her novel *The Violent Bear It Away*, such a creature as Eichmann must be logically excused on the ground that he is somehow "an accident of nature" no less than Rayber's own idiot child.[5] If action is forced upon society by the enormity of an evil deed, it is considered a corrective of nature, execution or incarceration thus being reduced from any relation to retribution.

For neither anger nor love find any rational role in such actions. Rayber Tarwater in spite of himself is so moved by love for his idiot son that he cannot kill the child, but he can understand his love only as aberration, an encroaching insanity.

Recently Walter Berns (*Harper's*, April 1979) has urged us to consider that anger directed against those who commit evil deeds at least "acknowledges the humanity of its objects: it holds them accountable for what they do. And in holding particular men responsible, it pays them the respect that is due them as men." The failure of his fellows to hold that degree of respect for him, who choose rather to explain him away as a mechanistic creature of nature, is the maddening pain in Miss O'Connor's Misfit. Good having been explained away, he has only his evil to give him any sense of being. Ironically, he's a better "Christian" than many who profess the faith, since his sense of loss is a sense of having lost the *good*. It would not be difficult to persuade the Misfit of the reality of original sin, as the grandmother discovers with shocking finality. Berns puts the conclusion to be drawn from our absence of anger: "If, then, men are not angry when someone else is robbed, raped or murdered, the implication is that no moral community exists, because those men do not care for anyone other than themselves." It is a conclusion that the Misfit feels forced to: "it's nothing for you to do but enjoy the few minutes you got left the best way you can — by killing somebody or burning down his house or doing some other meanness to him." Even then, "It's [*i.e., there's*] no real pleasure in life."

One is struck on reading Miss Arendt's characterization of Eichmann by its aptness to Miss O'Connor's Misfit. "A Good Man Is Hard to Find" is, from its title to its concluding words, a story whose texture of clichés develops a macabre comedy; but that story suggests that clichés are something quite other than a means of protecting one "against reality," in their origins at lest, though her characters pay a terrible price again and again for using them as a shield against reality. The relation of manners to mystery is a constant one in southern literature as it attempts to rescue cliché in its origins. The sense of community as a body in time and place — of members dead and dying and to be born — focused upon a geographical point, is strong in its anti-gnostic stance. For what is implicit and often overt is the attempt to reaffirm the order of creation as transcendent in its origins.

What we wish to remark here is that the language which entraps an Eichmann is one which Eric Voegelin would describe as residual symbols that have become opaque; it is this aspect of cliché which effects one's removal from reality, a recovery of translucence in those symbols leading one back to reality, a point Miss O'Connor repeatedly dramatizes. But most important to our concern, we must remember that the individual, in the very act of using language, participates in evil—bears false witness—and the incommensurate distance between the doer and the deed which is revealed in startling events awakens in us the realization that there is a mystery in evil itself, toward which we are often willingly drawn, since we do not will otherwise. The neutrality of the will is, alas, one of those comfortable illusions we cling to so that the tensions within the world seem relaxed. We wish in the words of a popular song to this effect, to go "rolling with the flow."

The mysterious attraction of evil is a principle in human nature that our southern writer has rather constantly addressed himself to as he bears witness to the reality of man in the world, for he sees in each of us some degree of participation that makes each in some degree a Misfit. I have suggested that there is a celebration of good in the drama of our desperate fight to establish at least some claim to evil against social and psychological and philosophical attempts to deprive us of that birthright. It is only through a blinding pride, which may exhibit itself as a banal disjunction through cliché from the reality of the evil in our deeds—as with an Eichmann or a Jones or a Manson—that we are able to deny our kinship to such arresting figurings of man as Miss O'Connor's Misfit. In the southern literature we have been talking about, we find ourselves already revealed in grotesque distortions that elicit both terror and laughter.

Our writer, then, is the prophetic poet, about whom I have written at length in a three-volume work *The Prophetic Poet and the Spirit of the Age*. I repeat in closing that he bears witness beyond the limits of art's projections of man's struggle within the *metaxy*, the "In-between." He knows this in his blood if not in his head, even as Haze Motes knows it in resisting his own calling to prophecy; even as so sophisticated a poet as T.S. Eliot comes to know it in his heart when he is at last able to make that gesture celebrated at the close of *The Waste Land*, that "awful daring of a moment's surrender / Which an age of prudence can never retract." I emphasize that distinction in closing, the old difference made between *reason* and the *understanding*. One is required to bring those complementary faculties of the soul into an ordinate support, each of the other, for the good health of the soul. The failure to do so brings us to a dissociation of sensibilities at a greater depth of the soul than those spectacles of the soul—our symbolic ordering in art or government. *Ratio ET Intellectus*, says the old scholastic formulation, grown out of Heraclitus through our principal thinkers into its scholastic formulation in St. Thomas. The loss of that relationship may set any man at any moment on the road away from reality. But when a whole civilization loses it, that civilization has secularized the spiritual faculty of the reason or of the understanding and becomes secular gnostic, whether it be categorized as rationalistic or romantic. There follows an inevitable abandonment of the dance for the race toward apocalypse, spectacles of which are everywhere about us, as in that encounter in Tennessee recently between the would be saviors of the snail darter and the champions of a water power Hawthorne would not understand. We have moved rapidly in this race of progress, from Monkey Trial to Minnow Trail in confusions beyond the art of satire.

If we learn this basic truth about Western man from our southern literature as we enjoy its various gifts, we will have begun to move toward a participation in community, the living body of humanity. As misfits all, we may encounter with the shock of joy a recognition of "a good under construction" in us, in Miss O'Connor's phrase. Her Hulga, we remember, was christened Joy by a mother given to cliché, and so changes her own name to the ugliest she can think of, as if that might change her nature. The story "Good Country People" leaves Hulga thunder-struck by the Bible salesman. That tempter, walking up and down the earth, is right about Hulga's futile attempt to raise nothingness to an absolute by reason. His prophecy fits us all in a special way; we're all born believing in nothing, a condition of the fortunate fall. The question is whether we have believed in nothingness "ever since." At that level, of course, there is no such thing as "southern" literature.

Notes

1. *Literature Against Itself: Literary Ideas in Modern Society* (Chicago: University of Chicago Press, 1979), p. 61. Professor Graff's book is a searching critique of the sterility in post-modernist criticism.

2. "Regionalism is ... limited in space but not in time. The provincial attitude is limited in time but not in space ... provincialism is that state of mind in which regional men lose their origin in the past and its continuity into the present, and begin every day as if there had been no yesterday ... what a difference — and it is a difference between two worlds: the provincial world of the present, which sees in material welfare and legal justice the whole solution to the human problem; and the classical-Christian world, based upon regional consciousness, which held that honor, truth, imagination, human dignity, and limited acquisitiveness, could alone justify a social order however rich and efficient it may be.... From now on we are committed to seeing *with*, not *through* the eye: we, as provincials who do not live anywhere." Allen Tate, "The New Provincialism," *Virginia Quarterly Review*, 1945.

3. "Existence has the structure of the In-Between, of the Platonic metaxy, and if anything is constant in the history of mankind it is the language of tension between life and death, immortality and mortality, perfection and imperfection, time and timelessness, between order and disorder, truth and untruth, sense and senselessness of existence; between *amor Dei* and *amor sui*, *l'âme ouverte* and *l'âme close*; between the virtues of openness toward the ground of being such as faith, hope and love and the vices of infolding closure such a hybris and revolt; between the moods of joy and despair; and between alienation in its double meaning of alienation from the world and alienation from God." From "Equivalences

of Experience and Symbolization in History," and unpublished manuscript quoted by John H. Howell in his "Editor's Preface" to Voegelin's *From Enlightenment to Revolution*. See also Voegelin's extended exploration of the idea in "Experience and History," Part II of *Anamnesis*, translated and edited by Gerhart Niemeyer.

4. I have treated this point at some length in Chapters 6 and 7 of my *Why Flannery O'Connor Stayed Home* (Sherwood Sugden, 1981).

5. There is a growing body of revealing literature, some of the most cogent of it from within the preserves of sociology and psychology, on the theme of these new sciences' obfuscations of the mystery of evil, the distortions that remove evil from individual responsibility into the abstract country of personal and social adjustment. For instance, Professor Donald Campbell, a recent president of the American Psychological Association, shocked many of his colleagues when he said in his presidential address:

> There is in psychology today a general background assumption that the human impulses provided by biological evolution are right and optimal, both individually and socially, and that repressive or inhibitory moral traditions are wrong. This assumption may now be regarded as scientifically wrong. Psychology, in propagating this background perspective in its teaching of perhaps 80 or 90 percent of college undergraduates, and increasing proportions of high school pupils, helps to undermine the retention of what may be extremely valuable social-evolutionary inhibitory systems which we do not yet fully understand.

If this late admission from an authority in the field still leaves the person entangled in "social-evolutionary systems" and the question of evil still rooted in "biological evolution," Professor Campbell does admit "social functionality and psychological validity to the concepts of sin and temptation and of original sin due to human carnal, animal nature." To remember sin and temptation in such terms is but small advance toward the spirit's territory, but it is a beginning. For a searching critique of psychology's deconstructions of reality that call forth Campbell's carefully hedged warnings, see Paul C. Vitz's *Psychology as Religion: The Cult of Self-Worship*, or the redactions he makes of his book in "Psychology: Advocate of the New Narcissism" and "Psychology: Enemy of the Family" in *The New Oxford Review*, April 1979 and May 1979.

Part III

On Fugitives, Agrarians and New Critics

8

Bells for John Stewart's Burden: A Sermon upon the Desirable Death of the "New Provincialism" Here Typified[1]

> The Georgia Review *published this long and devastating essay-review of John Stewart's study of the Fugitives and Agrarians,* The Burden of Time. *Montgomery here reveals his deep and detailed knowledge of the poetry of the Fugitives and the social and political views of the Agrarians. He also delivers (in sermon fashion) a stinging rebuke to Stewart and others (Ralph McGill and John M. Bradbury) who present an ignorant or shallow or simplified or prejudiced account of the Agrarians. In praise of the Fugitive-Agrarians (particularly Davidson, Tate, Ransom, and Warren), Montgomery notes that they were prophetic in their warning that industrialism (and the materialism, secularism, scientism, family dissolution, and governmental expansion that tend to accompany industrialism) would destroy old and worthy cultural traditions and institutions. Donald Davidson and Allen Tate were pleased to see Montgomery's able exposition of Fugitive verse and defense of the Agrarians. Tate, writing to Montgomery in September 1966, praised Montgomery's "mastery of the subject," and paid this tribute as well: "Your Aristotelian analysis of John Ransom's Bells for John Whiteside's Daughter is, I am sure, the finest criticism that or any other poem of his has ever had." Davidson wrote Tate in a letter dated October 17, 1966:*
>
>> Yes, I did see and exult in Marion Montgomery's *Georgia Review* article. It felt good (as Hemingway would say!) to find him so outright and thorough in his demolishment of Stewart and so very articulate about important matters. I thought

*This essay first appeared in *The Georgia Review* (20.2 — Summer 1966).

his treatment lifted his essay up out of the flame of personalities and mere argument into the realm of issues (large ones) worth the serious discussion he so brilliantly gave them.

While Montgomery has treated the work of the Fugitive-Agrarians in many of his books, two deserve mention: his Lamar Memorial Lectures, Possum and Other Receits for the Recovery of "Southern" Being *(University of Georgia, 1987) and* John Crowe Ransom and Allen Tate: At Odds About the Ends of History and the Mystery of Nature *(McFarland, 2003).*

I

"Regionalism is ... limited in space but not in time. The provincial attitude is limited in time but not in space.... Provincialism is that state of mind in which regional men lose their origin in the past and its continuity into the present, and begin every day as if there had been no yesterday.... What a difference — and it is a difference between two worlds: the provincial world of the present, which sees in material welfare and legal justice the whole solution to the human problem; and the classical–Christian world, based upon regional consciousness, which held that honor, truth, imagination, human dignity, and limited acquisitiveness, could alone justify a social order however rich and efficient it may be.... From now on we are committed to seeing with, not through the eye: we, as provincials who do not live anywhere."
—Allen Tate, "The New Provincialism," *The Virginia Quarterly Review,* 1945.

Given such a complex and inclusive attempt as Mr. Stewart has elected to make in this study of the Fugitive-Agrarians, one inevitably finds much to argue with in his book. But there is finally so much to protest that I conclude it a bad book indeed. There is an impossible chaos, not of the kind one encounters in certain books resulting from a failure of general organization, for the general form of *The Burden of Time* is acceptable enough: approximately the first half is devoted to the background of the Fugitive and Agrarian movements and to the history of the emergence of the groups, the second half to a detailed consideration of the work of John Crowe Ransom, Allen Tate, and Robert Penn Warren. The chaos I object to in the book lies finally in the mind of Mr. Stewart as it attempts to deal with literary works and with ideas. To some extent one can sympathize; the very multiplicity of men, works, ideas dealt with is formidable. The attempt for instance to treat exhaustively a John Crowe Ransom who is, in addition to being an accomplished poet, one of the central forces in a group of distinguished poets, a critic of art and of history and economics for 40 years, and polemicist in a metaphysical approach to contemporary society whose aim was the preservation of and integration of the individual. The multiplicity leads Stewart to those partial statements about ideas and poems on one page that do not find any complementary conciliation with partial statements made in other places. There is also a weakness at work, undercutting the larger appearance of order, that must be described as a lack of aesthetic acumen; much of the literary analysis in the book is either superficial or demonstrably wrong.

But the most fundamental cause of the book's chaos, which in sum gives one a mental and spiritual indigestion, is a provincial bias which does not allow Stewart to approach the ideas or the art or the poet or essayist in a manner which is at least initially disinterested. Cliché-riddled conclusion tends to be anterior to the particulars considered. Not that prejudgment is by definition wrong; the full and healthy growth of judgment should allow for conclusion sometimes immediately upon encounter of one's judgment with a particular idea. Surely the physician, after ten years practice, can diagnose virus infection without specimen slides; the dentist doesn't always require X-ray to discover cavities. One may learn to see *through* the eye and not merely *with* the eye, as Tate urges us to consider. But, alas, one may also see *with* the eye as misguided by the nose. If one is going to conclude at first whiff that an idea is sour, he must for his own sake do so with a proper appreciation of his nose's limitations; for larger sakes when he is in a position to deny needed sustenance to the hungry. Mr. Stewart, unless my eyes and nose deceive me, mistakes old beef for sour beef and prefers finally the kind of indefinite mush which is the general fare in our elaborate academic and political refectories. I propose now to examine in some detail the mess of potage Stewart serves us. In consequence, I shall go substantially beyond the limits of the usual book review, for the truth is that our birthright is at stake.

The great pity is that Mr. Stewart, like most of us, is caught up by what Alexander Hamilton warned of, a popular current, against which there is no correction by a permanent will because there is no longer any conception of an ultimate end. Thus when he is faced with the almost impossible task of defining that now ancient dog under our groaning table, The South, supposed by the generality to be the principal carrier of various viruses, he is scarcely prepared to evaluate those sources upon which he bases his judgments—as often as not rumor made moment's history by instant journalism. In pursuit of the question why such a harvest of poems and fictions appeared in the South since World War I, Stewart attempts a careful qualification of his evidence and judgment; but because his heart wants him to be on the side of the disinfecting angels, his head won't let him try whether those angels of the moment are caitiff or not. He moves from a sublime desire, nurtured in the academic and political laboratory, to a mission in the field. The result? A few tracks recorded, a scrap of fur, a worn down fang or two, partially restored with plaster. Finally there is little more substantiation of the beast, The South, than of that less infectious creature, the Abominable Snowman. There is a rehash of some old evidence, already presented with better clinical eye by the Fugitives themselves, and with conclusions quite contrary to Stewart's. Thus Stewart presents, from a decidedly provincial position, generalizations which are not perceptively related to the literature itself.

There is, by way of illustration, the question of whether the isolation of Tate, Warren, Ransom, Davidson, and the other Fugitives at Vanderbilt, as opposed to the presumably more liberated position of the expatriates of Paris or Greenwich Village, was good for the young Fugitives. Stewart concludes that the isolation was good. But he does so only after he has shown rather conclusively, as Louise Cowan has done before him in her *Fugitive Group*, that they were not isolated. Indeed, it is a question for a more searching study of the Fugitives than Stewart's whether the expatriates of the '20s, other than Pound perhaps, were as aware of the cultural and literary issues involved in the publication of *The Waste Land* as were Ransom, Davidson, and Tate. Such a probing would have to deal with such fundamental questions about our itinerant artists of the 1920s as those raised by Tate in "The New Provincialism," particularly that section of his essay which argues:

> Regionalism without civilization — which means, with us [southerners] regionalism without classical-Christian culture — becomes provincialism; and world regionalism becomes world provincialism. For provincialism is that state of mind in which regional men lose their origins in the past and its continuity into the present, and begin every day as if there had been no yesterday.

The early recognition of regional virtues by the Fugitives (which Stewart denies to them as being early) and by those men in particular who moved on to Agrarian discourse — Ransom, Davidson, Tate, Warren — shows them far less isolated from the larger world of complicated time and place that Eliot announced in his poem than the shocked reaction of William Carlos Williams or the nostalgic reminisces of young Ernest Hemingway over his private moment shows them to be.

Here, then, in Tate's definition of provincialism, as in other of the Fugitive-Agrarians' work, lies a significant center of concern in measuring the validity of their insight and accomplishments. For theirs was most certainly an attempt to cope with the eternal present without a provincial narrowness committing them only to the momentary. Stewart — and I am taking him as typical of a whole gaggle of writers and journalists as easily typified by John M. Bradbury or Ralph McGill — approaches such a question as the provincialism of Nashville, Tennessee, in the 1920s as if Tate were arguing that the artist should become Catholic or Davidson that the artist should live in a lonely cabin in Tennessee badlands. Handicapped by this view of the Fugitives, Stewart cannot see just how much and how early they become concerned with their own time; consequently he cannot see what light Davidson's sequence of poems, *The Tall Men* (1927), throws on Eliot's traditionalism. While condemning, even sarcastically ridiculing, what he takes to be Davidson's romantic, bookish view of history, which he concludes to be only a looking backward, Stewart fails to see that such escapism as he attributes to Davidson is precisely a facet of Eliotic romanticism under attack in Davidson's poems. Since very early in his career Davidson, while acknowledging that time leaves fragments, has considered history more lively than the butt-ends of our days and ways or sunlight on a broken column. Nor does he concede as inevitable that "Unnatural vices / are fathered by our heroism." He rejected early the deterministic concept of history that haunts Eliot's early poetry, both that aspect of it as applied by Charles Beard to American history and that psychological Pavlovianism applied to religion by Sir James Frazer in *The Golden Bough*.

Consequently Davidson reacts sharply to Eliot's early poetry, not because he fails to see the hollowness of the 1920s, but because he recognizes in that poetry a despair in Eliot himself, reflected in such surrealistic upside-down views of history as that in *The Waste Land*'s "What the Thunder Said." Until after *The Waste Land*, Eliot found no answer to determinism strong enough to command his commitment. But Eliot comes to see strongly "*through* the eye." The commitment of *Little Gidding* serves to underline the despair of "Gerontion," for by the time of the *Four Quartets* Cleo has become quite other than a woman with "her long black hair out tight" who fiddles "whisper music on those strings." History no longer has the strange look of *The Waste Land* in which

> upside down in air were towers
> Tolling reminiscent bells, that kept the hours
> And voices singing out of empty cisterns and exhausted wells.

Eliot's technique itself disguises the change in the poet — the kaleidoscopic "disembodied" voice in "Gerontion" and *The Waste Land*. The generous or awed respect of some critics in light of Eliot's genius and the incessant article mill requirements of other critics have contributed to a view of Eliot's whole work as if it were a steady unfolding of an initial vision. But the announcement in *For Lancelot Andrews* that he considered himself a classicist in literature, royalist in politics, and Anglo-Catholic in religion marks a significant development. It is, in fact, a recording of a commitment now strong enough so that history is capable of more than guiding us by our vanities through "many cunning passages, contrived corridors." Though Eliot's reading of Lancelot Andrews is older than "Gerontion," his commitment, "Costing not less than everything," is not. History, initially feminine and deceptive — Madame de Tornquist, Fraulein von Kulp, Madame Sosostris— transforms toward St. Mary in *Ash Wednesday*. By *Little Gidding* (1942) Eliot writes in a voice that no longer carries the ambiguity of whether it is the poet's or Prufrock's or Tiresias':

> A people without history
> > Is not redeemed from time, for history is a pattern
> > Of timeless moments. So, while the light fails
> > On a winter's afternoon, in a secluded chapel
> > History is now and England.

The point is that Eliot's final view of history is one that Davidson has already incorporated in his *Tall Men*.

In his flippant dismissal of Davidson as critic and poet, Stewart has done a grave disservice to a fine poet and to this complex poem. Had he examined such a technical aspect of the *Tall Men* as point of view and compared it to that of *The Waste Land*, and perhaps *Hugh Selweyn Mauberley*, he might have found the question of identity, courage, and risk contributing a richness in Davidson's collection of a separate order from Eliot's but at least as worthy, being actually closer to Pound's. Davidson's poem carries the consciousness of a poet in the city, but it is carefully made a definite person — not a disembodiment. The poet investigates the belief that history is *now*, as Eliot means the word in *Gidding*. It is the very process which Eliot is to describe as the end of all our exploring, which is "to arrive where we started / And know the place for the first time." To a considerable degree Davidson's collection encompasses Eliot's journey from Prufrock's tea party to the *Cocktail Party*. A personal acceptance of individual and cultural limitations informs Davidson's *Tall Men*, which acceptance allows action, as one doesn't find action in *The Waste Land*, though the journey motif considerably disguises the absence of action in the poem and leads critics on goose chases no less wild than those after the Tarot cards, in pursuit of evidence of "hope" in those early poems. I shall comment on this absence of action in Eliot's early poems in more detail when I come to consider Stewart's treatment of Ransom's poetry. For the moment, let it suffice to suggest that Davidson is acutely aware of the temptations of the waste land (compare, for instance, his "Conversation in a Bedroom" in which sequence the Ego is confronted by such temptations of history as Eliot dramatizes in *Murder in the Cathedral*). The voice of "An Intellectual" speaks:

> Out of the broken gospels, out of the desert,
> The parched, the shattered temples I heard a voice
> Chanting to a strident harp: *Oh, come, come in,*
> *Come in under the shadow of this red rock....*
> Whither I come, and solace now my heart
> With necrological beauties more permanent
> In the round glitter of skulls and rondure of bones
> Than all the old disease of life.

To which the "Ego" of the poem reacts, condemning the distortion of history implied, such "negative freedoms." For time is redeemed when seen aright. Which seeing involves a beginning from where one is. Green hills lie

> Where moonlight falls on honest grass
> And honest men who sleep or, waking, speak
> The tongue I speak and love.

Though "clocks will strike," time does not contain the past in the distorted manner of the Cleo passage of Eliot's "What the Thunder Said," in which

> bats with baby faces in the violet light
> Whistled, and beat their wings
> And crawled head downward down a blackened wall.

In response to this passage from the *Waste Land*, Davidson writes:

> With blithely tortured face he warps the night
> In shooting lines. Convulsive blackness crimps
> A blasted angular world where fungus growths
> Knit pile on pile of horrible beauty splashed
> With writhing human smiles.

The Tall Men is by a poet aware of himself as having been a soldier in France in World War I, an experience that stirred the mind to that blood knowledge of his own family's experiences in more ancient wars. Davidson's great-great grandfather's wife was captured by the Indians and carried into Canada and subsequently ransomed. One need hardly mention how closely aware Davidson was of his family's involvement in the American Civil War, but might recall the counterpoint in Eliot, the English Civil War, which is of more than passing relevance to Eliot's concern for the dissociation of sensibility and his early disaffection with Milton. One need hardly mention Davidson's unqualified commitment to literary and political principles he has never considered as ultimately lost causes, but needs reminding of Eliot's confusion, which is hinted at by his apologetic embarrassment on meeting Herbert Read in 1917, Read in uniform, Eliot an uncommitted civilian. (See Sir Herbert Read's "T.S.E.—A Memoir," *Sewanee Review*, Winter 1966, page 32.) One might consider that much yet is to be said of the early Eliot, as is further indicated by Read's recalling him singing in London "in a mood of solemn gaiety" the ballad we southerners call "The Unreconstructed Rebel." Looking back on those years Eliot wrote Read in 1928:

> Some day ... I want to write an essay about the point of view of an American who wasn't an American, because he was born in the South and went to school in New England as a small boy with a nigger drawl, but who wasn't a southerner in the South because his people were northerners in a border state and looked down on all southerners and Virginians, and who so was never anything anywhere and who therefore felt himself to be more a Frenchman than an American and more an Englishmen than a Frenchman and yet felt that the U.S.A. up to a hundred years ago was a family extension. It is almost too difficult even for H. J. who for that matter wasn't an American at all, in that sense. [*Sewanee Review*, Winter 1966, page 35.]

This, in the year in which *For Lancelot Andrews* was published with its now famous preface.

Davidson's clearer awareness of his origins carries a conviction in his poetry which he, and others, do not find in the literary conjuring of "Gerontion." From his personal action in World War I to the present day, Davidson has found himself daily involved with hollow, bloodless men in such an intimate way as to make his experience less speculative in its expression than Eliot's in *The Waste Land*. Engagement, freed of caution, tempts to excessiveness; there are some legitimate reservations to be made as to the literary merit of *The Tall Men*, though they are reservations implicitly recognized by the voice in the poem. Davidson himself advances criticism of his volume in *Fugitives' Reunion*. But reservations must be made on the basis of what the poem is, not according to what one wants it to be. Certainly the volume requires a critical perception keener than

Stewart's when he concludes that the *Tall Men's* complexities "would have appealed to the readers of Zane Grey."

Thus Stewart's inclination to a wrong conclusion because of insufficient understanding or misread evidence keeps intruding upon one's patience as he reads *The Burden of Time*. A damning instance is the repeated insistence that the Fugitives were unaware of themselves as southerners in their writing, a consideration introduced at times as if an apology for the Agrarian phase of Ransom and Warren in particular. Consider this statement of Stewart's theme:

> Ransom held most of the important tenets of the philosophy underlying his critical theories *before* he turned to thinking and writing on social problems. Even if one removed from his writing all mention of the Agrarian social image, his thought would still be all of a piece — so much so, indeed, that one can suppose that the parts which have importance for literature would have come into being in just about the same form without Agrarianism [page 203].

But this is having it however Stewart will. Did parts come into being *after* Agrarianism; is Agrarianism compatible to those early tenets? Is Stewart suggesting that Agrarianism is an aberration in Ransom? The truth is that Stewart doesn't like Agrarian ideas and is uncomfortable, sometimes angrily so, in their presence. One cannot write as he does above and reasonably conclude that it proves that "scholars may overestimate the significance of Agrarianism" in Ransom's, Tate's, and Warren's work. Nor is it convincing to assert as if self-evident that, though Warren soaked up the South in his boyhood, the southern material present in his poetry and fiction should not lead a reader to suppose that "the history of his own region meant more to Warren at this time than it actually did." One would not be entirely satisfied if the assertion were Warren's own, and certainly not when it is Stewart's. It is perhaps of some relevance to the art and polemics of Warren and Tate that they have their origins, as did Eliot, in a border state, but rather than moving East came South to Vanderbilt. This is by way of suggesting a point worthy of consideration, not an assertion as of factual conclusion. For I am forecautioned by the undocumented and unexplored assertions occurring too often in Stewart, sometimes presented as if established fact, as with his comment on the relevance of history to Warren's work, and sometimes as authoritative judgment requiring general assent, as in his reduction of Tate's essays and poems of the late '20s and early '30s to brilliant but chaotic utterances of a lively boy. On the Fugitive's early awareness of themselves, Stewart presents enough of the exchange in the early '20s between Davidson and the editors of *Poetry: a*

Magazine of Verse to show his conclusions inadmissible. But admiring the work of Ransom and Warren, Stewart is bent on rescuing it from its regional foundations toward claiming it for world provincialism. His attempt is so confused and over-bold as to require our looking a bit more closely into the matter.

II

One of the fallacies in Stewart's study of his subject is his penchant for oversimplification. (And again I remind the reader that I am considering Stewart as typical of a widespread provincial view and not as exceptional.) He looks at an argument by Tate or Davidson or Ransom, an argument out of some historical social institution perhaps, cites evidence of corruption in that particular institution, and concludes both that the institution is indefensible and that the propounder of the argument is ignorant of the full history of the institution. "One thinks of the Enclosure Acts and wonders how much Tate really knew about life under the *haute noblesse* of a Europe whose virtues he claimed for the South." One can arrive at such a naive distortion if he takes the evil of a system to be the whole, as the Agrarians did not, any more than they took the virtues to be the whole. And one may fail to see as well that a point propounded may be advanced primarily on its merit as it appeals to the reason, with history cited as secondary. Now such failure as Stewart's may be innocent or deliberate, but the result is almost inevitably to charge the abused argument with wanting "to turn back the clock." (One should remember Davidson's sharp insistence to the contrary in *The Tall Men*: "But clocks will strike.") When Stewart concludes that by 1930 Ransom, Tate, and Davidson were ignorant of English and European history, it is clear enough that he has considerably overstated his case, he depending upon his own shaky opinion, as in his questioning of Tate quoted above, rather than upon evidence.

When we look at Stewart himself as historian, we are made even more aware of inadequacy, for we see him presenting evidence which is pertinent to his investigation but drawing conclusions that are untenable in the light of the evidence he himself presents. If one goes one step further, he finds Stewart presenting partial evidence, some of it questionable, on the basis of which he judges the degree of knowledge possessed by the Fugitive-Agrarians. To illustrate this confusion, consider his preliminaries to a consideration of the Agrarian position. He begins by presenting the Old South as it really was, contending that there were two Old Souths, a conservative estimate to say the least. The one South was that of "reality," the other of "legend." Out of the conflicting existences came the recent burgeoning of southern letters. But the Fugitives, Stewart has already contended, were unaware of this complexity until they were middle-aged boys. In the first place, as Stewart has shown in the initial chapters, a revolt against the moonlight and magnolia South was a gambit of the Fugitives as poets. In the second, Stewart is unable to deal adequately with the legend half of his complexity because he does not deal adequately with the reality half, depending in part on questionable sources. To say, in characterizing the legend, that "Thomas Moore and Byron had taught southerners to pay lip-service to the classics" and that consequently southern academies offered a curriculum that included "some Latin and Greek" is to distort the reality, as if Stewart's investigation extended no further than a reading of *Life on the Mississippi* and the Grangerford section of the *Adventures of Huckleberry Finn*. The argument overlooks the firm classical foundations of, say, the University of Virginia and the University of Georgia. What a convenient simplification: otherwise Stewart might have felt required to go into the differences between two such institutions, Virginia's being more directly out of Renaissance England and Georgia's out of late 18th century New England. But such complexity would have upset the reality-legend halving of his cake. It requires no further pursuit of Stewart's legend concerning the role of the classics in southern education than to quote the Trustee Minutes of the University of Georgia (an institution founded by Yale men and modeled after that school). In the first quarter of the 19th century a student was allowed to enter, after academy training or private tutoring presumably, only if he was able "to read, translate, and parse Cicero, Virgil, and the Greek Testament, and to write true Latin in prose." Commencement exercises, according to the published programs, included formal orations by the students in French, Latin, and Greek. (See E. Merton Coulter, *College Life in the Old South*, page 35.) The classical languages unquestionably continued to be at the center of formal education in the South through World War I, as the attempts of the New England missionaries indicate, they devoting considerable energy after 1865 to teaching the newly-freed helpless Negro Latin and Greek. (See Willard Range's *Rise and Progress of Negro Colleges in Georgia*, Part I.) The importance of classical training to the Fugitive-Agrarian movement is testified to in some detail by the principals themselves in *Fugitives' Reunion*, a document which Stewart fails to avail himself of at points of his study where it would be helpful. Their direct testimony, recorded in May of 1956, particularly in the final symposium, embodies remarks by several of the group recalling their awakening in words quite contrary to Stewart's assertions.[2]

Also inadmissible as authority is Stewart's introduction of the frontiersman Patrick Henry, who is cited to prove that the literary culture of the southern planter came "from conversation, not from reading" (page 100). Again, the argument conveniently ignores the importance of such figures as William Byrd, John Randolph, and Thomas Jefferson. For, though all plantation owners were not versed in Western culture through direct familiarity with the languages of that culture's literature, many were; and those too are a part of the reality. Each age, each region has its dream of the Great Society that leads to romanticizing, and the romanticizing in the Old South was in large part by the frontier and Deep South parvenu who, like Sutpen, strives to emulate the Virginia Gentleman, though his women tend to pursue Heaven in the manner prescribed by New England Puritanism as injected by Wesleyan enthusiasm. The Virginia Gentleman was consequently a more considerable reality and power than Twain's presentation through the Grangerfords allows, or than Stewart is aware of. For dreams do have immediate social and political consequences, even as have ideas, from which one should be able to profit if critically alert. Tate, for instance, argued in 1935 ("The Profession of Letters in the South") that pioneering "became our way of industrial expansion, a method of production not special to us." Earlier (in "Remarks on the Southern Religion," 1930) he examines the development in the South before 1860 of what might properly be called agricultural industrialism, the appearance on the plantation scene of the precursors of Henry Ford. As Puritanism contributed to materialism in the East, to the discomfort of a Hawthorne, so did general Protestant evangelicalism in the South. The result: a destructive use of human energy and the land in the final interest of exchangeable commodity, Jonathan Edwards and John Wesley having finally been made pragmatic instruments. Such complexities of history lie under southern literature from the superficial observations of Twain, through the weak voice of protest in Sidney Lanier, to the profounder readings of the Fugitive Agrarians, and of William Faulkner and Flannery O'Connor. Curiously, Stewart charges Tate with being unaware of the particular phenomenon of industrial expansion as applied to the plantation, while actually producing a portion of Tate's essay (on page 126) which clearly shows that awareness. As Agrarians Tate and Davidson in particular began to say again and again, in defining values from the past worthy of survival, it is a misunderstanding to suppose that the spirit of the New South, as exemplified in Henry Grady, is a Post-Bellum development: the New South spirit is an old inclination freshly directed toward old ends. Eli Whitney proved to be the Deep South's Henry Ford: what Grady was subsequently interested in was a multiplicity of such minds to help attract capital, which capital could find advantage in the labor that had been abruptly divorced from the exhausted land. In other words, the old evil — worldliness — turned old means in a new direction. Its effect upon the religious and cultural life of the South was, and has continued to be, of primary concern to Tate.[3] One might consider him, in this respect, an angry and articulate Young Goodman Brown, whose initiation into the dark mysteries came quite early, as did the commitment he made as a consequence. In this respect he differs from Eliot, with whom he has many affinities.

III

The New South Spirit began to move relentlessly during the final decades of the 19th century, a new religious crusade led with fervor by Henry Grady, the tone of whose sermons on materialism has ever since colored southern politics. Grady's ringing words to the North, delivered on one of his invasions, sound very like Khruschev's more recent boastings about burying industrial America. "We are going to make a noble revenge ... by invading every inch of your territory with iron."[4] Thus the transubstantiation of the Old Deep South into the New. The pressure of merely surviving that led to such bold words left little room for or interest in ends. An occasional weak voice was raised.

> "O Trade! O Trade! would thou wert dead!
> The Time needs heart — 'tis tired of head:
> We're all for love," the violins said.

But Lanier's violins are hardly suited to the task that requires a John the Baptist. That Henry Grady's threat has been accomplished is nowhere more adequately illustrated than in the pained protest of then Senator John F. Kennedy in "New England and the South: The Struggle for Industry" (*Atlantic Monthly,* January 1954). His strong objections to the South's economic advantages at mid-twentieth century will certainly require future historians to consider that concern as it relates to his subsequent political biography. Certainly the public concern for the South's moral estate has strong economic undercurrents. It is equally certain that the New South philosophy has proved as little concerned with human dignity as was the infamous New England textile magnate's or the Deep South Simon Legree's. Unquestionably, the imitation by many prewar planters of a Jefferson or a Randolph was a token imitation, but in the same culturally and spiritually destructive manner as the magnates' and financiers' purchase of European art with a dream of refrigerating it in public mausoleums, the White House itself having recently served that end. The New South spirit turned towards imitating the Rockefellers and Goulds, while our Protestant fervor captured Rotary and Lion's Cubs. We are now, like the rest of the country, pretty well caught up in imitating the Joneses. For with the cry of Progress, we set ourselves on the road (in Jack Kerouac's now famous phrase for end-less motion). Indeed, because there were no ends considered beyond the acquisition of power (both financial and political power having been unjustly seized from the South), one could expect the accomplishment of little more than affluent aimlessness. It is an aimlessness characterized by the sophisticated concern for literature and art divorced of its past and removed from the present into a compartment: a small segment of the Sunday paper's "entertainment" section. There plays are promoted like circuses. Books are celebrated because they are just published, topical, timely.

The point of this castigation, which will hold for the general cultural concern of the region, with particular exceptions, is to call attention to what are still, after thirty or forty years, acute observations by the Agrarians on the causes of our regional decay into provincialism. Tate's essay, "Remarks on Southern Religion" (1930), is far more cogent than Stewart's denigration of it makes it appear when he caricatures it as dealing with "a fabulous North and a blundering monster called Protestantism." A reader must refer to the essay itself to see Tate's awareness of the effects upon the South of the secular, utilitarian spirit in it and then compare Tate's observations with his own of the immediate South. But one must do so, remembering that Tate's concern is, like Dante's and Eliot's, *with the effect on the individual soul of its own will and acts.* For effects are never the proper center of spiritual attention, though they often indicate false centers. One might consider this last proposition by observing the consequences of that force of the popular will in our society that has turned us to things as an end, the final effect of which is to turn the individual into a thing. (A pertinent analysis of this development is Eliseo Vivas' "Things and Persons," *Modern Age,* Spring 1965.)

From the beginning the Fugitives were aware of the complexity of modem industrial society, whose easy dream of cultural salvation was the importation of European art and literature, the extension of which dream is the television set in every home. The literal transportation of a castle by a moneyed man is followed by a group effort to preserve the movie set of Tara used in *Gone with the Wind.* Ransom returned from World War I, wrote a poem called "Old Mansion," displaying the expatriate southerner come home with a veneer of European sophistication upon his sensibility, a poem in its searchings into national provincialism much akin to the searchings one finds in Henry James, a spirit both Tate and Ransom have found congenial. Aware of the national provincialism, the Fugitives were aware as well of that local provincialism which misappropriated and distorted its regional substance, particularly in the interest of "business." Davidson wrote to the editors of *Poetry* in 1923: "We fear to have too much stress laid on a tradition that may be called a tradition only when looked at through the haze of a generous imagination."

The "haze of a generous imagination" is close to the center of Ransom's and Davidson's objections to *The Waste Land,* and much of the burden of the colloquy between the two older men and Tate, then in the East, revolves around it. Their debate is a working out of the complexities of tradition's relation to the individual talent and society. The poet, examining the poem itself, even though he might attempt to ignore the clash between the Old and New South daily about him, in the Nashville business world or in the persons of Edwin Mims and Chancellor Kirkland at Vanderbilt University, moves inevitably to larger concerns unless he withdraws into what Warren was to characterize later as "pure poetry." Davidson sees the cultural frenzy of town pursuing business and asks

> Why do they come? What do they seek
> Who build but never read their Greek?
> ("On a Replica of the Parthenon")

What he and the other Fugitive-Agrarians (Warren, Tate, Ransom) were doing was working out from a center — themselves as poets — to those larger concerns. Emerging into the harsh world of their own Reconstruction Period (and Stewart unwisely negates the importance of World War I on the group), they came to recognize themselves as possessed of a kind of traditionalism which, because of the peculiar advantage of their cultural origins and personal history, was unlike Eliot's, being less abstract, less bookish. While Eliot sought to restore what was lost, the Fugitives found themselves engaged in assimilating to art and argument what was still at hand but rapidly being lost. One representation of the difference I mean: contrast the sense of family one finds in the Fugitives and in their poetry to that loneliness of Eliot, and Pound as well. What the fortunate coincidence of the Fugitives' origins and encounter means to their development can be found well-stated in Davidson's "Thankless Muse and Her Fugitive Poets" *(Southern Writers in the Modern World).* One need only contrast the analogous writings of many of the expatriates to see a difference. In contrast to the Fugitives' encounter, it is as if Eliot and Pound attempt to choose their origins by an act of the will, through essay and art. Another indication is the history of these poets' movements: from St. Louis to London, from Idaho to Italy. The contrast serves to underline the advantage the Fugitives had: an anchor in reality that might prevent their intellectual lives ever to divorce from the present time and place and float away too easily into past glories.

While protesting the same decay that Eliot and Pound find in the modem world, the Fugitives do so from a point of different vantage. The immediate result is often a difference in literary mode, as between Ransom's "Captain Carpenter" and Eliot's "Love Song of Alfred Prufrock," for instance. Ransom sees, with a generous recognition of the weaknesses involved, a spirit which is nevertheless necessary to the modem world (as God's Fools always are); it is a spirit doomed by the world, but honorable, courageous, capable of an ultimate commitment against an overwhelming evil that costs "not less than everything." Eliot's poem, on the other hand, characterizes the poverty of a spirit who laments sadly being "at times almost the Fool." In Ransom's mode instead of a disembodied consciousness afloat in modern vacuums and defined by old signs and allusions, the poem functioning as an indirect commentary, there is a praising of foolish involvement in lost causes. Because there is a realism in Ransom's view which makes him aware that good causes are generally lost in the immediate world, the poet himself may possess a moderation necessary to his own involvement in the world. Ransom's poetry shows a poet less defeated than Eliot's poetry, at least up to Eliot's commitment to Augustine's city over the "Unreal City" that London stands for. Ransom is characteristically less elegiac than Eliot. More dramatic. Nor yet is he as rashly and harshly innocent as Pound in *Mauberley* and the early *Cantos*, who shaking the dirt of London and Paris from his feet in pursuit of a Utopian city he calls Dioce, loses touch with the world, till that overwhelming shock which is registered in the *Pisan Cantos*.

The self-awareness among the Fugitives helps a Davidson relate his experience in European trenches to Thermopylae, Hastings, Buchanan's Station, Appomattox, and feel confident as well that the world is not lost to Eliot's Prufrock or Pound's Mr. Nixon. Nor lost to the Sweeneys or the Grishkins as simply conceived as they are in Eliot's portraiture. (One might note that in the *Pisan Cantos* Pound agrees, commenting on "Grishkin's photo refound years after / with the feeling that Mr. Eliot may have / missed something, after all, in composing his vignette.") For Davidson looks to the future with expectations not unlike those one finds more recently expressed in Harrison Brown's scientific analysis of our prospect in *The Challenge of Man's Future* (1954), a work to which I shall later return. It is usual to find such concerns treated by the new provincial spirit such as Stewart's as

8. Bells for John Stewart's Burden

being a nostalgic looking to the past, for that new spirit is so immersed in the present moment that past and future are easily confused. Sadly, this emersion in the present moment is not of that high order of commitment that Eliot came to in the *Four Quartets,* a Stewart being rather drowned in present time than drowned out of it. More Phlebas than Heraclitus.

In considering the Fugitives' good fortune of origin and encounter, one should look somewhat closely at their city. Nashville in the 1920s was approximately the size of Pericles' Athens or Dante's Florence or Chaucer's London. Academy, city, country were close and often hardly distinguishable. The circumstances did not dictate or encourage isolation. Davidson remembers that "it was possible then for a young southern poet to pass from university to city, from city to university, without any great sense of shock." In *Fugitives' Reunion* it is made abundantly evident that such travel was possible within the university itself, among the various departments, in a way scarcely possible then in the large Eastern schools or since in any university one can name, *largeness* having become synonymous with *greatness,* thus providing the multiversity. Tate, distinguishing Fugitives from other literary groups of the time to be found in the universities of the East, says of those groups in contrast to the Fugitives,

> They were not groups in our sense, being associated only through the university and having a cosmopolitan range of interest without, I think, a simple homogenous background which they could take with them to the university where it might suffer little or no break in continuity. I would call the Fugitives an intense and historical group as opposed to the eclectic and cosmopolitan groups that flourished in the East.

Their being an "intense and historical group" committed them to the realities of the present in a way that has been facilely denied and unjustly described with the perjorative "academic," in the '20s by Chancellor Kirkland and now most recently by Stewart.

One of the present realities they were committed to was the diversity of personality and talent within the group. It is one of the remarkable aspects of the Fugitives that their growth as poets still allowed them to be generous-spirited even in the midst of heated debate among themselves over the merit of a phrase or an aesthetic principle. By way of contrast, recall the bitter squabble that developed among the Imagists, or the egocentric, jealous, self-promoting climate of the Paris circle that included McAlmon, Hemingway, Stein, Fitzgerald, and lesser lights. A Davidson or a Tate, respecting individual identity and peculiar talent, at once defined, by his concern, both his independence of and his relation to the other identity. What this means to aesthetic argument and critical evaluation can be readily seen by comparing the debate between Tate and Davidson (see Chapter Eight of Louise Cowan's *The Fugitive Group)* to Pound's attack on "Amygism" or his general correspondence with William Carlos Williams in the late 1920s and after. Where there is ample evidence of diversity of poetics in the Davidson-Tate exchange, there is little evidence of any power struggle. The question isn't whose knowledge is legitimate or absolute, but rather

> What shall we do who have knowledge
> Carried to the heart?

They were effective, then, as a group, resisting vigorously being cast in the role of their southern predecessors in letters, whether narrow "pure poetry" technicians like Edgar Allan Poe, plantation romantics like Thomas Nelson Page, or New South apologists like Walter Hines Page. (On the eventual expense of this resistance, to the group itself, see Richard Weaver's "Agrarianism in Exile," *Sewanee Review,* Autumn 1950.) Nor were they less relentless in opposing those who abandoned the past so totally as William Carlos Williams attempted in his first panic over *The Waste Land* or the puzzled and wandering Ernest Hemingway, whose refuge from the complexities of existence was style.

The Fugitives' concern for balance among individuals led to a concern for balance in the individual's society. Hence their inevitable objections to specialization as exhibited by the inordinate worship of science and technology. A parallel objection was to the belief that "poetry is an essence that is to be located at some particular place in a poem, or some particular event." The greater poets, Warren argued, are "impure" because they make a larger, doomed attempt "to remain faithful to the complexities of the problems with which they are dealing, because they have refused to take an easy statement as solution, because they have tried to define the context in which, and the terms by which, faith and ideals may be earned" ("Pure and Impure Poetry," 1942). Though late in Warren's statement of it, relative to the history of the Fugitive-Agrarian development, it is a principle in the early poetry of the group. As poets, they were committed to those political, economic, and aesthetic complexities that allowed no easy program. They must, as Davidson said in "Sanctuary," "Go further on. Go high. Go deep."[5]

IV

It is now time to consider the effects upon the Fugitives of their going further, higher, deeper into the complexities of existence as it revealed itself to them in the 1920s and to consider the validity of their vision. As we have noted, the modem concern for the Complete Man, a concern much remarked in Conrad, Yeats, Pound, Eliot, Huxley, Hemingway, led the Fugitives out of themselves toward a concern for the diversity of society itself and toward a concern for man as hero rather than as victim. As Davidson puts it, again in "The Thankless Muse and Her Fugitive Poets," "the natural step was to remember that after all we were southerners and that the South still possessed at least the remnants ... of a traditional believing society." The fruit of this remembering was the symposium *I'll Take My Stand* (1930), which was not a blanket condemnation of industrialism in favor of agrarianism, nor a condemnation of science in favor of the poet, as its early (and late) antagonists took it to be. The Agrarian position, as Ransom's "Statement of Principles" makes clear, was one of moderation, one in fact opposed to extremism, though its opponents, depending upon that native credulity which leads us to pursue *Progress* with the talisman *New* (whether followed by *South, Bread,* or *Razor Blades*), charged the Agrarians with wanting to return to a feudal society. The falsification of the stated position was easy since, given their moderate position (sometimes hidden in the confusion of debate, as when Ransom met Stringfellow Barr in Richmond in the fall of 1930), there could be no program of action. Stewart makes this absence of a program, the failure to provide a how-to solution, one of the two principal general failures of the Agrarian position. He might well have cited the Fugitive William Y. Elliott to support his point. It is Elliott, in *Fugitives' Reunion,* who expresses strong regret that the Agrarians did not make an effort to gain actual political power through those "Tracts Against Communism," the title Warren preferred to *I'll Take My Stand.*

A falsification of the Agrarian position itself, and of the subsequent attitudes of the principal figures in the movement, has been deliberately continued. Note as a glaring instance, since it had such generous acceptance by the public, Ralph McGill's *The South and the Southerner.* If one compares Mr. McGill's chapter on the Vanderbilt group with the transcript of the final session of the Fugitives' reunion, it becomes evident that McGill is no more adequate as historian than as literary critic, though he includes in his chapter as well a superficial evaluation of Allen Tate as poet. Stewart, unfortunately swept along by the same popular wave of the Utopian present as are Bradbury and McGill, concludes that "The importance of Agrarianism ... comes almost entirely from its relation to the imagination and critical writings of some members of the group." It is a comment short of the mark, though less bigoted and perverse than McGill's presumably deliberate falsification that, after its publication, "There was a determined effort to forget *I'll Take My Stand,*" and that by 1933, "Only Donald Davidson stood on the burned-out deck." One need only remark the publication in 1936 of a second symposium, edited by Allen Tate and Herbert Agar: *Who Owns America: A New Declaration of Independence.* The collection contained essays by Tate, Warren, Ransom, Davidson, Lanier, Owsley, Lytle, Wade — all of whom had contributed to *I'll Take My Stand.*

Stewart concludes that, "Looking back one sees those who continued in The Cause as caretakers of an abandoned estate." He cites Ransom's comment that his essay, "The South Is a Bulwark," is a "last act of patriotism," and concludes from this that Ransom showed "disaffection" with the cause. But as late as 1962, reviewing Davidson's new collection of poems, *The Long Street,* in the *Sewanee Review,* Ransom comments on the old cause as continued by Davidson with warm admiration. "But my admiration does not quite become emulation; there is a defect in my temper." These are hardly the words of "disaffection." They are more nearly an expression of self-disappointment. A more careful consideration of the complexities of the Agrarians' confrontation of the modern world would nevertheless show, I believe, that Ransom was not abandoning a position, but shifting his point of attack. Is not Ransom's literary criticism one facet of a general attack upon Leviathan of which Davidson's social and political criticism is another? Certainly such an essay as "The Concrete Universal" indicates Thomas Hobbes as a point of attack as does Davidson's examination of Charles Beard. It is premature to conclude that the effects of Agrarianism on Ransom are accidental, as Stewart does, just as it is the height of folly to conclude as he does that the principles of Agrarian debate were dead issues by 1936. The whole complex of urban problems shows far otherwise: juvenile delinquency, urban renewal, unemployment, leisure time on the hands of bored masses, and the general psychological effect of alienation concomitant in our structureless society with the condensation of population.

At the heart of the decay is the destruction of the institution most basic to Agrarian tenets, as it has been basic to the civilization of the West since Homer: the family as a stabilizing element of society. Even as I write, there is in the public prints much excitement over the Moynihan Report, which concerns itself with the causes of big city riots. Using Census Bureau statistics as a foundation, Mr. Moynihan (at the time of the report's compilation an assistant secretary of labor) came up with the startling and alarming conclusion that the Negro family has so far broken down as to be the elementary problem to be solved before any final "solution" to the Negro problem is to be accomplished. At the heart of the matter is the failure of the father as authority and the emergence of the mother as dominant figure. While such a development might suit a Robert Graves, it hardly accords with the desires of a Davidson or Ransom. These effects were foretold long since by Lytle and Davidson, and one remarks as well that Captain Carpenter is not the poet's version of Dagwood Bumstead.[6]

In the 1950s and 1960s philosophers, scientists, and literary men are engaged with the problems anticipated by the Agrarians in the 1920s and 1930s. A sampling of the evidence to indicate the immediacy of the problems might well start with the controversial debate between the humanities and sciences engendered anew by C.P. Snow's *Two Cultures* (shades of the Fugitive-Chancellor Kirkland conflict). Painfully pertinent as well are the examinations of our world by Hannah Arendt in *The Human Condition*, by Aldous Huxley in *Brave New World Revisited*; by the prophecies of Norbert Wiener's *Cybernetics*, Rachel Carson's *Silent Spring*, and Howard R. Lewis's W*ith Every Breath You Take*. The proliferation of scientific books on the mechanics of society, of literary and philosophical books on the decay of the concept of the hero or analysis of our relativistic concepts of treason and honor cry out to us from the paperback stands. We pray that the individual is victim, society the oppressive victor; for only then is there any salving of that personal social guilt we've been too easily convicted of. Still the problems rear themselves as the very monsters that Davidson, Tate, Ransom, Lytle, Warren, and Owsley foretold. Near panic results in the nation, as indicated by the rapid multiplication of government- and foundation-financed commissions that tinker and speculate on national, state, and local levels, predicting miracles through the multitude of loaves and fishes commandeered from the public. Indeed, there is such a groping of government-supported minds with the obstacles to the continuation of our civilization that the times want an army of Voltaires. How else deal with such absurdities as government support of Leroi Jones' militant racist theater alongside the public examination of the Ku Klux Klan? How else deal with the pursuit of equality of opportunity through preferential treatment or Secretary of Labor Wirtz's suppression of the Moynihan Report, the evidence it contains being common to the open eye for thirty years at least? In consequence of the confusion about us, the simplified version of Agrarianism reported to us by writers like Bradbury, Stewart, and McGill must be accounted either innocent delusion, disqualifying these spokesmen from our respectful attention, or deliberate betrayal, qualifying them for our strongest rebuke.

As feared by the Agrarians, we have now established in position of absolute power, amid the disintegration of our moral, spiritual, and intellectual fiber, the naive new religion embodied in the local tag "New South," our version of the perennial Great Society. Nor does there seem to be anywhere in a position of effective authority an awareness of the compatibility of chaos and old night with the vagueness of this announced millennium. We have abandoned the spirit and thought of that "Athenian Gentleman" (as Ransom called Aristotle in those Fugitive days), who was concerned with order at a point in history so much like our own. For we are in an age which is at once decaying, as Athens decayed before the frustrated eyes of Euripides, and giving birth to a new paganism such as the world has never before imagined. A *Medea* announced intellectual and spiritual confusions as to man's place in the world whose consequence was the destruction of Athens as subsequently catalogued by Thucydides. Euripides, however, does not argue Medea innocent of murder as she slays her own sons in the name of justice and in the face of what she recognizes as her "better reason." It has remained for our age to declare, in the name of justice, that Medea is innocent: the second U. S. Court of Appeals in March of 1966 established as a precedent of jurisprudence, that a person is not responsible for criminal conduct if, even though he knows an act to be wrong, he cannot control his behavior.

We are excitedly frantic over immediate effects of our new powers to change nature, exuberant over the prospects of willfully changing human nature, not only through social experiments but through the prospects of electric cathodes implanted in the human brain, selective evolution through DNA acids, and education through RNA acid injected to take the place of lectures and reading.[7] The recent eternals— the Dynamo, Evolution, Determinism — are now reduced by their offspring — Cybernetics, Controlled DNA Molecules, and Planned Economy — like Cronus overthrown by Zeus. To the new gods we refer, not the cycles of life in nature and the mysteries of mind as in the Old Paganism, but the annually acquired car, clothes, house, and improved tranquilizers. The symbol for worship in this brave new world? Man on the Moon, to replace the chaste huntress and the old conjunctions of Venus and Mars. The National Space Administration becomes the priesthood of the new Eleusinian mysteries, whose Persephone's nature is mechanical mind, mechanical body. We tithe New Gemini. Is it perhaps somehow relevant that we have chosen to call ours the Age of Anxiety. Without ends, how appropriate that our most celebrated accomplishment is to send our hero integers circling the earth for days with almost perfect mechanical precision. And while a splinter of formal philosophers and theologians announce that God is dead, how revealing our awe when Gemini 8 fails, as if we are suddenly confronted by diabolical miracle.

Concerning the line of ascent in the South towards such strange gods, the New South movement sought those gods through messiahs like Henry

Grady, whose tribe has increased like the division of cells. One inevitable consequence was that we too should lose a concern for ends. Abandoning the past for the present, we abandoned as well a desire for and power of foresight, which power and desire make possible to the eyes the larger prophesies of the future. The Fugitive-Agrarians objected to the destruction of a philosophical pursuit of science and the humanities, themselves preferring as values the development of the individual's mind and spirit to the pragmatic program resulting from the teachings of William James and John Dewey. What has resulted from that lost battle, as a careful look at any of the larger institutions of education will show, is the pursuit of utilitarian service to the body and medical service to the mind: the pursuit is expressed in the general shibboleth of "adjustment to the modern world," through "science" and "social studies." The initial battles between the Fugitives and the authorities at Vanderbilt were on these very battlegrounds, with Peabody Institute next door serving as an advance outpost of the enemy. Later, in the Agrarian phase, the attack was shifted against the regionally established temples: the Birmingham Mills and TVA. But the attacks have not been very effective since that time. For in the new idolatry, the means have been so pervasively established as ends, and there are consequently no suitable definitions of economic failure and social upheaval. The past is presented as dark and abandoned, the future diffuse with a magic radiance that intimidates the eye. But the fundamental end, once held inviolate, is long since lost. As Tate pointed out in 1930, in an essay Stewart characterizes as silly, the shift has been from a concern for individual salvation — whether that of the balanced intellect of Aristotle's concern or the purified soul of Dante's — to a concern for the salvation of Society, which salvation is superstitiously said to guarantee the individual. But in fact the reduced end has served to destroy the individual. The crippled creature that is each of us will not be soothed by the spectacle of Gemini as an annunciation of new Godhead, nor with Society as the true Second Coming, when we see the final economic and educational destructions advanced now in the name of the general good.

But putting aside the divine namings of godhead — Society plus Pure and Social Sciences equals Great Society — let us look at our situation as presented by a scientist in a work endorsed by William O. Douglas and Albert Einstein among others. Harrison Brown warns us, in *The Challenge of Man's Future,* of imminent collapse: either we must undertake such measures as absolute control of the birthrate, going perhaps to a system of regional quotas, and then go on to solve our industrial-urban problems through scientific formulae (brave new world indeed) or a general collapse will return us to those dark age horrors of agrarianism and the sweat of the brow. (He concedes that, in spite of the much-feared sweat, the meanness or nobility of the individual soul would have a chance to reassert itself.) Looking to the future, having studied "Vital Statistics" relevant to the human condition at mid-century, in particular "Food," "Energy," and "Things," he comes to "Patterns of the Future" deduced from the accumulated evidence (page 264):

> We see the possibility of the emergence of any of three possible patterns of life. The first and by far the most likely pattern is a reversion to agrarian existence. This is a pattern which will almost certainly emerge unless man is able to abolish war, unless he is able to make the transition involving the utilization of new energy sources, and unless he is able to stabilize populations.... There is a possibility that stabilization can be achieved, that war can be avoided, and that resource transition can be successfully negotiated. In that event, mankind will be confronted with a pattern which looms on the horizon of events as the second most likely possibility — the completely controlled, collectivized industrial society.
>
> The third possibility confronting mankind is that of the worldwide free industrial society in which human beings can live in reasonable harmony with their environment. It is unlikely that such a pattern can ever exist for long.

In the midst of such huge concerns as these, with which the Agrarians were much engaged, Stewart can say with assurance that "The New South has come to pass and it has turned out to be much better than the Agrarians had prophesied," words indeed spoken as if there were no tomorrow. One might as well, if he were a Ransom or a Davidson or a Tate instead of Harrison Brown, point to profound minds of the past: to a Pericles and his high assurances to Athens of its continuing glory as the *Medea* was being presented and the Peloponnesian War was getting under way, or to a Virgil's ringing confidence that Rome had accomplished what Brown says we must so that New Troy would last forever.[8] And a Tate would cite, instead of Brown's despondent final sentence quoted above, a traditionalist with ancient foundations who said, as a great beginning, "here have we no continuing city." (Hebrews 13:14)

What then shall we do who have such knowledge carried to the heart? Before Eliot sings in *The Rock*, "if the Temple is to be cast down / We must first build the Temple," the Fugitives were well started upon their Agrarian phase. Whatever Ransom, Davidson, Tate, and Warren were, they can certainly not be justly charged with being Utopians, expecting the iron gates to be closed on war or any society to continue perpetually. But with such happy intellectual innocence as to suppose them such, Stewart treats the importance of the Scopes Trial to the ideas and art of the Fugitive-

Agrarians. He says that, though Clarence Darrow "made a fool of William Jennings Bryan, the Spokesman for the Fundamentalists, Scopes was found guilty," as if the verdict were a gross miscarriage of legal justice. One must read Richard Weaver's analysis of the trial's arguments, in *The Ethics of Rhetoric*, to see the fundamental issue of that trial. For the issue was not Fundamentalism versus the true and lively word of science, as Stewart supposes it; the same legislature which outlawed the teaching of evolution as scientific dogma had also outlawed the teaching of the Bible in the public school: Weaver shows conclusively that Bryan's position was a dialectical one, the position of a responsible intellect, while Darrow's was indefensibly a rhetorical one, which exactly reversed his recent position as defense in the Leopold case. Far from arguing the Scopes case on its legal merits, and far from being involved on principle, as subsequent romantic treatments of Darrow's role would have it, Darrow distorted the issue for public consumption, centering his attention more on the journalists than on the jury. Bryan's blunder was, of course, precisely parallel to that of Meletus of Plato's *Apology*, in which famous trial scene Socrates is himself guilty of rhetorical evasion of the fundamental issue; namely, whether he, Socrates, had in fact violated the law (a curious circumstance for Plato to cast his teacher in, considering the burden of the *Crito*). Bryan, in allowing himself to be sworn as an expert on the Bible (as Meletus allowed Socrates to examine him as an expert on education), abandoned the real issue in favor of the circus performance that so amused the nation. Thus Darrow shifted the argument, through clever manipulation of emotion through emotional horseplay, from the issue of whether a law had been violated to the question of whether the particular law was a just one or not. Thus he made mockery of the legislative branch of government, whose concern it is by definition of our system, to correct the unjust law. Rhetorical abuses by the demagogue, characteristically expected in executive and legislative pursuits of elective offices, were shifted at Dayton to the judicial realm, though the presiding judge did not allow the shift to pass unchallenged, as the transcript of that trial shows. Through the journalistic distortions of the trial by people like H.L. Mencken, there came a confusion in the popular mind whose fruits are coming to harvest now with disturbing insistence: an instance is the doctrine that a private citizen has a legal (as opposed to moral) right to define what law is applicable to him. The doctrine of preferential treatment, instead of equal treatment, currently discussed as a necessary mode of correction of old social wrongs, is the inevitable consequence, and is indeed not a proposal but an accomplished fact, as the close inspection of federal institutions will illustrate. How those fruits turn ashes should be sufficiently indicated by the Birmingham Bombings and the Los Angeles Riots, effects as directly out of such causes as the Dayton Trial as American materialism is the result of Puritanism translated to Jamesean pragmatism. Typically, in searching for solutions to the racial problem, we look too narrowly at race. We fail to see that the concern for a breakdown in the Negro family's stability, which the Moynihan Report discovers, is more generally applicable than we are willing to admit and that political, social, and economic forces older than Franklin Delano Roosevelt or Lyndon B. Johnson strike deep into the issues. As Hawthorne pondered New England Puritanism, as Henry James pondered it — looking closely at Hawthorne and then at the emerging industrial society, finally from sanctuary in England — as Eliot pondered both Hawthorne's and James' reaction to changing America, himself early a refugee to England; so must we ponder, considering theirs and the Fugitive-Agrarian arguments and any others pertinent to our present confused situation. Lord Acton, examining "The Civil War in America: Its Place in History" some few months after Appomattox, said:

> The voice of European civilization, and the voice of the past alike, come to [the Americans] from another world. History is filled with records of resistance provoked by the abuse of power. But whereas in the old world the people produce the remedy, in America they produce the cause of the disease. There is no appeal from the people to itself. After having been taught for years that its will ought to be law, it cannot learn the lesson of self-denial and renounce the exercise of the power it has enjoyed.

A little earlier, Lord Macaulay, in an address to America, warned:

> Your republic will be as fearfully plundered and laid waste by barbarians in the twentieth century as the Roman Empire was in the fifth; with this difference; that the Huns and Vandals who ravaged the Roman Empire came from without and your Huns and Vandals will have been engendered within your own country, by your own institutions.

Frightening prophecy, this, in our Age of Anxiety, where inadequate means masquerade as ends: minimum wage or social security which are sold to the people by the government (who is the people) in cartoons, on television, and on post office walls. In an age in which items of manufacture are tranquilizers and ashtrays built to shatter when hurled against wall or floor to relieve tension, we should not be surprised by Molotov cocktails today against store walls from within which one bought food yesterday. Nor the subsequent tranquil dream of manna from government-operated skies tomorrow when statistical studies of the Watts area by economists and psychiatrists commend the operation. Nor is that individual, isolated maniac, daily reported in the papers, a less telling sign than the mob gone mad, though Manlius and the Sacred Geese of the Press seldom sound that alarm except in pursuit of a reader's easy tears or appropriations.

Because Stewart has underestimated, among other things, the strength of Greek and Roman culture in the South, and in Ransom, Davidson and Tate in particular, he fails to clarify the importance of the Scopes Trial to the Agrarian development. As it stands, the issue was far more fundamental than whether man is cousin to the monkey, which is what the journalists made of it and what it continues to represent in the excitable public mind. The trial was symptomatic of what was at stake — orderly government itself. And Ransom, whose training in Tennessee led him to concentrate on the Age of Pericles and Augustan Rome during his days at Oxford, could see that the decay of Athens described by Thucydides and of Rome by Suetonius, Plutarch, and Petronius was immediately relevant to the world whose center for him in the 1920s was Nashville, Tennessee. Ransom's vision of that world allowed him to deal directly with its immediate pressures and maintain his integrity as a poet. The sense of balance in his poetry — of idea to reality, of logical form to metrical, of particular concrete to general universal — owes a great deal to his training as philosopher, particularly to his study of the Greeks. Since Stewart does not adequately evaluate Ransom's knowledge of that civilization which extends to us from the Greeks and Romans and from old England, it is inevitable that he fail to do justice to Ransom's poetry, as we shall now see. In concluding with a consideration of one of Ransom's poems as it presents itself and as Stewart takes it, I intend to imply how intimately related are Ransom's critical, creative, and polemical aspects and demonstrate with Ransom as exemplum a complexity that Stewart has not adequately dealt with in his treatment of the major figures of the Fugitive-Agrarian movement.

V

In the hundred pages devoted specifically to Ransom's poetry and criticism, Stewart never satisfactorily integrates the background material explored in his first four chapters to determine how far and deep and high Ransom has gone. This assertion can be substantiated by reference to his evaluation of Ransom's "Bells for John Whiteside's Daughter." An early warning of the inadequacy of his study as literary criticism is the comment on this poem (on page 56) that here "Ransom skillfully manipulates stock figures and attitudes to ridicule the sentimental idealizing of childhood," as if the poem were satire. (The comment seems a distorted reduction of

Warren's careful analysis of the poem in "Pure and Impure Poetry.") In pages 220 to 222, Stewart explicates the poem in more detail, commenting on the confusion brought to the orderly adult world of the poem by the child's activities, she being a "non-conformist" to that world. "We are puzzled by the tone," he says, but the brief mention of diction and meter doesn't help solve the puzzle. A conclusion is reached about the poem however: "Ransom makes us look beyond the image of the storybook and valentine to a real little girl, who might be living next door." Stewart gets no further with an explanation of the poem's effectiveness because he discards as not pertinent certain clues, and neglects the relevance of background already prepared in the first half of his book. Tate remarked, in conversations recorded in *Fugitives' Reunion*, that the influence of the Greeks on Ransom's work is far more subtle than on his or Davidson's work. Even that "Athenian Gentleman," Aristotle, who in his own way was full of Ransom's "fury against abstractions" divorced of concretes, must not be dismissed as influence because of an occasional and limited objection to him by Ransom in later critical essays. And in addition to the classical influence, one must remember as well his early critical argument with Tate over Eliot's poetry, a debate central to Ransom's aesthetic interests. The debate is discussed as history in the early chapters but unaccountably neglected in the pages on Ransom as poet and critic.

Ransom's examination of Eliot's early poetry led him to conclude, as he wrote Tate, that there was a failure of form in "poem after poem." He wrote Tate also his conception of the effective poem, as contrast to what he considered Eliot's practice, a letter quoted by Stewart:

> The art-thing sounds like the first immediate transcript of reality, but it isn't; it's a long way from the event. It isn't the raw stuff of experience.... There must not be a trace of the expository philosophical method, but nevertheless the substance of the philosophical conclusion must be there for the intelligent reader.

Stewart wrestles unsuccessfully with an explanation of Ransom's sudden maturing in "Necrological" (which poem is inadequately explicated by Stewart in his *John Crowe Ransom,* University of Minnesota Pamphlets on American Writers, November 18, 1962), "Conrad at Twilight," and "Bells for John Whiteside's Daughter," poems coming so soon after the initial fumblings published in Ransom's first collection, *Poems about God*. But surely the key is here in Ransom's words to Tate. The poem *must seem to be* a spontaneous overflow of powerful feeling (and Ransom alludes favorably in this letter to Wordsworth's phrase "recollected in tranquility"), as exhibited in the Odes of Keats. Its form must be strict enough to prevent its being, or appearing to be, only "the raw stuff of experience," as one might consider Eliot's "Love Song of J. Alfred Prufrock." But even given strict form (which involves metrical, logical management through a strict point of view), it must not serve a predominantly expository philosophical intention, as "Sweeney among the Nightingales" may be argued to serve. Whether or not one grant Ransom that Eliot fails to find the right form, his arguments are directly helpful toward discovering what he himself is about in such a poem as "Bells for John Whiteside's Daughter."

As if adapting elements of the *Poetics* of Aristotle to his practice, Ransom concerns himself with the possibilities of a dramatic lyric. The poem is to embody an action performed and not stated or narrated, by means of a restriction of form that functions as a staging of the action. Thus the poem may give its illusion of immediacy. In other words, Ransom attempts to realize in the lyric a kind of action which is on a scale different from but analogous to that action described by Aristotle as executed by Sophocles. On the one hand Ransom has reservations as to the validity of the kind of summary of character one finds in Browning's "The Bishop Orders His Tomb" or Eliot's "Portrait of a Lady." On the other hand, he eschews poetry as contemplation, such poetry as one finds in Wordsworth's "Intimation Ode" or Eliot's later poetry. He is dissatisfied by what he calls "a mere cross-section of a brain at a given instant," and by poetry as philosophy or religion, though it should be noted that, in his statement to Tate, he requires such foundations to the poetry. Still he is equally dissatisfied by a poetry whose form itself becomes its end, one species of "pure poetry." Ransom says to Tate: "It is the formal preoccupation that destroys art, which must not appear meditated." Here, clearly, is an aesthetic concern for organic unity of the poem that is compatible to the *Poetics*, once more anticipating some of Warren's argument in "Pure and Impure Poetry." There is also a concern that "the work of art must be perfectly serious, ripe, rational, mature—full of heart, but with enough head there to govern heart." This to Tate in 1922, to which Ransom adds parenthetically that this concern "must be the trace that classical pedagogy has left on me." Classical pedagogy, both in manner and matter, would have introduced Ransom not only to the balanced mind of Aristotle but to the superlative uses of the concrete embodying the universal that one encounters repeatedly in the *Odyssey* and *Iliad*. The details of Hector's farewell to his son at the gates of Troy are more relevant to "Janet Waking" than a superficial look suggests. No wonder a reader of Stewart's analysis becomes exasperated then when Stewart concludes that, since there are very few allusions to "Odysseus, Achilles, Hector, Agamemnon, Oedipus, Creon, Aeneas, or the legends of Thebes and Rome," Ransom must have "put aside the classics when writing his poetry." One might as reasonably conclude that, setting down the title *Ulysses,* Joyce put aside his knowledge of the *Odyssey.*

The inadequacy of Stewart's perception here is of a piece with that already objected to and charged to his provincialism earlier, but it requires some further pursuit so as not to seem gratuitous literary judgment on my part. When a poet has assimilated his experiences, whether as southerner or as classical scholar, it becomes unnecessary to celebrate an awareness through the advertisements of allusion, those literary hiccups that mar the verse of many who gulp too thirstily at the Pierian springs after long wanderings in the desert. Such allusions in one's poetry — and this is the criticism Davidson directs against Eliot be it remembered in that complex poem Stewart characterizes as suitable "to the readers of Zane Grey" — may damage its authority. The general point on Stewart's failure as critic is that he does not see, either in the art or in the argument (of Davidson, Ransom, and Tate in particular), a view of traditionalism which makes possible an action of the mind on principles in relation to the immediate event without the necessity of a preliminary dwelling upon principle. Ransom's assimilation of Aristotle and of the concept of the family common to Ithaca and Nashville affect "Bells for John Whiteside's Daughter" and a dozen more of his central poems. And though Tate might disagree with the two older men on Eliot's accomplishment as poet, there is a firm agreement on principle. The "form requires the myth," Tate says in his "Horatian Epode to the Duchess of Malfi," a poem published early in the Fugitive days. It is a poem which itself might serve as an admirable commentary on what Ransom is about in his poetry, especially in regard to the inconclusive resolutions of his poems, an aspect of his poems one finds analogue to in Greek drama.) All three men feel that myth, to be effective in art, must be as intimate as breath; otherwise myth itself becomes a part of that "formal preoccupation that destroys art." As Davidson puts it in "The Thankless Muse and Her Fugitive Poets," "the images and symbols, in fact the total economy of the poem, require the support of a tradition based upon a generally diffused belief.... And since a tradition could not flourish without a society to support it, the natural step was to remember that after all we were southerners and that the South still possessed at least the remnants ... of a traditional, believing society." It is natural growth then when the most talented of the Fugitives— Ransom, Davidson, Tate, Warren — move on to Agrarianism.[9] Instead of a pursuit to become what they are not, a pursuit accompanied by some sense of panic in that fleeing of the desert signaled by Eliot's movement East from St. Louis to London and Pound's from Idaho to Italy, there was an exploration of what they were, in Nashville, Tennessee. And what they were they found already exhibited in some of their best poetry.

What this distinction means to the mode of Ransom's poetry can be quickly seen by a contrast of "Bells for John Whiteside's Daughter" to "Sweeney among the Nightingales." Eliot's adaptation of the ballad stanza allows a detached irony. The poem is static, an instrument for the weighing of failures, casting Sweeney against Agamemnon for instance. The correlatives in Eliot's poem function in the interest of philosophical conclusion, scene balanced by allusion, even as does the technique of the point of view. Eliot's concern is spiritual death, a concern which leaves more than a trace in the poem of "the expository philosophical method." Ransom's poem deals also with death, but in the manner of the Greeks rather than of Dante: his point of interest is with the ambiguity of acceptance of the inevitable, rather than with the spiritual solution of that ambiguity. Consequently both the ballad form and the correlatives it embodies function quite differently from Eliot's. To the point also is Ransom's expressed belief that death is the most poetic of subjects, by which he means the death of a particular person (not limited to a beautiful woman as in Poe) at a particular time, not a wasting of the soul into nothingness. He says, "there is no recourse from death, except that we learn to face it, and to get on speaking terms with it, and then have the characters who leave us and bereave us pass as magnificently as possible." The comment is closely directed toward the concrete reality of death; that is, the view is a dramatic one rather than a philosophical one.

The singular thing about Ransom's "Bells for John Whiteside's Daughter" is not that the reality enacted in it is that of the little girl "who might be living next door" as Stewart thinks, but the state of mind we might perceive our neighbor going through if we were attentive to his grief, given the unexpected death of his child. Thus the point of view in the poem is shifted slightly out of the parent's mind, the clue being the Browningesque title (compare "My Last Duchess"), so that the voice of the poem, the narrator's, is not literally the parent's. It is as if a close neighbor or kinsman looked over the father's shoulder. (Contrast Ransom's point of view in "Dead Boy," in which poem the words are those of an alienated kinsman, an expatriate southerner.) The slight shift in point of view allows for a firmness of the consciousness that deals with the ironic reality of a child's death, a necessary point of control to prevent either the sentimental Charybdis which Warren notes as contrast in James Russell Lowell's "After the Burial" or the Scylla of harsh satire of the adult's vision of childhood which Stewart takes the poem to embody. The poem presents, as an action, the shock of grief attendant upon the sudden impingement of that final disorder, death, upon the orderly consciousness of the adult. Thus the ballad stanza itself serves a different kind of ironically-presented disorder from that in Eliot's "Sweeney" poems. A reader experiences action similar to that found in a play: the disordering of the adult's mind, followed by a gradual return to painful order. Out of a state of shock, the voice of the poem moves to a dignity of grief; and the careful working of that movement, which is the poem's action, gives a dramatic unity to the poem.

To consider the poem's effect, and to some extent how Ransom's artistry brings it about: there lies behind the adult's voice a feeling of betrayal. The minor acts of violation by the child — the noises of yesterday that battered adult order, usually with little more than irritating effect on adult or goose (a nice juxtaposition of characters in the poem) — those minor acts seem suddenly more subversive, more nearly acts of conspiracy that call for something stronger than any initial "Alas!" This *brown study*, for which the child has abandoned her lesser wars, is louder in the initial instant of grief than her *bruited wars*, being as it is the final sound that time makes. But the disparity itself means guilt by association in the momentarily shocked and unbalanced mind of the narrator. It is against this shock at the depth of death that the poem happens, with the poem's voice fighting for formal control against the threat of emotional chaos. Thus the relatively strict ballad form (as opposed to the freedom of form in a poem like "Prufrock") serves the action in that it is at once appropriate to the reality of the sophisticated mind that is the narrator's and allows as well a form to the emotional action, rather than being a slice of emotional consciousness, "the raw stuff of experience." The action, that is, has a beginning, a middle, and an end.

Specifically, the first stanza establishes the state of shock in the narrator's mind: the interruptions of the expected meters in 1 and 2 help register the shock (for the poem assumes of the reader an experience of traditional meter regularity and such sophisticated manipulations as one finds in Keats' fourth line of the stanzas of "La Belle Dame Sans Merci"). The diction of the stanza is also involved in the shock. The understatement of *brown study* rings with a hollowness that allows for disappointment, irritation, puzzlement, being followed as it is by that Miltonic word of such catastrophic implication, *astonishes*. After this arresting by shock, there is a smoother recovery in the movement of the next three stanzas, toward the final resolution in the fifth stanza. Just enough anger is carried over to keep the remembrances of the child as she was when alive from becoming maudlin, in addition to which there is an elevation through disbelief. This elevation, with its tone of incredulity, attends the images and the sweep of a single sentence through the middle section toward the final stanza. It is, in that sentence, as if life itself is incredible in the presence of the hugeness of death, a nice inversion of the expected — that death is unbelievable in the presence of life, the state of mind from which the adult is initially astonished. The reversal is psychologically appropriate to an emergence from shock. The littleness of life is exaggerated: a child's annoying geese becomes a *war*. And through this disturbed attempt to name the disparity between life and death, the poem's mind moves on to the final stanza.

In the final stanza we are reminded that whatever tragedy there is belongs to the speaker, and not to the child, by an arresting of the flow of those central stanzas and a return to the irregularity of the initial stanza. There is not, however, a duplication but a counter pointing of that first stanza, thus establishing the limits of the poem's progress and resolving its tension. The speaker rises out of shocked confusion to acceptance. Such hesitation, appropriate to initial shock, as is carried in the first stanza by the meter of *little body* and *footfall* now finds an aesthetically pleasing resolution in the finality of *sternly stopped* and *primly propped* of the last stanza. Even the repetition of *brown study* in the end-stopped line of the last stanza has a different emotional value from its first use in the run-on line of stanza one. What such use of words and music do of course is produce as a reality a state of mind. But the poem is neither the raw stuff of experience nor a history of grief, as in the narrative moment of "Prufrock" or philosophical moment of "Sweeney among the Nightingales." It is a moment of awareness expanded to accommodate a dramatic beginning, middle, and end. Ransom's use of awareness is too close to what Aristotle means by *action* to dismiss the Greek influence out of hand. And his concern for death as a cause for a poem is one akin to that of Sophocles' *Oedipus the King*, rather than to Plato's *Phaedo* or Poe's "Philosophy of Composition." It is hardly suitable then to consider that Ransom, as he was assuming the position of influence among the Fugitives which they unanimously ascribe to him, "had no firm base of ideas from which to venture forth," as Stewart says of him.

Indeed, returning to the basic faults of *The Burden of Time* expressed initially, through which I presented John Stewart as typical of the New Provincialism, I can but conclude that it is Stewart who has no firm base of ideas from which to venture upon such a study as he has undertaken. Where a Ransom can play — upon such a basic cultural heritage as that from the Greek dramatists and Homer and upon such accepted form as the ballad stanza — a unique music, Stewart, swept by the popular current of the day, can do little more than echo the cries of the moment and deal hardly at all, though at great length, with ideas or art.

III. On Fugitives, Agrarians and New Critics

Notes

1. John L. Stewart, *The Burden of Time: The Fugitives and Agrarians*. Princeton: Princeton University Press, 1965. 552pp. $12.50.

2. On Stewart's abuse of historians, as well as of history: he says of Frank Lawrence Owsley, "The Agrarians may have admired Owsely's version of the wicked North, but professional historians looked upon it with laughter and scorn." Stewart offers no substantiation of the charge, either by concrete reference to historian or historical work. It is a procedure most suspect since Francis B. Simpkins, a professional historian (as was Owsley) whom Stewart twice appeals to as reputable is sympathetic to Owsley's views and cites Owsley as authority in his *The South Old and New* (page 497). For further substantiation, see Simpkin's *The Everlasting South*, particularly the chapter "Tolerating the South's Past."

3. Stewart is particularly negligent in his treatment of Tate's prose. He asserts that one of the failures "characteristic of all agrarian speculation on the relation of the writer to the times" is that it gives no "explanation of the alienation of the artist" since it takes "no account of forces having only indirectly or even no connection with the decline of tradition — mass production publication requiring huge sales, the development of a semi-literate market through public education, and the lingering Puritan mistrust of arts." One need only read Tate's "Profession of Letters in the South," the first few paragraphs of which deal with these forces Stewart names. And one might note as well that Davidson's contribution to *I'll Take My Stand*, "A Mirror for Artists," is replete with awareness of these forces, as indeed are the writings in general of the Fugitive-Agrarians, a natural consequence of their struggles in publishing the *Fugitive* magazine.

4. Henry Grady's account of the burial of a man in Pickins County, Georgia, delivered to a northern audience, electrified the nation and led to journalistic gushings not yet spared us. If one looks closely at the speech, it shows clearly enough that Grady is championing raw materialism; there is no hint of a concern with whether the dead man had mind or soul. There is only a concern that the South make money by providing the materials for future burials. The passage serves beautifully as a specimen carrying that odor of death that hangs upon the lips of the New South spirit. After cataloguing the foreign materials used, the South having provided only the corpse, Grady continues: "We have got [since that burial] the biggest marble-cutting establishment on earth within a hundred yards of the grave [for future tombstones]. We have got a dozen woolen mills right around it [to provide burial clothes], and iron mines, and iron factories [to provide nails for the coffins]. We are coming to meet you [the North]. We are going to make a noble revenge ... by invading every inch of your territory with iron." This is the spirit championed since by such latter-day Gradys as Ralph McGill, who as of this writing has still seen no connection between Grady's philosophy and the Birmingham Bombings and Los Angeles Riots.

5. Davidson's concern for delving into the modern situation by looking closely at history and prevailing philosophy is one aspect of his kinship to Ezra Pound, who just after World War I began such probings in earnest. Though their solutions to the modern world's problems aren't the same (Pound tending toward a reformed centralized power that Davidson rejects), they are actively committed to castigation of a civilization Pound described in 1920 as an "old bitch gone in the teeth." Both committed themselves early on fundamental issues in an engagement larger than literary, in consequence of which both are critical of Eliot. Davidson's arguments against historical determinism and against the Eastern financial establishment, in his *Attack on Leviathan* notably, find complements in Pound's essays of the 1920s and 1930s collected in *Impact: Essays on Ignorance and the Decline of American Civilization*. Both have been influential teachers, as the many public acknowledgments indicate. On their concern for the public's relation to art, compare Pound's "Possibilities of Civilization: What the Small Town Can Do" (1936) to Davidson's "Mirror for Artists" (1930). Pound cites Cesena, Italy, as an example of what a few spirits can do toward establishing and preserving a cultural heritage. He would have found John Donald Wade attempting at Marshallville, Georgia, what he prescribes: "figure out what you can do with the local plant ... Find out something not being done in New York or London." And one recalls the cultural revival of Nashville in the 1920s, but particularly a failure to ignore New York, which

failure Davidson castigates in various poems and essays. One significant distinction between Davidson and Pound lies in Davidson's awareness of a heritage in the South that Pound denies; speaking of America Pound says, "We ... have no families who have lived father to son in the same house for 2000 (two thousand) years," as if his journey into Italy would answer the absence. Davidson decided early the truth of the epigram Pound quotes for our guidance: "intelligence is international, stupidity is national, art is local."

6. Predictably, because of the political explosiveness of the evidence in the Moynihan Report, it was initially suppressed by Secretary of Labor Wirtz, but has since been used by a variety of public educators from Theodore White to the president of the United States. What Moynihan discovered is what Lytle and Davidson pointed out 30 years ago, though they were not so intent on general dissolution as to suggest preferential treatment. In another 30 years perhaps it will be possible to study Hitler's "solution" to the Jewish problem and the militant liberal's solution to the Negro problem objectively enough to see that both destroy the individual, white or black or Jew, though the one died more immediately and spectacularly than the others. I expect as inevitable a shock to many readers from my yoking of the two "solutions," given a society that is materialistic and secular. But the truth seems evident that the social revolt of the 1960s is in the interest of things, though much talk is made of freedom, human rights, and so on. The real desire is toward color television and a second car, via civil service sinecure.

7. Dr. James McConnell of the University of Michigan Center for Research of Mental Health, in reporting on experiments with RNA acid used with flatworms and rodents, made the suggestion presumably in jest. But the enthusiasm with which a reporter present seized the jest as his serious lead, to which his paper prefaced a catching headline ("Scientist Says Injections Might Replace Lecture," Athens *Banner-Herald,* March 6, 1966) serves to indicate what demand may be made of RNA by the "popular will," particularly in an election year.

8. Again, it is evidence of the failure of Stewart's study that Virgil, Horace, and Latin poetry in general are ignored, though no full treatment of Davidson is acceptable that doesn't deal with this influence as it affects both his poetry and ideology. See John Crowe Ransom's review of Davidson's *Long Street:* "The Most Southern Poet," *Sewanee Review,* Spring 1962.

9. It is interesting to observe a continuing community of minds among Ransom, Davidson, Tate, and Warren, as separate from the other Fugitives gathered at Vanderbilt for the 1956 reunion. More is involved than simply deference to their superior talents and accomplishments as the four come to occupy the center of the stage to answer questions posed by some of the others present or debate a question concerning Fugitive accomplishment or Agrarian argument. Warren's participation bears looking into, he being the one of the four who seems most estranged. Davidson remained at Vanderbilt, teaching and writing; Ransom at Gambier had the *Kenyon Review* and his garden; Tate, though mobile, had the Church and Dante to steady him. Warren, the most restless of the group, had no such anchors, as the quality of his fiction since World War II seems to me to reflect. But it is Warren, in the final symposium of *Fugitives' Reunion,* who seizes finally upon the rambling attempt to establish what the Agrarians were about and talks with somewhat angry fervor about that spirit that moved them in the late '20s, with Ransom, Davidson, Tate approving his statement. The extent of Warren's disaffection with his old position is not clear, though on the "Today Show" (May 17, 1965), in connection with the release of his *Who Speaks for the Negro,* he repudiated his essay in *I'll Take My Stand* as being written while he was going to school in the South shortly before he saw the error of his ways. Still, the manner and the matter of his recent collections of poems, *You Emperor and Others* and *Promises,* indicate that the repudiation was not so thorough as his television statement would have it.

9

The Agrarians: Here and Now

> *In this brief essay Montgomery discusses the southern Agrarians' address to existence, focusing on the philosophical and theological implications of their criticism of modernity. Here, as elsewhere, he puts the word "southern" in quotation marks, signaling that he does not restrict the epithet to a geographical region south of the Mason-Dixon line. This "southerner" is distinguished by "his address to place, to the concrete portion of the created world it is his good fortune to inhabit," by his membership in a community of fellow creatures (a Burkean society that links those living, those who have died, and those yet to be born), and by his awareness of "the continuing presence of the past." But more than this, Montgomery's point is that the Agrarians (and other "southerners" like them) insist that man as the steward of nature and the maker (of arts and crafts, of houses and gardens) should live and work in harmony with "the Cause of existence." At the conclusion of the essay Montgomery summons that good "southerner" Alexander Solzhenitsyn to restate the Agrarian position. In his Harvard commencement address, Solzhenitsyn traces the West's spiritual confusion to "rationalistic humanism or humanistic autonomy: the proclaimed and enforced autonomy of man from any higher force above him." In two essays in* The Men I Have Chosen for Fathers *(University of Missouri, 1990), Montgomery expands upon the connections between the Agrarians and the great Russian novelist and social critic. See "Solshenitsyn at Harvard" and "Solzhenitsyn as Southerner," pp. 128–171.**

I should like to characterize, briefly, a certain type of "southerner" as a corrective to a very limited response one still encounters to the southern Agrarians. My "southerner" may or may not actually live in the southeastern United States; indeed, the attempt to isolate him geographically has been one of the more devious maneuvers to discredit the larger vision that lies at the heart of *I'll Take My Stand*. Wherever my "southerner" lives,

---

*This brief essay originally appeared in *The Hillsdale Review* 3.2: 12–17.

the distinguishing characteristic that marks him is his address to place, to the concrete portion of the created world it is his good fortune to inhabit. His characteristic address to place, to be detected by sensibility and not through the measure of statistics, gives him a surer sense of his own being than if he were committed to placelessness. It is possible, of course, to be committed to placelessness, through an act of will, which in the last analysis of its effect upon *person* becomes not simply a denial of place but a denial of one's own being. There is a considerable body of such placeless souls among us, of whom Solzhenitsyn speaks when he says: "Spiritually all intellectuals nowadays belong to a diaspora. Nowhere are we complete strangers. And nowhere do we feel quite at home."

Given the limits of our worldly existence, my "southerner" may find himself in exile from place, as does Solzhenitsyn, a man who would at once appreciate the "southernness" reported by Professor William Havard of Vanderbilt: "Where do you live?" asks the surveyor. And the middle-aged black man replies, "I *stay* in Chicago, but I *live* in Alabama." The willful denial of such a distinction by the members of our intellectual diaspora has a most seductive spokesman in Milton's great poem *Paradise Lost,* but one feels confident that one who *lives* in a place will not be taken in. The words from Milton's unhappy intellectual characterize the modernist drift in the world since the Renaissance so succinctly as to make them a suitable epigraph to the study of much of our philosophy, theology, and politics since Milton framed the cry of spiritual agony in a spirit capable only of *staying* in the world:

> The mind is its own place, and in itself
> Can make a hell of heaven, a heaven of hell.

On the other hand, the "southerner" of whom I speak, the person to whom some place separate from his own mind is of importance, discovers in his acknowledgement of a place other than his own mind that he thereby becomes member of a community of creatures, a community larger than his private moment and wider than his mailing address, though his participation in that community will very likely show itself at the local level. In consequence, he will feel his "southernness" in such a way that he will recognize a "southernness" in others far removed from him — removed by both time and place. There occurs, then, a recognition of removal, of separateness, that is far less destructive than our modern sense of alienation. For the discovery of such separateness is at once an elevation beyond time and place, whose reciprocal effect paradoxically is a firmer anchor in time and place for our "southerner."

To put the point again, my "southerner" discovers a transcendence of time and place from *within* an immediate community, however sparse its membership at his personal intersection of place in time. (Wherever two or three are gathered together, we are told.) He comes to such discovery precisely because he has come to understand with heart and mind the importance of old time to the contingency of his particular moment: He discovers the continuing presence of the past. And he discovers that the importance of place lies in his immediate community's consent to both the virtues and the limits of any person's existence and of the existence of all that is other than himself. The *here* and *now* become, quite possibly, numinous. (I must set aside the importance of grace on the point, only reminding the reader of the importance of the "local gods" in our literature of place, from Homer through Virgil and even down to such a troubled modern as Ezra Pound.)

If one gains some recognition of this quality of the "southerner's" address to existence, he will better understand, I believe, why the so-called southern Agrarians were and are much larger in their concerns in *I'll Take My Stand* than the provincial reading given them by certain critics would allow. For some of their readers still attempt to reduce them or dismiss them as merely a brief, local phenomenon of the rural South in the 1930s, a flickering across our national consciousness at the beginning of the Great Depression, a flickering long since darkened by the wandering priests of Progress who cast psychedelic lights of self-interest against a future never-never land. It should be clear by now, of course, that the fact of the Agrarians' coincidence at a place (Vanderbilt University) in a moment of our history (the 1920s and 1930s) is not a sufficient explanation of their growing appeal to an audience widely dispersed and various in its local callings. The importance of southern history to that group, as they saw themselves and as they have subsequently appeared to others, can hardly be exaggerated. But in that emphasis, which can be and has been used to isolate them, one may miss a larger point: in discovering a continuity in their own past and in their own place, they discovered themselves also citizens of a community more enduring than that brief history of a conjunction of persons which led to the landmark symposium, *I'll Take My Stand*.

Our growing hunger for history, after such long neglect, may be exploited into a fad, but only because it touches a deep general hunger more valid than any modernist's temptation to preserve the past in the amber of sentimentality — as when we declare a building a "national monument" and thereby rigidify our past. Most of the Agrarians came to know that, as Flannery O'Connor was to put the point in relation to herself as a southern writer: "To know oneself is to know one's region. It is also to know the world, and it is also, paradoxically, a form of exile from the world."

The Agrarian tributes to this understanding appear in the several arts through which they continued to bear witness—some as poets and novelists, others as historians and economists, and so on. For what they recognized in consequence of this discovery—some of them more deliberately than others—is that man as artificer, as maker of "things," whether of poems or arguments or objects, is most fully man when he is most consummately artist. As that good "southern" poet from England, David Jones, discovers for us in his poem *Anathemata* (his pilgrimage through his Welsh inheritance which parallels and complements the Agrarian recovery): man as *maker* is the more fully a witness to the first cause of being. With this recognition, one looks at the work of his own hands, whether it is a poem or a house or a garden, as a thing set aside, set above that which is only natural through an act of praise called art, the mode of our being that is most human. (I mean here to include in *art* our activities as various as the scientist's laboratory work and children's games.) What one makes, says Jones, is a thing "lifted up ... made over to the gods." This point of recognition was increasingly for the Agrarians, as it has been for many of their followers, a rediscovery—a recovery of an ancient wisdom about man's place in nature. It is a recovery that reaches beyond and deeper than the recent and more spectacular panic of the emerging religion of Environmentalism, a new Paganism paradoxically sired on nature by technocracy, in which for the most part self-interest is set against self-interest. (Naderism, from the Agrarian position, appears a confused chaos of alarms and sallies from no firm base in reality; that is, it lacks metaphysical grounding.)

What follows from the Agrarian recovery of this ancient ground is a conviction that man as maker, whether of poems or of nature civilized as in crops or nature reconstituted as in machines, participates in a continuing and much larger action of creation. He does so as long as he realizes that his concert of being, his tribute of making, must be in harmony with that larger action of creation. (The mystery of man's having been created in the image of God is ancient ground indeed, though perhaps no older than the recognition of a music of being, of all creation's tribute to its source.) As maker, man participates in the being of the world; as maker, he recognizes that the Cause of the world is in steady presence, requiring of man an ordinate relation to all being. Now within this recognition lie the roots of his concern for both the joys and responsibilities of stewardship. In the exercise of stewardship (the position contends) man is more closely involved than as mere caretaker for the absentee lord of the world's estate, a presumption which would leave man at his best as only a passive, vestigial Adam in a continuously decaying Eden. (See Faulkner's Ike McCaslin.) But he is also less than the ultimate lord of creation, the center of a power he is tempted to dream as an absolute of his own devising. (See the analysis of such dreamers as revealed in the work of Eric Voegelin or Gerhart Niemeyer.)

With this recognition of the limits of his active and passive participation in being for the "southern" Agrarian, the meaning *of family*, of *community*, of *law* and *art* and *work* and *play* takes on dimensions of meaning otherwise merely arbitrary. A concern for or contentment with sheer survival in nature on the one hand or for an absolute dominance over nature on the other must be rejected. One's sense of order within this recovered vision is an active sense of his ordinate homage to being itself, homage to the person of man and to the creatureliness of all that is not man.

And because this ordinate homage to being has as its principal measure a relation to the cause of being which men call God, one finds a ground beyond the arbitrary on which to found the necessary control of those private deconstructions of the self which our fathers named pride, envy, avarice — those insatiable foragers on mind let loose by the will when one declares the mind its own place. The public control of those ravenous beasts (pride, envy, avarice) which feed so implacably on each person's being is reflected in the world most persuasively in our manners, rather than in law purged of manners. For manners are an outward show of a respect for law, a sign of recognition that law is ordinately related to existence under the aegis of the Cause of existence. Through manners, in which personhood is recovered, law is seen as formulation of principles derived (through grace) from existence and its Cause, not as the primary cause of community or instrument of the deconstructions of nature toward gnostic dreams. This is to say that manners keep law from becoming at last the gnostic tyrant of the popular spirit which such "southerners" as Eric Voegelin and Solzhenitsyn and David Jones recognize as progressively destroying the foundations of civilized order in the West.

In his now famous Harvard speech, Solzhenitsyn remarks of the West that "Any conflict is solved according to the letter of the law, and this is considered to be the supreme solution." But, he adds: "Life organized legalistically has ... shown its inability to defend itself against the corrosion of evil." It has failed precisely because the letter of the law is insufficient to deal with the flexibility of evil. The letter of the law, in removing the spiritual dimension from our social bonds (by denying, that is, the existence of evil), has become vulnerable to the very real existence of evil, as it has also obscured the very real existence of good. It leaves our social institutions helpless before the confusing presence of Faulkner's Synopses or O'Connor's Misfits, whom we meet daily, or the larger manifestations of denied evil, less regular and alas increasingly less arresting — an Adolf Eichmann or Charles Manson or Reverend Jim Jones.

I am myself quite convinced that this good "southerner" Solzhenitsyn is right in pointing to the worldly cause of our spiritual disorientation: "rationalistic humanism or humanistic autonomy: the proclaimed and enforced autonomy of man from any higher force above him. It could also be called anthropocentricity, with man seen as the center of everything that exists." That is precisely the position defended by Milton's Satan. And in relation to these other "southerners," the Vanderbilt Agrarians, it is well to remember that Robert Penn Warren suggested calling their symposium "Tracts against Communism." In doing so, Warren was recognizing the spiritual dimension of the Agrarian position, so sharply counter to the general Western understanding of "agrarian reform" in our century. For "agrarian reformers," as recent history has demonstrated so tragically, assume the world's body and the minds of men (other than their own) to be the prime matter out of which to build ideological edifices, some of which now confront us more menacingly than they did at the time of *I'll Take My Stand:* such reformers are eager to assume this pendent world.

Our confused response to the cry of "human rights" as a principle of international diplomacy continues to show that we have not learned, as a nation, the spiritual dimensions of human rights. But our divided response to Afghanistan or Angola or Cambodia or (more recently) to Cuba and El Salvador underlines the urgency: we as a people must come to a clearer, deeper realization of man's responsibilities to the world's body and the inhabitants thereof. Very slowly we are waking to that necessity, and an excellent point of departure for the recovery of the ancient grounds of community in nature is the testimony of *I'll Take My Stand*. It is a more hopeful point of entry upon those grounds than our appeals to the United Nations—or even appeals to our Congress as that body is presently peopled.

10

Misunderstanding Criticism

> *In this essay-review Montgomery reviews Cleanth Brooks's* William Faulkner: First Encounters *and* The Presence of Grace and Other Book Reviews *by Flannery O'Connor. He discusses the New Criticism practiced by both Brooks and O'Connor, and the dangers to poets and critics when they misunderstand this criticism. The New Critics have been blamed for separating art and life, and some of them did. Montgomery defends the southern practitioners of the New Criticism (Cleanth Brooks, Robert Penn Warren, John Crowe Ransom, and Allen Tate) from this charge. He does find that modern criticism, devoted to scholarly detachment, to academic "objectivity," separates the critic from his subject and from the larger life revealed in the writer's work. But he is pleased to note that Brooks avoids this pitfall in his study of the South's greatest novelist. Flannery O'Connor claimed that the New Criticism of Brooks and Warren is a rearticulation of Thomistic principles, and Montgomery agrees, seeing these principles evident in Cleanth Brooks's work.*
>
> *St. Thomas is also a presence in the thought of Montgomery's fellow Georgia writer Flannery O'Connor, and Thomism in her writings is a focus of three of Montgomery's books:* Why Flannery O'Connor Stayed Home *(Sherwood Sugden, 1981),* The Trouble with You Interleckchuls *(Christendom College Press, 1988), and* Hillbilly Thomist: Flannery O'Connor, St. Thomas and the Limits of Art *(forthcoming from McFarland).*

At some point in one's encounter with the imposing work of William Faulkner, one will want to read Cleanth Brooks's larger studies, *The Yoknapatawpa Country* and *Toward Yoknapatawpa and Beyond*. But the general reader should start with *First Encounters*, a prologue written after Mr. Brooks made the long journey and returned to share it, generously and considerately. One starts here not simply to learn how to read Faulkner's

---

*This essay-review originally appeared in *Chronicles of Culture*— 8.5 (May 1984): 22-24.

great work; the deeper lesson is how to move beyond Yoknapatawpa, to understand the relation between life and art. Mr. Brooks, who has been called "the best critic of our best novelist," knows that literature provides a resonant ground for those serious social pleasures though which we pay homage to the community of man, to our strengths and weaknesses, individually and in concert. The end of such social encounter is not simply knowledge but understanding. Reading this "little book" (as Mr. Brooks calls it) is like listening to good conversation about life itself between a great artist and his best reader. It is to learn what it means to be civilized — and well-mannered, for Mr. Brooks includes the reader in the colloquy as equal to the serious pleasures.

By such tribute to Mr. Brooks, I suggest that he is very much "southern," but I intend "southernness" as a much more inclusive term than the provincial understanding of it when it is applied with pejorative undertones. There is an important point at stake, given the growing tendency among students of American criticism to misunderstand Mr. Brooks as "New Critic." Mr. Brooks's "southernness" is of more ancient lineage than a superficial anchor in geography, politics, or history (though he is more than superficially anchored in the historical South); thus, his conversation has an added dimension as it touches upon the fabric of Faulkner's own "southernness." Mr. Brooks understands that one must make discoveries about "southernness" for oneself, out of one's own experiences as aided and abetted by the witness of one's forefathers — in this instance Mr. Brooks himself talking about theme, character, plot in selected stories and novels of a great novelist. It is our good fortune (and Faulkner's) that Mr. Brooks is himself southern; he knows firsthand the language and customs Faulkner draws upon and often assumes common to his reader. Given the inevitable lapse from old ways and words, Mr. Brooks can provide a continuity that helps us avoid misunderstanding. *First Encounters* is in a significant way a companion to that "New Critic" text that revolutionized the teaching of literature in the academy, the famous or (in some quarters) notorious Brooks and Warren *Understanding Poetry* (1938).

How refreshing are Mr. Brooks's delight in *The Hamlet* and his eagerness to share its rich fullness, while being considerate of the reader's rights of discovery. It is as if Mr. Brooks has practiced his art for a long time to be prepared to render homage not only to a great artist, but to our shared life. That ordinate homage is a gift to us. Alas, this book is of a kind made almost impossible by modern academic concerns for civilization which require the habit of detachment from existence, a detachment which is called "objectivity" but which most often can provide only sterile abstractions of art or life suited to the mechanics of publication, lest the scholar perish in the academic marketplace. (If we were wise in our concern for civilization we might discourage young scholars from publishing books. To publish out of one's gifts rather than as a necessity dictated by a job description might produce at last such wise works as this, in which one has a civilized host serving our mutual humanity to its good health.)

Mr. Brooks as "New Critic"—and indeed that whole amorphous movement—appears to be, increasingly, misunderstood and blamed for a range of ills from the "deconstructionist" fad to the deaths of poets like John Berryman and Robert Lowell. New Critic porridge can be deadly, of course, depending upon the partakers. The "southern" members of that movement, however, are too often misrepresented by some who properly lament literature's turning against itself in deconstructionism or bewail the suicides of gifted poets. I think we may get at the point best by turning to Flannery O'Connor's *The Presence of Grace*, a collection of her brief reviews, contributed for the most part to her diocesan paper, *The Georgian Bulletin*. She is speaking to a more restricted audience than does Mr. Brooks, to Georgia Catholics.

Miss O'Connor's reasons for writing these reviews are interestingly complex. She is concerned with "the generally low level of Catholic taste" for one thing, in art, history, theology. She playfully refers to this work as acts of penance, but there is a serious edge to the play, given her recognition of how ineffective the reviews are likely to be. They do allow her to pursue her interest in Old Testament studies as a dimension of her fictional concern with prophecy; in disciplined descriptions of work by Maritain, Gilson, Voegelin, and others, she confirms her understanding of art and history. For those who savor the compact incisiveness of Miss O'Connor's writings, this collection is a pleasure.

She castigates a new novel as "fictionalized apologetics" which "introduces a depressing new category: light Catholic summer reading." She observes elsewhere "the clerical gift for bringing forth the sonorous familiar phrase of slowly deadening effect." Zen, she observes, since it is "non-conceptual, non-purposive, and non-historical," is therefore "admirably suited to be exploited by the non-thinker and pseudo-artist." She advices her local audience that Caroline Gordon's *How to Read a Novel*, "along with Maritain's *Art and Scholasticism*, should be studied by any Catholic group making public pronouncements about literature." In reviewing a novel by Julian Green, she laments that "Spokesmen for the deliver-us-from-gloom school of Catholic criticism have found that this novel commits the unpardonable sin: it is depressing." She, to the contrary, declares it written "with great deftness and delicacy and with the moral awareness that comes only with long contemplation on the nature of charity ... it offers no solutions by the author in the name of God," being "completely lacking in false piety." Above all, she warns her southern Catholic audience to protect itself against the "assumption that there is a brand of criticism special to Catholics rather than that any good criticism will reflect a Catholic view of reality."

The collection, being the work of a gifted an devoted observer of humanity, is both a delight on its own merits and a rich mine for those students burdened by term papers and theses, though she would most likely regret such necessities. Her interest in Hazel Motes of *Wise Blood* or young Tarwater in *The Violent Bear It Away* is reflected in her remarks on grace, especially her concern for distinctions between Catholic and Protestant understandings. One discovers also additional evidence of her own indebtedness to the New Criticism, her uses of which make interesting juxtaposition to that of her contemporaries like Berryman and Lowell. In a generally perceptive essay in *The American Poetry Review* (May/June 1983), Marjorie Perloff examines those "*Poètes Maudits* of the Genteel Tradition," finding them poisoned by the "brooksandwarren" (Lowell's word) approach to poetry. She finds these middle-aged waifs inheriting from Modernists a principle "codified by the New Criticism ... the rigid separation of *art* from *life*." "If Lowell hadn't existed, surely the New Criticism would have had to invent him." Of Lowell, who turned the personal to poetry regardless of its violations of persons, Miss Perloff mimics his self-justification: "For wasn't poetry, as Ransom and Tate had taught him, wholly unrelated to life?" Well, no. It is one thing for Lowell to have misunderstood; it makes him a pathetic figure in his own poetry. But it is serious critical error not to distinguish the wayward student from his teachers. Certainly Ransom, Tate, Warren, and Brooks teach no such thing. (One should read Tate's essay contemporary to his influence on these displaced poets, "The New Provincialism," to begin the distinction.) What is taught, at least by the "southern" members of the New Criticism, is not that art is unrelated to life but that it is one aspect of human life. This lesson was unlearned and thus illustrated by the pathetic confusion in the lives of Lowell, Berryman, Blackmur, Schwartz, and their kindred. It is worth reflecting then that Flannery O'Connor and these poets share the same teachers but come to very different understandings about art's relation to life. The fault Miss Perloff lays at the teachers' door is in the poets, as may be briefly demonstrated by looking at the "Letter to Teachers" preface Brooks and Warren supply to that most influential New Critic book, *Understanding Poetry*.

In the "Letter" the argument is that if poetry is to be studied as literature, "one must grasp the poem as a literary construct before it can offer any real illumination as a document." It must be read as human artifact before one can with any safety see its proper correspondences as a document to life. Thus the three principles of the anthology:

1. Emphasis should be kept on the poem as poem
2. The treatment should be concrete and inductive
3. A poem should always be treated as an organic system of relationships, and the poetic quality should never be understood as inhering in one or more factors taken in isolation.

The letter closes by quoting with approval Louis Cazamian: "More important [to the student of literature as opposed to the student of history], and much more fruitful than the problems of origins and development, are those of content and significance. What is the human matter, what the artistic value of the work?" These matters, of course, grew out of history no less than from immediate human experiences, in recognition of which one may not overlook such poems in this revolutionary text as Donald Davidson's "Lee in the Mountains" and Tate's "Ode to the Confederate Dead." Whatever its origins — immediate or remote in experience — art is not here separated from life. And the celebrated concern with paradox by these critics in their text is one manner of homage to the mystery of life, lest the work of art be reduced to a "document" whereby life itself is reduced.

That our latest generation of lost poets misunderstood their teachers on this point is rather conspicuously documented by their lives. Indeed, their common problem is a failure to separate life from art in significant ways. Remembering Santayana on the question, we may say with Miss Perloff that they are the last sons of the Genteel Tradition. Removed from the larger mysteries of life, they reduce both art and life to the circumference of the personal, excluding in subtle ways other persons. Increasingly, they are unable to distinguish their own life from their art. The illusion they suffer, which gives them a limited energy, is of the vortex, with art overflowing from the personal. The reality they suffer, however, is that of the maelstrom, with the ego self-consumed. There is a religious intensity of testimony in them, but it is the crying out of the lost souls in the desert and prophecy only indirectly. Their work has the force of entropy. Freud, their priest, combines with the New England Puritanism in them as they attempt to rationalize their predicament, giving them a sense of doom which becomes too often a wailing self-justification.

Flannery O'Connor, to the contrary, sees in the New Criticism a rediscovery of artistic principles articulated by St. Thomas; confirmation she finds in Gilson and Maritain, particularly in Maritain's *Art and Scholasticism*. She finds it also in that very "southern" writer Caroline Gordon's *How to Read a Novel*. These rediscovered principles are conspicuously present in Mr. Brooks's book. (In her letters to would-be writers, Miss O'Connor repeatedly recommends Brooks and Warren's *Understanding Fiction*, sending her copy to one correspondent and remarking that it is "full of my juvenile notes.") The heart of this mater is the distinction between man as creator and God as Creator, between man as Artist and God as "artist." If art is not carefully distinguished from life in the light of this distinction, it becomes inevitable that the poet confuse himself with God. Since he cannot create ex nihilo, he can but feed upon himself.

The consequence of such confusion is our general decline into the new gnosticism about which Eric Voegelin (one of Miss O'Connor's authors) warns us. For man's assumption of himself as the god of being touches not only poets but scholars and politicians and theologians as well. The consequence of the error in the poet is that pathetic self-consumption toward nothingness reflected in sad, wayward poets like Lowell and Berryman. They may survive more as epitaphs of the age than as abiding poets; that they recognize this likelihood is repeatedly revealed in their lives and letters, but nowhere more conspicuously than by the sardonic (not tragic) irony of their poetry. That sort of sad failure is why it is important to value art as praised and practiced by Cleanth Brooks and Flannery O'Connor.

Part IV

On Individual Authors

11

For Andrew, in Celebration

> *Here Marion Montgomery pays tribute to Andrew Lytle, perhaps the liveliest of the southern Agrarians. Noting Mr. Lytle's wit and humor and liveliness in his creative and critical work as well as in his personal encounters with others, Montgomery recalls Lytle's 1985 lecture "The Habitable Garden" at the University of Georgia and the social gathering in his honor at the Montgomerys' Crawford home. At this festive gathering, late in the evening, Mr. Lytle and others must have recalled Lytle's admonition in the Agrarian Manifesto I'll Take My Stand: "Throw out the radio and take down the fiddle from the wall." Actually, those gathered sang old folk songs to the tune of a guitar, not a fiddle.**

When Andrew Lytle was invited by our department to visit us as the John Olin Eidson Distinguished Scholar in English last year, the Athens *Observer* announced in its calendar of events: "Andrew Lytle, yes, THE Andrew Lytle speaks on the craft of fiction." The wonder and pleasure implicit in that emphatic adjective, I trust, proved gratifying to this distinguished gentleman, whose fiction and essays have not always been afforded the general respect they require. That his virtues as a man of letters have been long treasured by some is evident; that his audience will continue is assured in the writing itself; that it will grow is signaled by the increasing concern abroad in the land for rediscovering the grounds in which his literary virtues are built and to which he bears witness. It is to that ground that I speak, rather than to his work itself, and I think the most direct way to its recovery lies in recognizing its presence in the man himself. And so I'd choose to celebrate the fullness of person we name with respect and affection THE Andrew Lytle.

But such recognition requires, as he has taught us, a balance between private affection and public respect and deference, lest order itself — not

---

*This tribute to Mr. Lytle was published along with others in a special number of *The Chattahoochee Review* 8.4 (Summer 1988): 61–64.

only in the realm of letters but in the *res publica*—be set awry. He makes the point in *A Wake for the Living*:

> Not to know the difference between the public thing, the *res publica*, and the intimate is to surrender that delicate balance of order which alone makes the state a servant and not the people the servant of the state.

The loss of a clear vision of this distinction erodes both public and private things, causing disintegrations in the social fabric of community and leaving a randomness in personal concerns.

Such is the decay some of us lament as "modernism," which Mr. Lytle has engaged at many levels and for many years: in his analysis of fiction as various as *War and Peace* and *Madam Bovary;* in his long pursuit of the meaning of family and community to be found in the history of his region; and in a culmination of those concerns by dramatizing family and community strengths and weaknesses in the most arresting of his own fictions, *The Velvet Horn*. And he has also given us more directly and more personally the sum of his long concerns in a critical commentary upon our world, *A Wake for the Living*. Here I mean *critical* in one of its special uses. For in sum the work is a joyful celebration of his own engagement of the diversely created world and as such a reminder that we are, as a society, at a crucial turning point in our relation to creation. His genial irony (witness the title) alerts us to the fact that much more is at issue than the memoirs of a distinguished literary critic and teacher and editor and fiction writer. The book is not simply a recalling and summation, but the continuing act of engagement. It is not a signal of the end of a life but a confident testimony of a continuing life which may be more fully entered upon through vision.

In the introduction to his lively *Wake* there is a key sentence, out of which we may discover the importance of the proper balance between public and private things. That same concern is, of course, rather central to that first collection of essays with the mischievous title, *The Hero with the Private Parts*. (A second collection is in the offing.) The mischief lies in the discomforting reminder of our inclinations to Manicheanism through any idealism that overlooks the mysterious realities of life in this world. He might have reminded us that heroes are not divinities by speaking of "heroes with feet of clay," but that approach itself hints Manichaean separations. And so he approaches matters of high seriousness with wit and humor to remind us of truths about the complexities of our existence in the world. The most silent of those truths is that the abiding concern for balance between the public and private things has more at issue than merely making community tolerable at our worldly level.

11. For Andrew, in Celebration

There are limits upon public and private concerns, then, a most crucial point, lest public things become an absolute imperative reducing community at last to a provincialism — a condition that seems endemic in modernism despite its confident commitment to the progress of secular millennialism. And limit is also important at the level of the private, lest as individuals we make that most fatal of mistakes, the one that tempts us to believe that each private person is his own and only true light. And so to that sentence in the *Wake* in which this complex truth is focused: quietly, confidently, and with an ordinate humility. "Now that I have come to live in the sense of eternity, I can tell my girls who they are." Telling his daughters, telling over the sad and happy account of their heritage. But also sharing with us at the public level of letters in the interest of our public and private good health. That is what his *Wake for the Living* is about.

Lest we misunderstand the fullness of the prophetic intentions of that work, lest we take as more apocalyptic than is warranted the funereal and elegiac suggestiveness of his title — this *wake* for those of us almost dead in life — we must remember Mr. Lytle's own act of living in the light in of eternity. For words like *elegiac* and *funereal* are inadequate to the witness he bears in his memoirs. He celebrates and accepts both life and death, as at an Irish wake, though without that notorious Irish abandon. What that means is clearer from a personal recollection, which I trust manages a proper balance between the private and what may be shared in public. When Mr. Lytle visited us in the spring of 1985, he gave publicly a very challenging paper on the possibilities of "A Habitable Garden," a speculative, metaphorical reflection upon the world since Adam. He also read one of his stories, with his engaging wit and humor — those sure signs of a resonant intelligence. He redeemed the time between those public appearances with class visits and with lively engagement of students and faculty wherever encountered — mornings, afternoons, nights. And then his visit to us came to an end.

I remember, and shall, a final gathering at Crawford. We were a motley flow, a Chaucerian assemblage of God's plenty, including the very old (among them several of his old friends) and the very young, with the several stages in between. In the midst of the festive farewell, as spry as if young — which he continues to be — and kindly wise as if old — as undeniably he is— Mr. Lytle. Talking into the night with a range of high and low topics, with a genuine pleasure in our presence as only those comfortable with life can manage. Telling stories about a pet turkey, recalling those who have been his friends and companions and who are to most of us large and shining names in our letters. Later he sang old songs with us, deep into the May evening, with the crowd at last beginning to thin, but Mr. Lytle never wavering.

I remember most poignantly a moment, at the shank of the evening when the guitar was being passed around as we sang old mountain songs and hymns and worksongs, that my grandson asked Mr. Lytle whether he knew "I Am an Old Confederate." No. And so, sitting on a piano stool by Mr. Lytle, the ten-year-old led us—those of us who knew or half knew the words. It was a ragged if enthusiastic rendition. Our young leader anxiously attentive to the particular words, to getting them right because they carry a history he as yet does not understand but understands in consequence his double responsibility to the words: both for the history they carry and his obligation to come to terms with that history. The rest of us, variously incapacitated by voice and knowledge, seeing that very old man and that very young boy caught up by Troy and Roncevals more locally taken. Despite our ragged show, Mr. Lytle seemed much taken and applauded us. Whereupon the boy withdrew and copied out the words, asking some of us in whispers how to spell some of the mysterious words—*Point Lookout, Freedman's Bureau*. At last he presented the document to Mr. Lytle, who received it with that dignity proper to receiving valuable gifts, with mutual manners as old as Homer. That was a ceremony near his leave-taking. How better conclude festivities? Back to Athens, then, and on to Monteagle on a Tennessee mountain. Back to the vegetable garden he had already planted, having already gathered his firewood against the always-coming winter.

At the last, he and I stood beside the car that would take him back to Athens for the night and then on home. A young graduate student seeing to that courtesy stood by. A dark night, no moon but plenty of stars, with the heavy smell of honeysuckle and privet, a new spring world all about us. We embraced and spoke farewells, knowing how tenuous if delightful in its wonder all this world is. I have not seen him again, but trust I shall. Meanwhile, I honor him for his delight in God's creation with all its rough and smooth variance, a delight that is his because he has "come to live in the sense of eternity." It has been his special gift as a man of letters to share much of that delight with us, whether we may have been close to him or not. Through that gift he will be long among us.

12

How to Get Here from There: A Tribute to Madison Jones on Our Passage Through Gehenna

> *Using Dorothy Sayers's essay "Why Work" and St. Thomas Aquinas' teaching on artistic principles and integrity as his point of departure, Montgomery praises Madison Jones for staying at home at Auburn University (not becoming a wandering teacher of creative writing) and for devoting himself to the good of the thing made in his fiction. This is the primary responsibility of the poet, not "rectifying humanity," as some poets and critics have presumed. "The artist is responsible 'to reason in making,' his responsibility being to the perfection of the thing he makes." Montgomery places Jones in company with other writers, especially southern writers such as Flannery O'Connor, Donald Davidson, and Allen Tate: All of them share a vision of human nature in which "the person is a created rational soul incarnate, through whose freedom as such a creature flows our history in a range of strengths and failures turning on the tension between love and self-love." The orientation to love of others rather than self is part of a tradition that reaches beyond these southern writers to Homer, Socrates, Sophocles, Aristotle, Virgil, Dante, Chaucer, and Shakespeare. Montgomery places Madison Jones in this worthy company.**

There is something awkward about public tribute to a man for the body of his works, especially when that tribute is not accompanied by Nobel or Pulitzer emoluments, which at least keep open his prospects. It becomes even more awkward in our Age of PR, when public comment genuinely held might serve only to make the skeptic more skeptical. The public's confidence in public words has eroded considerably since Ezra

---

*Along with other writings devoted to or honoring Madison Jones, this tribute originally appeared in *The Chattahoochee Review* 17.1 (Fall 1996): 43–51.

Pound put the danger more cynically than skeptically in skewering Arnold Bennett:

> I never mentioned a man but with the view
> Of selling my own works.
> The tip's a good one, as for literature
> It gives no man a sinecure.

But then Madison Jones has not only endured, he has survived the literary endangerment of his gifts. It is in praise of his deportment of those gifts that I venture on tribute.

When I received invitation to this special issue of *The Chattahoochee Review* celebrating Madison Jones, I happened to be reading an essay by Dorothy Sayers from the 1940s called "Why Work?" In it she warns that "It is not meet for us to leave the service of our [making of tables, if we are carpenters by gift] to preach the word." We should stick to table-making, not for our safety but as a moral responsibility to our peculiar gift as carpenter. In addition to which, good work does its own preaching. "It is the work that serves the community; the business of the worker is to serve the work." Not comfortable words to us, who are taught from the cradle that we can "be whatever we want to be," regardless of the limits of gift. Even our peculiar gifts are increasingly rejected as "undemocratic," though we have now succeeded in rejecting God as cause and must turn for culprit to cultural history, and in the latest desperation, to genetic determinism as rescue from any sense of having failed moral responsibility to our gifts of nature as this particular person.

Such thoughts were being stirred in me, then, when I was asked upon this venture, and I was struck at once in recognizing that Madison Jones is admirable in his devotion to his own "table making," his calling as fiction writer. He has from the beginning committed himself to his work as a responsible craftsman, concerned to make a good table, so to speak, which balances firmly on the floor, its legs suited to that balance so that it does not rock or tip over. And this is also to say that in his making, he responds to the realities of human nature, including his own, in deploying dramatically our common humanity as present in this moment of history and in the light of history as he can know it. Otherwise, any table he might make would not satisfy him as the primary judge of his own table-making.

One evidence that such is his virtue as "maker" is that he has not been an itinerant carpenter, though in the history of the South that actual calling was an honorable one, when good oak and hickory and the like native wood was at hand along the wandering carpenter's way. Madison has not joined the academic wanderers, a peculiar species in our age, speaking (or so I believe) the disintegration of the academy itself. A far remove in time and place from the Medieval wandering scholars, bearing more or less lively words as gift, and giving rise to a still viable — though now increasingly ignored — literary heritage. If circumstances sometimes require the wandering scholar — *homo viator* as poet, as with Dante — that has not seemed the primary cause of our wanderers' wandering, as Dorothy Sayers anticipates in her essay. There has been rather a pragmatic advantage, for instance, to the "creative" writer in teaching creative writing hither and yon, according to sudden institutional recognitions of advantages of such programs in attracting students to a "well-rounded" program, in order to justify the public largesse.

The dangers in self-enlargement through moving to higher and higher stations in the academic landscape have been, since World War II, accompanied by an accelerated deracination of the academy itself. It has been in competition for "names" rather than devoted to substantial character in discrete persons as faculty who support intellectual gifts. If one is poet or novelist, one can of course rationalize academic hopscotch by arguing such wanderings an advancement necessary to the perfection of one's own gifts as poet or novelist. One might even argue that a deracinated wandering, reminiscent of the Medieval troubadour poets, is even in the interest of the communities visited, on which visitation the poet brings the true and lively word to an otherwise isolated and benighted institution. In that drift of thought, how easy to become confused about reality. How easily one may come to believe himself the cause of his gift and thus distort a reality, even through the subtlety of his own gifts with signs— with words. That is, one may come to believe himself responsible *for* his gifts, rather than responsible *to* them, in which new formulation all the difference between illusion and reality perceived *through* gifts turns on the lowly preposition. One thus becomes savior of community, rather than servant to community.

And this is the point Dorothy Sayers speaks to in her essay when she observes that "to aim directly at serving community is to falsify the work; the only way to serve the community is to forget the community and serve the work.... The work takes all and gives nothing but itself; and to serve the work is a labor of pure love." Such a devotion of responsibility to one's gifts flows over to community as love, even though that community misunderstand — as did Socrates' community, for instance. (Socrates was a first victim in Western history, I'm diligent to remind us, of "teacher evaluation" gone awry.) One's primary responsibility is always to the perfection of his peculiar gifts, regardless of the diversity of gifts to each person. And in that devotion, the person participates in community ordinately, proportionately. The argument here is as old as St. Paul's address to the nature of community in respect to discrete, individual gifts in 1 Corinthians 12.

Though we may have seemed to abandon our concern to honor Madison Jones in such argument, we need only to be reminded of his constancy of devotion to his gifts, which devotion he exercised steadily, in relation to one place, Auburn University. In doing so, and without an intention to do so as primary, he is exemplum to our concern. Through his work in devotion to his peculiar gifts, and with a devotion beyond either self-interest or the interests of community (though he is not indifferent to either), he has held as primary, as the fundamental principle, a moral obligation of stewardship to his own gifts. How contrary to the general supposition about our gifts: our arrogant presumption easily absorbed from the spirit of our age that one owes it to oneself to rescue community, not through good works according to gifts inherent to our personhood, but through a vague intention to the "general good." That our academies have adopted this principle to justify their own existence at the close of our century measures the decline of the academy, its abandonment of intellectual integrity as its own primary reason to exist, at the expense of community. What Miss Sayers, and Madison Jones, know is that such a presumption is a deportment of sentimentality above the "good," enlarged to a vagueness by good intentions, thus paving a way to Hell, as old wise minds have reminded us all along. As for such old wise patrons of intellectual integrity in relation to the discrete gifts of our personhood, it is no accident that Dorothy Sayers is still remembered by some of us for her devotion to one of them, through her own considerable intellectual gift: to Dante, in translating the *Divine Comedy* and providing incisive explications of the vision caught by that great monument to unaging intellect. Our own recourse to her here is first of all made in order to emphasize a significant virtue she shares with Madison Jones as fiction writer, as a maker of his own imagined things. His has been a concern for the good of the thing he makes, and he has long recognized that responsibility as the moral responsibility of the artist. St. Thomas Aquinas on the point reminds us that the artist is not responsible for rectifying humanity, for "art does presuppose rectitude of appetite," a responsibility proper to the gifts of the philosopher or theologian as opposed to the artist. The artist is responsible "to reason in making," his responsibility being to the perfection of the thing he makes.

In our day, the "pure love" required of the craftsman for the thing he makes has been increasingly set aside in favor of techniques of making, whereby in the end there is an imposition of intentional form upon the made thing in the interest of technique itself, as if technique assured "originality."

It is a species of our religion of technology adapted to the production of art, more conspicuous in the popular media, perhaps, and especially in television art. But we cannot escape its increasing dominance of the academy itself. Indeed, the shifting of our concern for making within the academy might be symbolized by the growth and elevation of journalism as the principal academic "science" of making, with signs always defended as intending to the "general good" of society, of course, as is argued by other disciplines as well. Not to be outdone, English Departments (and Drama Departments) within the academy have shored against their own erosion by evolving "Creative Writing Programs," in which technologies of making are pursued, gradually abandoning a grounding of intellect in reason larger than technical justifications of any making. The distance between "good literature" and the public mind, nowhere more lamented than in Creative Writing Programs hungering for an audience, has at least this partial cause for the separation. (Technology better adapts a machine to use than it can a poem.) On this point, I am always reminded of what one of Madison Jones's old friends, Flannery O'Connor, says. Asked whether "creative writing" can be taught, she responded that, yes, it can, and that what results is the kind of writing we must then teach people not to read.

I am of their generation, and of their persuasion as revealed in their works, so that perhaps there is reason to recognize this companionship in valuing my own testimony here. And in making this tribute I may even be seen as violating the precept I just advocated, the primary responsibility of the artist to the good of the thing he makes. But then, I am not writing a poem or a story but advancing an argument about our gifts as persons, some persons being gifted in making imagined things—poems and stories. In the interest of my argument, and in praise of the implications in such devotion to gifts as peculiar to each person, I would not set a more general perspective to the argument, considering the nature of our age, in which community is in an accelerating decline. Those conditions can but exacerbate the poet's making, in that he lacks a sufficient community devoted to his principle concern with the good of the thing he is making. (Art's issue is not at last how large but how perceptive its audience.) In this respect, Dante had an advantage over our own poets in this attempt, an advantage remarked by some of them, including T.S. Eliot and Flannery O'Connor. On that circumstance of the poet's responsibility to his gifts then a few words more.

The poets I extol—Eliot, O'Connor, Madison Jones in our immediate concern—share in an understanding of the nature of the person, an understanding now generally rejected. And so his position as poet is counter to the evolved conclusions about human nature now dominant, the position established by Modernism as it has risen since the Renaissance. It leaves the poet troubadour I celebrate quite other than a wandering minstrel increasingly obsessed with his own self-interests, the Modernist effect upon the poet. He is rather like the old Psalmist, whose lament anciently was that "by the rivers of Babylon" he is tempted to sit down and weep, wondering "How shall we sing the Lord's song in a strange land?" Madison Jones's lament in this context gains a frictional context to his making, as in his praise of community even as it is drowned by a TVA project for instance. The very closeness of his dramatic sense to the circumstances of community in our day could only get in the way of any advantage to him personally through his art. He does not go with the flow. He has certainly never been a "popular" novelist, nor for that matter has he been valued critically in the academy on the other hand. But he has not abandoned his vision of human nature, nor his obligation as maker in responding to that vision (the "matter" with which he makes) through his art.

Madison Jones knows this well enough, as he also knows the temporary cost of such knowledge, the truth in Dorothy Sayers's words: "We may say that the best Art should be recompensed at the highest rate, and no doubt it should; but if the artist lets his work be influenced by considerations of marketing, he will discover that what he is producing is not Art." It will be only a species of preaching an acceptable word to the Modernist choir, now installed in the academic tabernacle at last as priests of an Ambiguous Progress. The "popular spirit of the age" (especially of our own age) is easily excited to hear, or see through popular media, news about a famous painting (declared famous by expert testimony). It has just sold at public auction for several million dollars, if you can believe it. For the clever media expert in the sciences of "popular spirit," there are fillips possible which stir sentiment into sentimentality (perhaps even unto high Nielson ratings in certain media). As for the painting, it brought only yesterday the highest purchase price yet for a still life. Better still, the artist in life received only a pittance for the finished work. Or perhaps he swapped it for bread and wine. And how sensational if it can also be said, in closing, that the artist died in poverty in an attic or wracked by self-sought disease on an island in the South Pacific. Ah art! Ah artists!

As for the seeming triumph of the modernist secular, now established, "church" and its frictional difficulties to the poet or the philosopher in our day, I believe we are reaching its dead end. It was born out of Cartesian Idealism. And that Idealism has led inevitably to a sentimentality about the lonely "self," the Alienated Self of popular secular myth. This sentimentality washes over our vague public concern for the amorphous self in a condescension to persons, usually justified as to the common good. For the Modernist directors of the common good (whose portrait Eric Voegelin gives us in *Science, Politics, & Gnosticism*) would require a reconstitution of personhood itself. If we scratch beneath the laving surface of sentimentality, as we may do with the razor or laser of careful words, what we discover is self-love being generalized as if the common good. In truth, it is in justification of the autonomy of the self-laving self. Each person is thus sovereign, having no persuasive orientation to community beyond the self and its absolute "rights" as a sovereign autonomous "state."

That it does become so generalized in a pretense to an enlarged "tolerance," at the heart of which lies only this self-love, nevertheless speaks some hope. For that means that the constriction of love about the lonely self still carries within it, though diminished, a residual intuitive sense of disquiet, a recognition that the self's dislocation speaks the possibility of its orientation beyond the imminent collapse upon its own increasingly empty center. And this is to speak of the necessity of reason in recovering orientation. Dante, on his famous journey, had first to recover a suitable "academic" discipline of his own reason, under the tutelage of Virgil. Only by that preliminary recovery of the self to its nature as a reasoning creature might it rise beyond self-love. That was the sharpest lesson learned by Dante in his descent into Hell. The motto he found engraved over Hell's door, incidentally, seems more and more appropriate as school motto for our own academies: "Abandon hope, all ye who enter here."

If a residual sense in us of a dislocation within the Modernist vision of humanity carries in it a disquiet hinging upon self-responsibility for the dislocation, that disquiet is most welcomed. For it hints at the possibility of a hinging, of the turning of the self beyond its closing circumstances. Again, the Modernist strategy recognizes more than it will acknowledge the implications of such unrest. For it maintains that such disquiet must be relieved, not by confession, contrition, and amendment, but by a vague generalized sense of guilt from which the self is exempted by its acknowledgement of "general guilt." Clever intellects have become adept at manipulating this misdirection of love — Dante calls it Perverted Love, this self-love escaping self-responsibility. We may observe that such generalized "guilt" emerges as thematic in our literature in this century, its most immediate source (I contend) out of Puritanism metamorphosed into pragmatism in our national social and political history. That early literary realist, academically considered a "Romantic" novelist, Nathaniel Hawthorne, realized this manipulation early on, and it is of significance that Hawthorne has been one of the "fathers" of our century's "southern Renaissance" in letters. It is in this quarter of our literary landscape, then, that a formal criticism well locates that literature, including Madison Jones's own works. It is a recognition specific to Flannery O'Connor. And it was a recognition also to that young Yankee from St. Louis, T.S. Eliot, who made his own torturous escape from the Modernist position in which he was educated as "philosopher" before he can became poet and at last mystical poet.

I intend here only to call attention to Hawthorne as a "realist" quite unlike Henry James, or James's immediate literary successor, James Joyce, who appropriated the emerging science of psychology into traditional concepts associated with personhood ("epiphany," for instance), thereby disguising the self-love dominant in his own *Stephen Hero*. And so it is in Hawthorne's company that we find Madison Jones, though indebted in technique to James and Joyce. Similarly, we find his early mentors such as Donald Davidson and Allen Tate and Andrew Lytle in Hawthorne's company, sharing a vision of human nature. For these, the person is a created rational soul incarnate, through whose freedom as such a creature flows our history in a range of strengths and failures turning on the tension between love and self-love. In a world in which strengths in this creature have become termed failures and failures strengths, the public spirit thus disappointed in its nature, intuitively recognizing distortion, is increasingly dominated by a cynicism, a cynicism which finds at our moment as proximate object of its disquiet the machinations of the state and of the academy as servant to the state. Yet entrapped by its inherited Cartesian Idealism, the philosophical "science" of alienation, it as yet knows only its disorientation from human nature. No wonder that more and more frantically it seeks external causes of that dislocation — some temple against which to hurl random bricks in rejection of Modernist reductionisms of nature, and especially of human nature.

That such a suspect principle is operative in our day has been shown by a number of works, as popular as Allan Bloom's *The Closing of the American Mind* and as demanding of intellectual attention as Eric Voegelin's *Science, Politics & Gnosticism* and his *The New Science of Politics*. The shared dangers to the community of persons rising from such a principle we now acknowledge more and more, but in response to its symptoms, not fully aware of the disease itself. The social fabric is everywhere in collapse as family decays, with a growing violence regardless of personhood, from car-jackings to pornography. Still, a chaos of thought is our response, the likely end of which chaos has been prophetically anticipated from of old, whether we turn to the works of Plato or the Old and New Testaments as points of departure now abandoned explicitly by the academy. These possible points of departure for the person or his community, each in contingency to alternate and antipathetic ends, stir tensional desire in both person and community. Shall we govern the "self" and community by those old virtues through which we discover an end larger than person or community? Or shall we, through self-love, gratify and magnify person and community. That inclination is evident in a current popular shibboleth: "We're Number One." But still standing, in resolute opposition to such self-love, there is a community of the living and the dead, a presence to us acknowledged as "tradition": Homer and Socrates; Sophocles and Aristotle; Virgil and Dante, names to remind us of a multitude of sustaining witnesses. Closer home, Chaucer and Shakespeare; T.S. Eliot and Faulkner; Walker Percy and Flannery O'Connor. And among them, Madison Jones.

And so we return to Madison Jones as maker, as a writer of fictions in this line of descent. As maker of fictions, he holds steadily within this deeper current of a traditional vision of the person as a created rational intellect incarnate. He does so, without sacrificing his primary gift as maker of fictions, his responsibility to the good of the thing he makes. He has not been content to sit down by the rivers of Babylon and weep, arrested by the question as ancient as humanity itself: "How shall I sing the Lord's song in a strange land?" He has sung and sung and sung toward perfecting his gifts of song. More steadily, I suggest, than we have heard and heard and heard.

13

Remembering Who M.E. Bradford Is

Montgomery's title echoes the title of one of Bradford's books: Remembering Who We Are: Observations of a Southern Conservative *(University of Georgia, 1985.) As a literary critics and a commentator on politics and culture, Bradford was always careful to make distinctions, to ensure that words were rightly used and rightly taken. Montgomery sums up Bradford's concern: "When signs are disoriented from reality we become incapable of significant action—that is, action signifying through effect our recognitions about the truth of things independent of the signifying action. It is a virtue in our deportment towards the world which Mel spoke of as piety." Montgomery emphasizes Bradford's concern for the permanent things and for the particularities of history and nature as encountered in time and place. He calls Bradford a "Traditionalist as Rememberer," one concerned with linking the generations: "the dead, the living, and the yet unborn," to use Edmund Burke's phrase.*

Bradford knew, studied under, and wrote about a group of men who variously made their mark as Fugitive poets, Agrarian social philosophers, and New Critics: Donald Davidson, Allen Tate, Robert Penn Warren, John Crowe Ransom, Andrew Lytle, Cleanth Brooks, among others. From the New Critics he learned how to carefully explicate the text as a thing existing in itself, but like the best of the Agrarian-New Critics, he was able to comment on the text's connections to nature and history, to theology, philosophy, economics, and politics. The second half of "Remembering Who M.E. Bradford Is" treats in some detail the history and thought of the Fugitives, Agrarians, and New Critics, and Bradford's relation to them. The tribute closes with a comic yet poignant account of Montgomery's last meeting with Bradford.*

**This tribute originally appeared in* Modern Age—*41.2 (Spring 1999): 99–116—five years after Bradford's untimely death.*

13. Remembering Who M.E. Bradford Is 143

> ...We spoke of much else besides [our business of the day]: of friends and mentors and the rumors of both — their fortunes and misfortunes, their origins and our own; of illustrative stories, many of them drawn from outside the narrow confines of the academy; of adversaries, ancient and modern; of our delight in the progress of one another's work, and reports of our personal lives; and most particularly in the rehearsal of common bonds antecedent to our professional identities, visible as much in the manner of our speaking as in its content — in idiom, in humor, in certain hyperbolic gestures, verging on swagger, panache, and familiarity.... [W]e cultivate the arts of memory, and thus hope to preserve to our posterity the bond which has heretofore (and I borrow from Burke) linked together among us "the dead, the living, and the yet unborn."
> — M. E. Bradford, "Not in Memoriam, But in Affirmation," *Why the South Will Survive* (1980)

I

The traditionalist as rememberer, of whom M.E. Bradford (1934–1993) is one, is a rarity in our day, and most especially when as gifted as he. Such a one devotes his intellectual energies to sorting the good from experience, in the broadest sense of the term, in order to restore the good to a continuing viability in the community. Bradford chose to do so as rhetor, a term he used with piety towards that high calling. Through the disciplines of the rhetor, and towards the fruitful cultivation of memory, he dealt with social, political, cultural circumstances as he found them mired in the spectacle of Western history in our time. His gifts as rhetor were both formidable and effective: formidable, as his honorable adversaries, ancient or modern, must perforce admit; effective, because of a more lasting aspect than the mere arrest of words on a page. In an age when truth is reduced to number, such words are ordinarily counted and listed in a summary of a life, a "bibliography" accounted biography by an age too hurried to deal with more than print-bites.

Even by such measure, Bradford's was a notable life, made the more so in the burst of words as he rapidly and more rapidly approached giving up words altogether. There is a spectacle of spiritual energy in his prolific last days. But to rest our attention on spectacle is to miss the significant ends towards which he spent that energy. It is those ends he would have us remember. As rhetor he adapted distinctions proper to that art, and he was guided in doing so by an intellectual inheritance that is ours, with which we may face the always-changing circumstances of time and place. By the discipline of distinction, intellectual order is restored. Its necessity now seems more pressing upon us than even upon him. For we find circumstance feeding chaos wherever we turn — crime in the streets, in the homes; betrayals in low and high places; the litany of grievance seems endless. A rhetor such as Bradford recalls to us how intimately related to order is the grammar of things, the fundamental distinctions about the world and man in that world.

Through our careless and sometimes studied abuses of distinction, spectacle itself is abused. We need only consider the corruption of our signs, our language. When signs are disoriented from reality we become incapable of significant action — that is, action signifying through effect our recognitions about the truth of things independent of the signifying itself. It is a virtue in our deportment towards the world which Mel spoke of as piety. In that deportment, whereby we acknowledge the things of creation to be the very things they are, we respect spectacle itself, though we do not confuse it with the essence of things. This is a lesson Bradford understood, in part from Aristotle.[1] As he knew, significant action is necessarily accompanied by spectacle. It cannot be otherwise. What we know as intellectual creatures is always initiated by the spectacle of things, mediated through the senses. It is the price we pay for the gift of existing as rational intellectual creatures.

Spectacle carries over into the signs we use, into our words and gestures of recognition, our more or less mannerly deportment to other rational creatures. Bradford's own significant action, his thought, continues as a vital effect *through* the spectacle of his words, by which we may remember him beyond personal grief at his death: effects *through* words rightly taken, and so *beyond* any arresting spectacle clinging to the works themselves, whether in memorable phrase or that larger numbering, bibliography. Given both a gifted and devoted rhetor, there lies within the spectacle — those books and essays bearing his name — principles that are more abiding than name itself. He subscribed to those principles, finding them certified by history and literature. What his words attempted, and what we would well emulate, was to recall fundamental truths that sustain us, each in his personal quest for the abiding. That is our obligation to truth as intellectual creatures, on our way as *homo viator,* as wayfarer in the world. One such truth, quite unpopular in our day, is most ancient to the human condition. Because of our given nature, now fallen as a "self" forlorn (ours is called the Age of Alienation), we can only begin with spectacle as our first response to existence in our quest for significant action. As rational souls we can act only through spectacle, through the accidents attending existential things.

Bradford embraced this ancient truth about human nature. Indeed, he found it most memorably illustrated in his personal experiences from boyhood onward. He saw it also as a truth held longer in the South than in other territories of our national identity. It is a principle exhibited in some southerners' dependence on rumor, anecdote, story. It is no accident that it was in South Carolina where there gathered the wayfarers about whom Bradford speaks in our epigraph, though in truth it might have been in any place and any time. That is a point recognized in Aeneas's journey to Evander, the Arcadian, seeking help in his war against the Latins. The two delay their pressing business of the day to talk of family bonds antecedent to the grim business at hand, remembering who they are so that they understand what they may be to each other. It is no accident, also, that the southerners whom Bradford especially valued as men of letters were students of Virgil. We might recall in particular Allen Tate's "Aeneas at Washington."

The conversationalist such as Aeneas or Tate or Bradford is much given to story accompanied by "certain hyperbolic gestures, verging on swagger, panache, and familiarity," whereby one imitates the possible or probable responses of human nature according to its encounters with reality, a preparation for engaging whatever pressing business that lies before one. This deportment emerges from an active remembering. In part, it is both an act of acceptance of human limitations and a celebration of human potentialities, to be repeated tomorrow in a more public or more private quarter—potentialities for both good and evil. And we might add that this often ritualized remembering by a wayfarer reflects in degree the storyteller's recognition of his own propensity to failure, even as he may hold with dogged passion to a desire for transcending human failure. One might well consider whether this is the locus of what is called "southern humor." This sense of humor, by recognizing the gesture as hyperbolic, as verging on a swagger at the edge of the tolerable in manners, may modify what might otherwise become an ironic action of mind towards the world, a retreat from it in which irony turns sardonic as the wayfarer descends towards despair.

Getting to the truth of things beneath spectacle is the abiding challenge to man as intellectual creature. It was the challenge Bradford embraced, whether he was talking about a story by William Faulkner, a political action by Abraham Lincoln, or social confusions shadowing our regional natures. As Traditionalist and Rememberer, he would recover principles through that challenge. He was concerned with what T.S. Eliot speaks of as the "permanent things." He, too, viewed the permanent things in relation to his own circumstances, on behalf of his contemporaries and those to follow. Thus his labor was made always in relation to *where* and *when* he appeared in creation as wayfarer. Bradford discovered himself wayfarer in the American South, and through the experience of his growing years there — his experience of the South's geographical and historical and cultural history fusing with his own present moment — he was prepared to prosper when he went to Vanderbilt University as a graduate student in English. There he found himself in a climate of critical concern for literature amenable to his dawning interest in the permanent things. Perhaps he was more fortunate than many of his contemporaries who also went away to college to major in "English" after World War II. He was prepared for, and could learn from, local mentors who were a special breed of the "New Critics," that is, from people like his teacher Donald Davidson, who knew virtues deeper in the academic discipline of criticism than might be acknowledged by or welcomed by academics elsewhere who tended to a criticism purified of history and nature.

He learned not only Aristotle or Homer or the succeeding giants of Western literature borne into the present by the spectacle of their lingering words, but also from Davidson, Tate, Cleanth Brooks, and Andrew Lytle. These mentors were personal contemporaries, manifest presences in his life. That they were so adds an aura to his words about them and their work. Robert Browning, a poet who struggled with current adversities in a world antagonistic to remembering, dramatizes a recognition of the aura attending the cultivation of memory. The speaker of his "Memorabilia" addresses an unidentified wayfarer in a moment whose circumstances are not fully revealed. That stranger had actually seen "Shelley plain"; the speaker asks with excitement, "And did he stop and speak to you, And did you speak to him again?"

Browning's tone is exactly right. It echoes what many of Bradford's students must have sometimes felt on hearing him talk about his talking with Davidson, or Tate, or Brooks, or Lytle. Browning's speaker realizes, without being able to articulate the relation except by a story of his own which pops to mind, that such encounters touch us with a mystery of generation beyond the tyranny of time and place, through our gift as intellectual creatures. He sees in his chance meeting of one who had seen and spoken to Percy Bysshe in the flesh an analogy to his own encounter on an empty heath — a lesser encounter, but somehow a part of present experience. He had once found a molted eagle-feather which he carried away for remembrance — not the eagle itself, but palpable evidence that an eagle existed in the local, empty world. Of such encounters, to which past experience is brought, are metaphors made by the imagination and remembered by the telling. And by that telling, generation is bound to generation. And by memory imaginatively used, the bonds may be strengthened. That means that our signs — our words as literature — are crucial to intellectual life.

II

Through signs rightly taken and rightly used, through images and metaphors and analogies understood, we try to accommodate what we know to an increasing immediacy of knowledge, wherein experience in the here and now is enlarged by experiences witnessed by others through signs, though those others may be by now remote from us. Slowly, our "self" (as we call the soul in the 1990s) responds to other selves, and with a growing confidence that persons *there* and *then* are real persons to us *here* and *now*. They are more than molted feathers or name as artifacts empty of meaning. It is the recognition of an actual presence of the distant and the past, known through the mystery of our own intellect, that we pursue. We gain an immediacy which speaks of an encompassing life of generations. That is a movement of intellect beyond its arrest by wonder, so that ours is an active intellectual life in this world. Otherwise, we become pseudo-traditionalists. The pseudo-traditionalist, stalled by wonder, succumbs to a limited and limiting reduction of persons past. That act of response to the offering of the past is to clasp partial recognition to one's bosom as did Browning's young speaker his eagle feather. Great, complex — and therefore ambiguous — human minds become as feathers in the present moment. History becomes but the molt of human actions in that state of mind towards history we call nostalgia.

Alas, it is the pseudo-traditionalist who is presented as traditionalist by a modern intellect which would be liberated from history and the residual monuments of history, what Ezra Pound calls "two gross of broken statues ... a few thousand battered books." The modernist intellect, sworn enemy to tradition, survives only so long as freed of even these remnants, knowing its very survival as modernist, as autonomous mind, depends upon abolishing tradition altogether. Tate catches this mind in his essay "The New Provincialism" (1945). The "new provincial," he says, would extend "his own immediate necessities in the world [by assuming] that the present moment is unique." His is "that state of mind in which regional men lose their origins in the past and its continuity into the present, and begin every day as if there had been no yesterday." Given an encounter between this provincial and the pseudo-traditionalist, distinctions become the first victims. Little wonder that it is difficult to call an orderly hearing for the Traditionalist as Rememberer.

The provincial mind is able to maintain its provincialism, at the expense of orderly community, by reducing the accidents encountered through circumstance to make them seem substance. The pseudo-traditionalist does the same. The difference is that the one concentrates upon present spectacle divorced from nature and history; the other, upon past spectacle insufficiently mediated by nature and history. Both take the *appearance* of things or ideas as reality. The Traditionalist as Rememberer would understand and practice a cultivation of memory in the present moment, bringing forward new growths out of the abiding truths in existence itself. It is with spectacle that we must begin our journey towards understanding, but spectacle mistaken for substance is the death of understanding. Discovering this error helps explain just why the intellectual community at this point of history is so largely comprised of creatures of the air. In the old Scholastic's description, or in Allen Tate's (see his "The Angelic Imagination"), we are victims of an "angelism," suspended betwixt and between realities. We become lost and tethered, floating over a desert intensified by our error, the desert of appearances.

Another perspective upon reality became increasingly available to Bradford as he set about his graduate work at Vanderbilt University. It opened more and more as he accepted the necessities of his wayfaring by rejecting the temptation to float randomly. He could see words in our day reduced to *insignificant* spectacle, words freed of any measure by reality, thus becoming the tenuous tether of mind by accidents of reality. Through the virtues of the "New Criticism," as Bradford encountered it in practice at Vanderbilt, he discovered a possible address to our modernist confusions. By it, he intended to escape both the modernist entrapment in the present and the pseudo-traditionalist entrapment in the past. The young Fugitives had warned of both dangers as they set out. In the first issue of *The Fugitive* they announced that, in their intent as journeymen poets, they fled "from nothing faster than from the high-caste Brahmins of the Old South."

To take signs as if themselves substantial by severing them from substantial reality, whether the reality of the present or that of the past, converts sign to prime matter for the making of a subjective little world sacred to the self alone. It is the danger in nostalgic romances, destructive of life in the made thing, the poem or novel. It is also the danger in the more general rejection of reality through arrogant subjectivism, the attempt remembered for instance as the Symbolist Movement in our literature that proved seductively destructive to a poet like Eliot, from whom Tate learned that valuable lesson. In this indulgent behavior, whether through nostalgic longing or subjective revolt, we become oriented not *to* or *by* our *intellectual*, but by and to our *animal* nature. That has been the dominant direction in art since the turn of this century, yielding sentimentality on the one hand or rebellion against being on the other. The one would cling to a vaguely remembered world; the other would throw out the world and make its own.

But how might our necessary encounter of spectacle be enlivening, be restorative of spectacle itself as ordinate to the truth of things? Not an easy undertaking in a world which sees spectacle as the end of intellectual desire — a world in which competing species of spectacle are advanced as the real, the true, the substantive. Intellectual engagement in such a world partakes of the surreal, not the real. I remember Bradford remarking once on this difficulty. He was invited to give a lecture at an Ivy League school (probably on Abraham Lincoln, a popular topic assigned, given his notoriety). He was expected to wear horns and perform his dance, he said, and he expected to oblige. "To them I'm the beast of the Apocalypse." For many, Bradford was a comic caricature, writ large but safely reduced as a "provincial southerner" by those who had not read or pondered Tate's essay on themselves as provincials, nor read carefully enough the fiction of Flannery O'Connor.

And so he would not only wear his Texas Stetson in Ivy League halls— and in the large, imitative state institutions. He would also say apparently outrageous things about that Cromwellian, Abraham Lincoln, as expected. But with an added dimension: He was always studiously attentive to his texts, always careful to anchor what he had to say in the history of Lincoln, in Lincoln's historical circumstances as affecting our own, involving history antecedent to Lincoln and history precedent from him. As many of his antagonists, friendly and unfriendly, remember from question and answer periods following lectures, he was gifted with almost total recall, had read voluminously, and so brought the unexpected but factually precise rejoinder to the defense of his position.

The risk of approaching a serious concern through what appears a comic spectacle to the careless, at the podium "verging on swagger, panache," was not without its danger to his position, just as it is a danger to use irony or whimsy with the literal-minded. But he took the risk. Not to do so might leave others of his diverse audience in an arrested deportment of mind towards his topic. The heart in him and his concern for neglected principles might otherwise be overlooked. He was a truly generous spirit, a disposition not always recognized by those who took his manners as simply an exaggeration of a residual "southernism." Thus mistaken, he was denied some preferments in both the academic and the political arenas, incidents recorded elsewhere. Meanwhile, he continued his concern for our possible loss in embracing unexamined shibboleths, a concern that affected his deportment before us. The paralysis of unmoving minds gives an illusion of order in the formalities of institutions of government, or of the academy. This is not to say that he could not himself be fiercely mannerly on occasion, nor that he was not tempted to conclude that some of us were held by invincible ignorance, which fear is the true rhetor's temptation to despair.

III

How did Bradford come to his late harvest of books and essays? The number of books currently "in press" is arresting. His had been a long journey to such an issue. The Traditionalist as Rememberer labors to sort the good from experience in attempting its rescue as presently viable, but unless by grace he is given extraordinary vision, he may not come to harvest in due season. Not at each point of his experience does the sojourner through the seasons of his own becoming distinguish degree in the *good*, at least not clearly. From experience, we relate wisdom to age. And so we commit to the careful cultivation of history, valuing the seasoned husbandman.

What is required is a steady intention to the good, a good will, in the light of which the husbandman is justified as keeper of community. Also, the wisdom of the old is that we keep the good actions of intellect, sorted from the lesser. It is not for the reputation of that remembered one primarily, but for the contribution of the good he does that lives after him, saved by our sorting to the continuing good of community. One's harvest, even one's late harvest, may not be free of tares. Aristotle and St. Thomas Aquinas are not valued for their precise views of physics in relation to the existential world. But to discard all their harvest by faulting their science is not only silly but also consequentially destructive of reason itself. Reason tells us that Ptolemy in the light of Galileo, Galileo in the light of Einstein, perhaps even Einstein in the light that may dawn tomorrow are succeeding lights, though partial. We remember and honor each, not for their errors, seen from our own enlightened position, but in recognition that they contribute to cumulative light never perfect in its intensity, even in our enlightened age.

An intention to the truth of things is the initiating and continuing principle shared with our stumbling fathers, as they seem to us. An intention to truth, to a rightness about the good of literature in service to intellect, is an initiating principle for some of those New Critics whom Bradford emulated as literary critic. They considered that, when mind is reasonably awake and well-intended to things other than itself, it knows when it has encountered a poem that commands a closer and a more respectful attention. More is present than the spectacle of that poem as it engages mind in the ear or from the page. And so the critic focuses attention first upon the virtues apparent in the poem at the level of its spectacle. The best criticism of literature lies in coming to a clarity of mind whereby response to the poem is made in respect to that poem as a *being*, a *very*, a *made* thing existing in itself. Through its spectacle, then, we move towards a possibility of glimpsing substantive being. The precisions of structure in detail, or the apparent simplicity of the lyric cry of the whole poem, engage us in the riddle whereby spectacle holds a something within it. Or the intricacies of its ambiguities may eventually reveal the poem's anchor in the complex reality of the world, especially in relation to the active, responding mind that holds the poem beyond or deeper than its accidents. Or one may engage the subtleties of irony growing out of the poem's limited power to comprehend the mystery of substantial realities.

Such were the early considerations about the text itself, developed marvelously by those New Critics, among them the men whom Bradford chose as mentors. But the New Critics he chose tended to be as much interested in history and philosophy and theology as in textual explications of the received canon of Western literature. The critical movement as a whole had been allowed into the academy after World War II, sometimes reluctantly, by the presiding chieftains of academic departments. As a larger movement it was not so fully dedicated to the encompassing concerns Bradford moved towards, having in it as a limit an obedience to the text itself. With that limited, and eventually limiting, critical concern as largely defining its role, "literary criticism" was gradually accepted as a respectable academic discipline. Yet it brought with it, by its elected limitations, problems which we are still sorting out in trying to reckon literature's claims upon us. The point is that that sorting got underway early at Vanderbilt, to Bradford's benefit.

To use such a charged and disputed term as *literature* to name collectively those things we make with signs, those works which Yeats, in a memorable phrase, calls "monuments of unaging intellect," requires here a pause for distinctions. This is especially necessary, given the state of the critical mind as we encounter it in current feather factories, the academies, where those monuments are either sorely abused or rejected. This intentional abuse or rejection of the term's largess to the human spirit is, ironically, effected through an insistence on inclusiveness of all spectacle of words as equally valid, by a relativism which asserts categorically (in a logical inconsistency) that anything in words must be accepted as "literature."

What is afoot is a new overrunning of literature by randomly surging ideological battles, battles increasingly localized to the personal survival of the critic as warrior maintained at public expense. The economic status of the "newest critic" of the 1990s seems increasingly his primary concern. With this difference noted, the critic's primary concern for his own economic status (see the recent history of Professor Stanley Fish and his cohorts at Duke University), we nevertheless find the circumstances of current criticism in the academy strongly reminiscent of those facing the academy in the 1930s. In both instances the conditions are largely created by political invasions of the academy. In the 1930s a critical consensus about the nature of literature developed against those invasions, sufficiently unified as a movement to mount a counteroffensive, the movement now called the New Criticism. (The term is credited for its academic popularity to John Crowe Ransom, who in 1941 published his *The New Criticism*.)

Certain members of the movement in the 1930s, those we shall call Agrarian-New Critics, were intent on the pursuit of words rightly taken and rightly used towards truths lodged in human experience, truths high and low in the orders of being, whereby the dimension of spectacle in a poem allowed an enlargement beyond the limited arrest of mind in the text itself. It is a point Cleanth Brooks and Robert Penn Warren remark in the introduction to that influential textbook, *Understanding Poetry* (1938). What distinguished these critics in particular from the ideological appropriations of literature to political uses was their continuing respect for the poem as a thing in itself, a reluctance to arrest it to secondary uses in the conflicting quests for power. But they were also reluctant to disjoin the poem from larger resonances it necessarily carries because of its dependencies in history and nature. They tended to exhibit a certain humility in recognition of the limited comprehension of human intellect itself, a deference to more cogently reasoned explications than their own.

There might well be larger ends at issue in the reading of a poem than exhaustive explication, but those ends must be pursued through and out of the integrity of the poem, not imposed upon it. That was a principle already articulated in the preface to *I'll Take My Stand* (1930) in relation to the social, political, cultural, and economic circumstances of the nation: The essayists objected to attempts at a recovery of cultural community made by proponents of industrialism as directed to consumerism, whether those proponents were among the capitalists or the socialists. Those untoward attempts, they said, resulted from the expediencies of a forced "pouring of soft materials from the top" into the cultural matrix. The most promising mechanism to the attempt was through control of the academy's applied and theoretical sciences, especially including the "soft" sciences such as sociology and political science. The attempt was to impose essence forcibly, to exercise what Eric Voegelin was subsequently to name a "New Gnosticism." "Gnosis," he says, "desires dominion over being" in its modernist manifestation. The Agrarian-New Critic of the 1930s, as literary critic, resisted manipulations whereby language was made the instrument for pouring gnostic ideology in "from the top," whether to justify a process advocated by a radical capitalism or by a radical socialism, the common strategy to control learned from Nominalism.

In retrospect, we see how some of the young Fugitive poets at Vanderbilt in the 1920s developed naturally into their Agrarian position and subsequently made reputations as New Critics. The continuity in their development is important, lest we confuse our Agrarian-New Critic with the New Criticism in general, a mistake one finds in Gerald Graff's work. Along the way the Agrarian-New Critics were joined by likeminded souls: Cleanth Brooks is a conspicuous member from an older generation, as Bradford is of our own. The Agrarian-New Critic held as a dominant principle, requiring of him an enlargement of mind, a position at sharp variance from the modernist ideologies of gnostic intent, ideologies in conflict politically from both the left and the right. These gnostic contenders moved from within the social body in sharp and ever sharper antagonisms which have reached a climax and collapse in the 1990s, whose spectacle revealing failure on both sides is the collapse of Soviet Russia and of Eastern Europe, the signal of that so-called "end of history."

Bradford's old teacher and friend Donald Davidson reminds us in a telling poem about Nashville's attempt to commercialize a piece of Western culture, the building of a replica of the Greek Parthenon as tourist attraction, that such manipulation is doomed. Such a monument erected for gnostic purposes, to promote consumerism, does not carry the Greek mind into a presence at Nashville. It is but "blind motion," a "dim last / Regret of men who slew their past," leading them to raise "this bribe against their fate." It is a "pouring in from the top" in a pretense of cultural piety, whether erected by the so-called "right" in relation to commerce or by the political might of the "left." The point is relevant to the attempts to foster culture through governmental agencies, attempts increasingly controversial, in which controversy Bradford was himself involved. It is with a poignant irony, then, considering the history of his treatment by the political establishment as candidate for the directorship of the NEH, that we learned in the evening news at about the time of his death that the Nashville "Parthenon" is now in such decay that it is not only an eyesore but a growing hazard to public safety with the collapse of inner city order. Davidson's "shopgirls" no longer safely loiter "where willows crowd the pure / Expanse of clouds," to embrace "a plaster thought, / And eye Poseidon's loins ungirt," though at last we hear with them more certainly "the brandished spear" of Athene and increasingly are moved by that "bright-eyed maiden's rage" over violations.

A work of art reduced to commercial ends, as with the "Parthenon," or used for bolder political purposes such as the Marxist uses of literature in the 1930s, has as effect the reduction of persons, shopgirls or critics, to integers. The dream of process as god develops machinery for the programming of reality by gnostic intent, whether a machine in service to a "free enterprise" manipulation of persons or a socialist manipulation of persons. Given the shallow reading usually accorded the Agrarian-New Critic, it needs reiterating that his address to consumerism as the enemy of the human spirit is equally directed at the political left and the political right. Despite assertions to the contrary, the Agrarian-New Critic in *I'll Take My Stand* does not reject process, commercialism, or progress. Rather, he demands a relation of these concepts to the highest good of the human spirit.

IV

The principle underlying the Agrarian-New Critic's position as literary critic, shared generally in the New Critical movement at large, may be simply put: Some poems are better than other poems. He judges them as things existing in themselves, made by that intellectual creature — man. The problem term, of course, is *better*, since it commits intellect, willy-nilly, to judgments in relation to hierarchy, a most heinous devil term in the 1990s. The intellect gives degrees of consent to a poem's being the thing it is. But judgments of degree are required beyond a criticism of a poem in a scholarly journal devoted to explication. We may even be required at last to judge a person as maker, in the light of our diverse gifts as makers of good and less good things — poems or cars or institutions. Some poets are better than other poets; some statesmen are better than other statesmen. In these enlargements upon questions of degree, it is apparent now, as it was also often acutely apparent to Bradford during his career in the academy, that to be an Agrarian-New Critic is to hold an endangered position, with no lobby devoted to preserving this endangered species of the critical mind.

The Agrarian-New Critic holds a dangerous position because of an almost universal antagonism towards any position hinting at judgment based in degree. It is a bold position at any point of history, but reactions to such an intellect at this point of history are highly exacerbated. Relatively speaking — that is, speaking in the shifting light of history — it was less shocking to the generality of the body politic that some critics in the 1930s held that Robert Frost's "Birches" was demonstrably a better poem than Joyce Kilmer's "Trees." Today, to judge that Frost's inaugural poem at Kennedy's installation is demonstrably beyond Maya Angelou's at Clinton's is to risk at least academic lynching. The popular media will not even hint at such a possible truth.

Of far more importance than "professional" risk, however, is the danger in such judgment to the critic himself, for he must either die intellectually by turning away from judgment or change, grow. The little word *better* opens literary criticism beyond the confines currently prescribed to it, in the direction of philosophy and perhaps even unto the realm of theology. It is even possible that there is a moral dimension latent in literary judgment, as there may be in the act of reading at all. Moral judgment redounds upon the judging intellect for good or ill, or threatens the complacent intellectual establishment of the moment, or even both. In the 1930s it redounded upon both, and our Agrarian-New Critic responded by an active opening of his mind to larger concerns. That was already a direction taken by some of the Fugitive poets, leading them first to their Agrarian phase.

They began to make interesting, sometimes startling, discoveries about the meaning in their intellectual actions which led them beyond spectacle of such action, their poems committed against the usual current of poetry in their day. They found themselves accompanied by shadowy presences out of the past who seemed to become more palpable. Amenable companions to thought were joining them, sometimes from unexpected quarters of the history of the Western mind. And they discovered they had been accompanied all along by less congenial presences out of history. Descartes, for instance, was increasingly recognized as dislocating them in their journeying. Their reaction to the radical subjectivism practiced in the Symbolist Movement or the subjectivism feeding popular sentimentality in verse might both claim descent from the implications in *cogito ergo sum*. Plato, Aristotle, St. Augustine, St. Thomas Aquinas proved to be more or less companionable as they dawned to another way of seeing mind in nature, not because they were old but because these were open-eyed. In addition, those forebears were discovered to have been "New Critics" themselves. They were conspicuously akin in their respect for distinctions involving degree as appropriate to the reading of texts.

Those ancient companions were in quest of the truth of how things stand to human intellect. Not that Descartes was not concerned for truth. But Descartes, as did many of his followers, tended to a self-isolation, one stage of which is a concentration upon text as a reflection of the isolated self. It became evident as well that some of those older doctors of the mind, though concerned for the general health of ill-fallen intellects, were primarily concerned for the truth itself as the only proper medicine to intellect. That truth might be pursued from within texts, including the "text" of nature, for the common good, a pursuit into but beyond — out of the text, lest intellect become mired in mere spectacle and lose truth, which is the mind's purchase upon the essence of things. Nor was it to be denied that such labor as theirs prepared a way for a distinct literary and artistic flowering of Renaissance monuments to unaging intellect, Dante's *Divine Comedy* being a singular blossom. Could these ancient critics of being bear parallel in the modern critics whose concern became more and more the unexpected phenomenon called the "southern-Renaissance" of letters?

From our perspective at century's end we see that among some of the Agrarian-New Critics and their allies there was a growing concern for degrees of the good. That concern led important members of that movement back to Dante both for support of their critical position and as a measure of their accomplishments in letters. We need only name Allen Tate and T. S. Eliot. We might even add that irascible and often convoluted traditionalist in modernist robe, Ezra Pound, who sometimes seemed unwilling to forgive Dante his greatness as poet. Nevertheless, the New Critical movement, as it emerged in the 1930s, tended to defer questions buried in the term *better*, questions engaging philosophical or theological concerns. The immediate battle was too pressing to entertain potentially divisive concerns from within the movement. Their foremost engagement must be with conspicuous forces attempting to seize literature for political and economic ends. Those forces demanded the literary critic's alliance as the cost of a continuing support. Literature became hostage in the mounting battle between factions of modernist materialism, left and right. The New Critics meanwhile proved more effective against the Marxist attempt to seize literature from within the academy, in places, but less successful in withstanding an outside, usually local, intrusion.

It was more successful within the academy's small preserve, the department of literature (especially "English" departments), but with an attendant irony in light of what literary criticism has become in the 1990s. While Marxism was kept somewhat at bay from literary departments, there was less success in other humanistic disciplines — in sociology or in political science departments, for instance. The New Critic, though embattled in departmental wars within the academy, maintained his position in literary studies. But he did so in part by avoiding the potential divisiveness within his own critical movement, the incipient divisiveness raised in declaring one poem or novel better than another. He was required by the exigencies of local circumstance to oppose attempts to exclude literature altogether from the curriculum.

He fought a Parthian strategy, increasingly ineffective, as the history of academic curricula from 1950 to 1990 will show. And it needs noting that his struggle was less with departments of the hard sciences than with those of the "soft" sciences, by then comfortably established in humanistic studies. The hard scientist — the chemist or physicist or biologist — must be at least precise in the denotative uses of the sign. For the "soft" scientist, the denotative in signs, anchoring sign to external reality as a governor of subjective responses to the actual, may easily become a liability. Indeed, the "soft" scientist might for his own survival as academic require a liberation of the subjectively connotative. That statistics are used so differently in particle physics and in social studies is a metaphor to the point. Nor should we forget popular uses of the Heisenberg uncertainty principle in speculations about the self — a principle popular for a decade now in literary criticism for its scientific aura.

There was a danger in the New Criticism inherent in its emphasis upon the text, a danger analogous to the uncertainty principle in physics — the uncertainty of subjectivity in intellect, which subjectivity the modernist reckoned must be rescued as a higher reality, superseding "objective" reality. By the limited emphasis on the text, the critical intellect may isolate itself from questions of the larger dependencies of the text in history and nature. But without the critic's awareness of that involvement, excessive attention focuses on accidents until accidents begin to appear to be made substantive by the attention itself, depending upon the critic's ingenuity. There grew a closing of mind, making the literary critic vulnerable to another invasion, increasingly imposed upon departments of literature from outside: the assignment to "English" departments of the responsibility to teach elementary grammar as salvational to the establishment. It intended to do so by operations performed upon numbered sentences that required proper punctuation or correction of subject-verb agreement or pronoun references. Exercises poured in from the top. To put the point thus is to recognize the gradual transformation of universities into secondary schools, whatever the discipline, and certainly so at the undergraduate level. What might not be recognized is a double assault upon literature itself, the dual forces antagonistic to each other in the political sphere but jointly committed to a pragmatic use of sign. If the Marxist and the commercial materialist were enemies to each other, they were not natural enemies, and they proved to be allies in the erosion of humanistic studies, the liberal arts. Both advanced an insistent demand that signs be used to pragmatic economic and political ends. Thus institutions once devoted to the liberal arts were gradually transmogrified.

V

Bradford entered the academy at this stage of its decline. He was one of many who learned from the New Criticism how to read a text, but he learned better than most, fortunate in the university he entered. Meanwhile, literature was besieged from within the academy; it was also being impressed from without for pragmatic service. The commercial world needed undergraduates who were proficient at a sixth-grade level in the mechanics of words. Bradford's chief mentor at Vanderbilt, Donald Davidson, had published a textbook addressing necessities beyond those limited demands, his now-famous *American Composition and Rhetoric*. First issued in 1939, with other editions as late as the 1960s, it steadily declined in use. It was occasioned, Davidson said, by his realizing that when one attempts to teach the elementary in our age, he ends up wrestling to recover the student's mind challenged as wayfarer. Such a match was hopeless if attempted with the workbook method which was growing in popularity at the time. Davidson's text would remedy the deficiency by offering an anthology of superior prose, approached by a superior analysis that would reveal why some paragraphs are better than others.

In other institutions, perhaps two or three novels might be allowed in the usual Freshman courses, which were otherwise largely dissociated from literature. The workbook approach to grammar and composition bore vague analogy to laboratory courses, and in time would develop the likeness more markedly. For English departments seemed more apt to maintain their academic territory through the emerging "science" of composition. Other disciplines happily yielded to the claim. And by the late 1950s English faculties had become expert advisors for other disciplines as to where to place a comma. Indeed, English faculty found themselves on call as experts to colleagues who might need advice on subject-verb agreement or pronoun reference in scholarly sentences destined for specialized journals. The humanities accelerated in their decline, one suggests ironically, alongside the decline of texts like Davidson's *American Composition and Rhetoric*, which was originally a Freshman text but which became a text for advanced composition at the senior level before being abandoned altogether.

Amid such changes, the teacher-assistant, his Freshman "English" class dismissed with the charge to correct faulty pronoun references in the dissociated sentences of Exercises 13 and 14, might typically make off to his own afternoon seminar taught by senior faculty removed from Freshman and Sophomore "English." There degrees of irony and types of ambiguity could be sorted as his important work, his principal reason for being a part of the university's conglomerate of specializations as we burgeoned into mega-versities. Thus in the academy, as illustrated here symptomatically, there developed intensive training of graduate students more and more specialized. Steadily the literary critic, the graduate student turned Ph.D., found himself isolated, even from his immediate peers, in proportion to his specialized interest in literature. Still, he was highly favored in professional journals devoted to his concerns. We could well discover evidence of this fragmentation in higher education by surveying the variety of specialized journals in disciplines other than "English."

Against this brief account of formalized training in this century's academy, we find Bradford writing for an astonishing variety of publications and speaking before a variety of audiences. Clearly his interests cut across the confines of separate provinces. And clearly he was an encouraging figure for us as we note the long list of books and essays lamenting the death of mind and the withering of liberal arts. Beginning with James E. Conant's *Education of American Teachers* (1963), we see many leading towards that surprisingly sensational protest, Allan Bloom's *The Closing of the American Mind* (1987) and Dinesh D'Souza's exposé of the scandals of academe, *Illiberal Education* (1992).

Considering this milieu in retrospect, we wonder whether the New Criticism in its response to literature did not somehow imitate its antagonists on either hand. The Marxist attempt to force literature to serve social program exacerbated a tendency indigenous to the New Criticism as it moved to authority in matters literary: the tendency to isolate criticism from the larger arena proper to intellect, confining its attention to the text alone. There was the further inclination to retreat from the outside world, the world of getting and spending, the world that increasingly demanded process training in punctuation if English departments were to be justified. This "service English," this textural pragmatism, tended to establish "consumerism" as an ultimate goal, requiring the liberal arts to train students in the processing of signs towards that end.

Thus beleaguered, literary criticism might well be tempted to isolation in the text as text, the last refuge in literature. If the exercises justifying academic criticism were sufficiently esoteric, at least the consumer-oriented world which paid the freight might be given pause. That world seemed easily awed by the esoteric in sciences other than criticism. Bradford chose to address this error of direction. He understood the importance of economics and myth, of politics and commerce, to the mind in its ordinary services to community as well as in its extraordinary services. He understood as well that the labor of mind, if estranged from an ordering vision of higher ends, was not enough. And this at the time when the estrangement of art from reality seemed widely assumed in the world of social commerce. Left and right joined then (as they did in little else) to complain about those who seemed content to write, at public expense, books about books, those critics isolated in their "Ivory Towers."

The uncertain and even strange specialization of the literary critic is difficult to justify to a pragmatic world. That is one reason why Allen Tate called a collection of essays in defense of his critical role *The Man of Letters in the Modern World, Selected Essays, 1928–1955* (1955). He would have us understand, among other things, that the man of letters embraces letters larger than mere "fictions" taken as entertainments for the world-weary, unoccupied mind. His critic provided society with an ordered insight of proper ends. Plato reminds us, Tate says, that a society without arts "lives by chance." For the New Critic to have stalled the Marxist and kept somewhat aloof from commercial consumerism was not enough. While the New Criticism had carried the day in literature departments in its brief moment, it had failed to establish a concern in different academic disciplines for the larger virtues to mind signified by *letters*. From Tate's and Bradford's position, it was as necessary to the literary critic to know the political dimensions of Plato and Aristotle as for the sociologist or political scientist to know Homer and Dante. For in the common knowledge thus established there exists a mutual responsibility for lucid discourse, the right use of right words, equal responsibility for language's mechanical usages, whether comma or subject-verb agreement.

We have generalized the New Critical movement as it was to emerge in the academy from the 1930s onward, a movement whose members shared techniques of reading texts but were not united in declaring common ends to which good reading points. To appreciate Bradford's position relative to the movement, we have noted certain growing digressions within the movement, digressions setting in early but portended within the Fugitive-Agrarian community even before the critical movement emerged. Their bringing to criticism Agrarian concerns which could not avoid philosophical and theological considerations meant that estrangements among them were inevitable. Friction developed between Donald Davidson and Allen Tate on the one hand and John Crowe Ransom (and to lesser degree Robert Penn Warren) on the other. Ransom seemed increasingly restive with his Agrarian position, although much later he would speak sympathetically about his earlier stand taken with his Fugitive friends, with a tone of nostalgia. Fundamentally, however, he preferred to be thought of not as an Agrarian-New Critic, but simply as a New Critic. For his was a position essentially Cartesian, by way of Kant, a position intolerable to his friends Davidson and Tate.

13. Remembering Who M.E. Bradford Is

It is out of a rarified version of the New Criticism, here suggested as Ransom's later position, that the Newest Critic of all emerged in the academy in the 1990s, and surely with irony upon irony, given the historical context we have limned. The Newest Critic now inherits the academy, respected among diverse disciplines, even as he is gradually revealed as the bastard offspring of the purified New Critic and the Marxist long in the tooth. With a concern for the text as text, as an end in itself, he nevertheless trades on a scientific aura summoned to his gifts with the text (often considerable gifts). His ingenuity with the text is accompanied, as occasion requires, by ideological borrowings out of Marxism. His criticism is defended in terms amenable to social, political, economic egalitarianism. Thus his position as literary critic seems secure in troublesome times. He addresses the text itself in a manner supposed to placate the popular spirit. That is, he pronounces every text the equal of every other text. What is lost first of all is that old respect for the text as a thing in itself, the point of departure for his New Critic progenitor.

The academy has largely succumbed to this reduction of intellectual order, which in the hands of the Newest Critic turns our signs towards an absolute zero, towards a disorder. In this resulting chaos of common understanding about words, the Newest Critic would establish his hegemony of mind on the authority of his expertise in the science of language. So enticing become his arguments, buttressed as they may be by a residue of ideological afterthought and by semi-scientific speculations about language itself, that he promises to prevail. He trades on our innate, given desire for justice towards all things, in an age in which the measure of justice is acceptable as "just" pronouncement about things only when all degrees of the *good* are denied to them. The consequence of this assault upon intellectual responsibility is that the shoddy thing — poem or argument — must be accepted as elevated to dominion, without acknowledging, however, that the strategy denies the egalitarian intent.

The academy, operating at this moment under the rubric of the "politically correct," is busily perfecting a process of intellectual amnesia: The student has eradicated from his memory by process as education the truth of things as he actually knows them by his existential experiences, things he actually knows by the fact of his being alive at this moment and in this place. The hope of his rescue lies in a commonality in the members of the body politic, another residual gift deeper than ideological residues which is complementary to the innate desire for justness towards things in themselves. It is a gift of intellect long called common sense. Long ignored, it has been suppressed with the consequent possibility of a variety of explosions. We have even now to deal with those explosions in provinces of society itself which seem far removed from the academic world, though the betrayals of intellect itself are more than coincidental causes. The disintegration of the family, the turmoil of the inner city, whatever the symptomatic spectacles associated with such occurrences, are related to the deconstructions of language. Donald Davidson would take the point, as Bradford did, and as we must.

VI

We have been describing the intellectual state of the nation and of the academy as Bradford was to leave it to us. It is a description from the perspective of a friend, a Traditionalist as Rememberer. The view towards the truth of how things stand with us speaks a strenuous battle ahead for any who would consent to service in the academy or to the service of community. The spirit of community which the modernist mind would have us embrace is largely defined by persons who have lost an understanding of the principles we have been suggesting, so that what they call order we call disorder. Our good fortune is that we survive to remember those principles which Bradford knew well. The contemporary ground to our remembering seems shifting under us, whether we stand in the academy or in the public square. We may seem threatened more than we imagine Bradford to have been as he set out as *homo viator*. He helps us recover the point from which we must move by his reminder, said in many ways: We must begin here and now, and we do so by cultivating memory in the ground we inherit by existing at all. In remembering Bradford as literary critic, we speak of that point in its relation to art and history, a part of our inheritance. But even as we depend by our existence at a point in nature out of history, so too does the poem, or any made thing in itself.

Aristotle considers this point of dependence of a thing we make with our words in relation to that thing as it exists, a made thing dependent on its maker. Its existence is caused by art's disciplines acquired through history. Because our making — whether of a poem or a house or a garden — is so intimately dependent on our actions as maker consequential to our understandings of art and history as disciplines of mind, we may confuse those disciplines. Thus Aristotle makes distinction. Art and history are distinguishable from nature, the existential complex of existences in the here and now. But they are also to be distinguished from each other. Art is concerned with the possible or probable; history with the actual — past or passing. But such distinctions are cogent to understanding only in relation to a *where* of nature at a *now* of our intellect's response to the contingencies of time and place as these affect us. These are contingencies which we try to understand by attention to history and the practice of our peculiar art.

We cultivate the present with our emerging understanding of the truth of things; the most effective tools to that cultivation are art and history. Through the remembering of history we move towards art. The past and passing affect what is to come, the possible or probable, whatever species of made things we are given to making — poem or garden or institution. By these operations of intellect in the here and now, we discover that existential reality speaks to intellect the more fully as intellect is prepared to hear by the disciplined listening to the truth of things. And that disciplined listening is best induced by our remembering through our making.

To understand why a poem or a house or a garden is good, why one of them is better than another of the same sort, or why among categories there are differences independent of degree (their existence in the orders of being): that is the necessity demanding of us distinctions, even unto degree. And through understanding by distinction we appreciate the possible-probable as imaginatively engaged by intellect. We do so, recognizing as well that intellect is limited in its desire to understand by the complex realities of the whole of creation. Given such understanding we are the better attuned to Faulkner's concern through words to explore the human heart in conflict with itself, which we discover through art that speaks to our own heart's conflicts with itself. We may come to understand as well T.S. Eliot's or Walker Percy's attempts at a different level of the truth of things to reveal the sign in its relation to intellect as it struggles with the relation of sign to the qualities and accidents of existential reality, including their own minds as makers. How poignant Eliot's cry in his last great poem:

> *Every phrase and every sentence is an end and a beginning*
> *Every poem an epitaph. And every action*
> *Is a step to the block, to the fire, down the sea's throat*
> *Or to an illegible stone.*

It is by recovering the disciplines of memory, then, that we shall best bear witness to who we are and in doing so honor Bradford. We shall do so if we are not misled by the intoxicated air we breathe in this modernist moment. Above all, in holding to degree as implicit in the orders of being and not of our own making, we must not submit to the absolute moral judgment which the adversarial modernist would impose upon us: the moral judgment that there is no moral judgment, and that morality is relative and so infinite and so necessarily without degree. In that absolute the moral dimension of human existence disappears like the smile on the Cheshire cat. The abolition of morality is the abolition of man.

But in a closing moment, let us set aside our high concern for the low estate of the academy and the public square and recall Bradford as a presence to us. I recall my last meeting with him — not the actual words we spoke but his conduct in the circumstances. He was by then (October 1992), as I had noticed a few months earlier with some alarm, unwell, though far from ready to surrender his labor of words despite the clear prospect before him, his coming encounter with Truth as we must all come to it. I welcomed an invitation to meet with him and others in Baton Rouge, to talk of the Agrarians and the English Distributists. There was to be an initial evening lecture, and afterward conversation such as he describes in our epigraph. Alas, my own plane was delayed, so that it was midnight when another friend met me at the airport, the key to my reserved room in hand. We arrived at the guest complex. Beyond a numbered door lay a promise of hot bath and sleep before my paper the next morning.

We found my room; the numbers matched. But at that point, fumbling with my bags and the key, we heard a loud objection from within. The door swung back as we pushed. There stood Bradford in his underwear (it was a muggy Louisiana night), in *my* room. He had been sitting at a desk writing, papers sprawled out. Though rudely interrupted, he at once ushered us in, dignified in his bearing beyond the spectacle of his dress, or lack of it. He picked up the phone and sorted the matter out with dispatch, arranging a room for me across campus, even at that late hour. His courteous concern, his energy summoned to my convenience, his whole bearing, I remember in relation to his appearance as both tired and ill. His was the deportment of a gentleman to one caught by untoward circumstances of the world; the deportment of one who knows who he is and bears himself supportive of others who, disoriented by circumstances, may not be so sure of who they are.

That was my last meeting with this Agrarian-New Critic, in the flesh as we say. Meanwhile, remembering that encounter I must learn to sit and talk the better of high matters, among gatherings that summon those absent from us, of whom Bradford is now one. We must consider how we may bring high matters down to earth, in the service of an orderly rescue of myself as person and of ourselves as community. Let us be quick to add that we must not neglect a concern for low matters even though comic to our encounter, since what we think of as low or insignificant matters again and again prove highly important. In our moment's life as intellectual community, even in a hotel room far from home, from whence we sojourn and towards which in its highest manifestation as home we move in our wayfaring, we may yet value the delight in our deportment as company along the way in talk which may even verge on swagger, panache, familiarity through idiom that is fundamentally respectful of the truth of things—and through humor in this comic circumstance, in which we recognize ourselves. We thereby recognize our limits as guardians of the truths such as we sometimes praise through words partaking of hyperbolic gesture.

Always in such circumstances we are at a point here and how, to be eventually remembered as then and there. And always, it may be a long time before we are together again in the flesh, though by memory we recover the moment. Well-recovered, it is to our continuing health. At such moments, though the concern may seem trapped by low matters, such is the mystery, that they may become transformed in service to the high. Even a concern for feathers may speak the reality of eagles beyond what we may first imagine. That shall be tomorrow's concern, encouraged now by Bradford's continuing talk that would stay us by degrees, his concern for the better as it may be discovered in the here and now when cultivated by the arts of memory. Such is the labor required of intellect as its service to the largeness of reality, a reality permeated by the mystery of all mysteries. Not the mystery that anything should cease from being, but that anything should be at all. That is the mystery setting us on our way. A tree or rock; a poem or music; our self or family or community. Even New Critics or Newest Critics. Aristotle or Cicero or Burke or Homer or Dante or Chaucer. Or M.E. Bradford.

Through this mystery of mysteries lies our quest to know who we are in truth, requiring that we hold this moment's remembered story of fortune or misfortune to dear friends, ancient or recent, now absent from us. I shall remember, "Y'all come on in and let's straighten this out." I shall remember that midnight encounter with a gentlemanly soul, a patron of community in the world, rousted out from the words he was setting down on paper. I shall remember his rousting out those who could find lodging for a wayfarer from Crawford, Georgia, fallen upon minor misfortune in that strange place. I, a friend, had come a tedious, almost weary, way for that meeting, which neither of us could know was to be our last, this side another gathering of shade with shades.

Next year, or the next, many of us will no doubt be caught off guard for a moment by a young student who happened upon words bequeathed to us by this rhetor. "You mean you actually *knew* Mel Bradford? In *person*?" That is my hope. On that occasion, answering *yes* as well as we may, we may be amused in gratitude, remembering: Here we pick up a molted feather, an eagle-feather in the midst of "blank miles round about," as Browning's innocent says in losing his innocence on his journey across the heath.

Note

1. I have in mind Aristotle in general, but particularly the *Poetics*, in which he distinguishes the *action* in *Oedipus the King* as Oedipus's recognition of the truth of his circumstances, mediated to us through spectacle: the costumes, setting, above all the words spoken. In the *Poetics*, Aristotle distinguishes history from poetry, the one concerned with the *actual*, the other with the *possible* or *probable*. Recognizing the limits imposed by the actual upon the imaginative uses of the actual is the poet's principal challenge. He is, consequently, a *maker* and not a *creator* by limit.

14

Walker Percy and the Christian Scandal

This essay discusses Percy's qualified political liberalism, his concerns with sentimentality, his reading of Existentialist philosophers, and his view of man as wayfarer, especially as reflected in his first novel The Moviegoer. *Percy, like Flannery O'Connor, believed liberal sentimentality leads directly to the gas chambers, largely because liberal sentimentality is divorced from reality: It is separated from the source of tenderness, Christ. Drawing upon several published interviews with Walker Percy, and examining Percy's The* Moviegoer, *Montgomery discusses Percy's view of human nature and the modern predicament, emphasizing that any serious discussion of this requires a metaphysical perspective — a perspective not always explicitly stated in the Percy interviews, though it is certainly implicit in Percy's fiction. Modern man as wayfarer is not a mere* self, *not an autonomous individual: He is a* person *anchored in a specific time and a specific place. And this is what Percy's protagonists try to come to terms with: personhood in place. The essay relates Binx Bolling's moviegoing to Plato's cave and, more importantly, to the Mass. While the movies fail to engage the real or to certify place (to use Binx's terms), the Mass does, for in the Mass the Word made flesh certifies time and place and sanctifies the person. As Montgomery puts it, "The ersatz food of art divorced from its relation to the creating Signifier through being, God, the Cause of moments of time and points of place, at this juncture of my next step on the journey, is poor food indeed." Montgomery treats Percy's interest in place and person more extensively in* Eudora Welty & Walker Percy: The Concept of Home in Their Lives and Literature *(McFarland, 2004). St. Augustine Press has "in press" Montgomery's* With Walker Percy at the Tupperware Party: In Company with Fyodor Dostoevsky, Gabriel Marcel, T.S. Eliot, Flannery O'Connor, and Others.*

*This essay appeared in the April 1993 issue of *First Things.*

In Washington, where he was to give the eighteenth Jefferson Lecture in the Humanities on May 3, 1989, Walker Percy also gave an interview to Scott Walter for *Crisis*. This is almost exactly a year before his death, and both the interview and his lecture, "The Fateful Rift: The San Andreas Fault in the Modern Mind," reflect not only his journey up to that point, but a continuing concern for the meaning of the journey and to a degree a continuing ambiguity in his understanding of intellectual experience. He still shares with Binx Bolling an amused wonder in the presence of experience, still somewhat divided of mind as to the dependability of immediate experience, a condition suited to the novelist. Perhaps the point can best be presented by noticing the divided sense in which Percy uses the term *liberal* in his interview.

A problem arises in his discomfort with the liberal mind, with which he nevertheless shares causes. "I agree with them on almost everything: their political and social causes, and the ACLU, God knows, the right to freedom of speech, to help the homeless, the poor, the minorities." But the liberal position on abortion and euthanasia is "a mystery, a bafflement to me." Their "hearts are in the right place," but "they cannot see the paradox of being in favor of these good things and yet not batting an eyelash when it comes to destroying unborn life."

First of all, there is a question here as to whether we are dealing with a paradox or with a contradiction. But a more troubling question is whether the "liberal" whom Percy has in mind addresses the causes he accepts enthusiastically in the same manner of intellectual deportment to those causes as Percy does. For this "liberal" may in actuality deport himself to good causes and bad without discrimination, so that his attitude toward abortion or euthanasia is neither paradoxical nor contradictory. In other words, it is possible that one may deport oneself, even to good causes, without one's heart being "in the right place." That is the climactic recognition of T.S. Eliot's Thomas Becket at the edge of martyrdom, who in horror steps back from the most subtle treason to the soul, that is, doing "the right thing for the wrong reason."

These words of Percy's about his "liberal" friends and acquaintances occur after some talk in the interview about *tenderness*. Mr. Walter has asked whether Percy meant a tribute to Flannery O'Connor in Fr. Smith's words in *Thanatos Syndrome*: "Don't you know where tenderness leads? ... It leads to the gas chamber." He'd like to give Miss O'Connor the credit, Percy responds, but it wasn't a conscious use. He had in mind his own experience of the German people as "extremely sentimental," possessed of a "tremendous tenderness." And he emphasizes here, as he does in other interviews, the comparison implied in his last novel between the Western liberal and the Weimar Republic liberal in relation to the effects of Weimar tenderness as executed in Nazi Germany and our own obsession with the right to abortion. "Nothing offends the American liberal more than being compared to the German liberals of the Weimar Republic." He cites *The Defense of the Destruction of Life Without Value*, by two "liberal Weimar doctors," emphasizing that it appeared in what was "probably the most liberal democracy in Europe." What Percy knows is that the "whole notion [of euthanasia and abortion] is very reasonable without the Christian ethic." To talk of "the sacredness of life," unless "you really mean it," cannot but support the improvement of life by the systematic eradication of people whose "quality of life" is inferior. One can, in defense of the sacredness of life, be suddenly in the position of executing the program of the liberal Weimar doctors, which of course comes to pass under Nazi rule, under "national socialism"

We may begin by correcting the citation of Flannery O'Connor, who is very careful in what she says of *tenderness*. The quoted passage is from her introduction to *A Memoir of Mary Ann*. Castigating a "popular piety" such as associated with liberalism in its political and social rhetoric, she says that we "mark our gain in sensibility and our loss of vision," in that having lost faith, "we govern by tenderness," a tenderness "wrapped in theory." And then her precise words: "When tenderness is detached from the source of tenderness [i.e., Christ] its logical outcome is terror. It ends in forced-labor camps and in the fumes of the gas chamber." The important point is that tenderness is not the problem in itself, for tenderness properly oriented is a desirable deportment toward creation. But when that manifestation of disoriented tenderness occurs again as dissipated into an almost universal acceptance of abortion, Mother Teresa is right to say (as Percy quotes her): "If a mother can kill her unborn child, I can kill you, and you can kill me." Since Mother Teresa spoke these words, we note, euthanasia as a public policy has been submitted to plebiscite in our own country. The issue, then, is not tenderness, no better example of which is among us than Mother Teresa's, but the distortion of that sentiment by separating it from its source in Christ, which separation Flannery O'Connor characterizes as sentimentality.

The general sense of experience in our age, the most common bond among our separated selves, is the sense of a derangement, and Percy (among others) finds this an effect of the Cartesian displacement of consciousness. What we are left with, let us say, is a residual element of sentiment, an intuitive inclination to tenderness, that finds no proper orientation in respect either to nature or to human nature. Tenderness separated from the source of tenderness thus supports a "popular piety" that goes unexamined, a piety in which liberalism in its decline establishes dogmatic rights, rights that in an extreme — as presently in the arguments for abortion in the political sphere and for "popular culture" in the academic — become absolute dogma to be accepted and not examined. To examine that dogma might perhaps serve to restore tenderness to its proper source. Indeed, the attempt at that rescue and restoration is the disturbing aspect of Percy's fiction, disturbing to the "liberal" mind in its common manifestation among us.

What is somewhat discomfiting about Percy as dialectician — and the dialectical is the principal aspect of his fiction, as well as central to his other work, including his interviews — is his seeming inconstancy in holding the advocates of tenderness to account in their various causes, even those separate from euthanasia and abortion, those other causes to which he himself is committed. Those are causes he tends to ally himself with — but precisely out of his commitment to the "source of tenderness." Despite his confession of sympathy to shared causes, he does not actually "agree with [the liberals] on almost everything." To help the homeless, the blacks — that is, minorities as abstractions — to defend free speech with Pavlovian tenderness, is far from Percy's own ground of defense. He has been incisive, for instance, in castigating that species of abortion and euthanasia practiced upon language in the name of semiotics, a destruction of language now raised to an academic principle.

To do the right thing (to clothe the poor and comfort the widow) for the wrong reason is the greatest treason. But it is most destructively a treason to the would-be comforter's own soul. With this, Percy would undoubtedly agree. Walter, in the course of his interview, asks Percy his reaction to Allan Bloom's *The Closing of the American Mind*, remarking Bloom's original title, *Soul Without Longing*, and recalling Father James Schall's quip that the title should be *Longing Without Soul*. (Of Bloom, Percy remarks, "I suspect he is a nihilist.") If we take Father Schall's pointed jest and explore it in relation to Walker Percy's own long journey, we see the heart of Percy's concern, a concern central to his fascination with the mystery of sign, of language, in relation to the reality we experience either by a deportment through ordinary sentiment to reality or a deportment of sentimentality, that is, a manner divorced from reality.

What we might say is that the modern condition of the person is of a soul longing for its recovery as soul, longing for an escape from the reductionism of *person* to mere *self*, to consciousness disoriented from reality. And we find Percy wrestling with this condition not only in his concern for semiotics, but in his own ambiguous address to himself as southern writer. In taking up this strain of his thought, his "southernness," I must make it clear at once that I myself am centrally concerned with "southernness," by which I do not mean a limited historical or geographical reduction to the local accidents of place. My own position is that we are born provincial but if blessed in our labors by grace may become regionalists. That is, we may at last come to some accommodation in our necessary journeying, our wayfaring in time and space, in relation to the present realities of explicit time and space that are always conditions to our actual existence as persons. Much more is involved, I contend, in respect to Percy as "southerner" than his inclination to credit to his "southernness" only the texture of his fictions, as he is inclined to do. On this question, there is much more to say. Meanwhile, however, we take up his response to Scott Walter's question about himself as southerner.

In discussing the loss of culture, manners, belief—once associated with the American South as stereotypical, in contrast to the North as the "land of industry"—Percy remarks the dissolving of those differences, though in some degree they once obtained in our history. He says, however, that now his grandchildren are "like the kids in Dubuque, Iowa." That this sea change has occurred, I believe, is an effect of "liberal" sentimentality, by which I mean to suggest at once that the Iowa children suffer as well as the Louisiana Percy children. The "Christian scandal," Percy says in this interview, is its "emphasis on individual human life." Without that scandalous emphasis, anything goes, including the gas chambers. The importance of encounter of person with immediate existence, the accommodation to *this* place and *this* time, which is so heavy a theme in recent literature of the American South, is exactly the issue, though reduced in its implications whenever frozen in our accounting for it by a reduction to mere history or geography. That is, the concern requires a metaphysical perspective beyond the account of history or naturalistic geography.

The liberal response of tenderness, then, which makes the Louisiana child and the Iowa child hardly distinguishable in their manifestations in time and place, begins with a denial of personhood in its fundamental actuality. Put briefly, sentimentality is a distortion of proper sentiment as oriented by the realities of time and place and thus a distortion of significant creation. It begins with a dislocated emphasis on egalitarianism, a shifting of perspective from the essence of personhood to the accidents of personhood in a reductionism of discrete entities to identities of each other in the name of "equality." It is accomplished though a nominalism in service to pragmatic attempts to restructure the accidents of existence, under the mistaken supposition that accident is substance. Thus the dislocation of sign from reality by nominalism makes ready the manipulations of gnostic intellect. Required: an assault on and dislocation of the sign in its relation to the actuality of the signifier (the sign user) by the removal of meaning in sign. Through that subversion the proper relation of personhood to the present reality is destroyed. There is no better instance of the point than the effect of the media in reducing the diversely known by actual personal experience to a putative sameness. To hear the media tell it, the Des Moines child and the Louisiana child are identities, not persons, a manipulation possible through the sentimentality attaching to an abstraction, "child." That distortion involves, in its reaches, even the reduction of the voice of signs, the reduction to a common "accent."

Indeed, in the leveling of "North" and "South" following the most recent invasion of the South by the North as the new "land of industry," there develop "schools" devoted to removing "southern" accents from employees. Now in this dislocation of a person from the immediacy of place, he is left with mere "feeling" toward whatever object of attention is not the self. Feeling replaces the possibility of a full communion in being itself with that which is not the self. To suppose, then, that the actual South known by the novelist and used by him makes him a "southern writer" only insofar as he uses that knowledge as a matter convenient to his form is to misunderstand the complexity of place to the soul. It is to misunderstand the nature of man as a wayfarer who must learn not only to be *at* a place but *in* a place as well.

And that is the tensional conflict in Percy's Binx Bolling in *The Moviegoer*. Here lies the center of the mystery of our existence as person, as wayfarer in time and place, Percy's continuous theme. About that theme he expresses himself ambiguously as often as not. The ambiguity enriches the fiction, surely. And expressing himself so, he associates himself with his protagonists in a complexity echoing the relation of James Joyce to his Stephen. What is meant by this cryptic analogy we may discover in turning to Binx as Percy comments on him in another interview, one in which he talks with French critics in a trans-Atlantic conversation on December 3, 1986, in which Judlyn Liffy of Worldnet conducted a televised exchange between Walker Percy and a gathering of French scholars. The occasion was the inclusion of *The Moviegoer* on the reading list in English and American literature for that year's examination in Agregation d'Anglais for future teachers. Percy, he was told by the panel's moderator, Professor Claude Richard of the University of Montpelier, was included with such notables as "Shakespeare, John Donne, Oliver Goldsmith, Alfred Lord Tennyson, and Dashiell Hammett." To be on that reading list, Professor Richard said, "is, in France, like ultimate recognition." With that preparation, Professor Richard propounded the first question, the one Percy had to contend with from his early recognition as novelist to the end: "Do you consider yourself as a southern writer and, if so, what features of your work do you regard as peculiarly southern?"

After a mannerly response to the honor of being included on the reading list, Percy answered the question that would never go away. It would not go away in large part because it was a question gnawing at the root of his own intellectual blossoming, a question he had come to but uncertain terms with in an earlier interview, the now-famous one with himself. There he both asked the questions and answered them, in a self-interrogation that rejected questions about his "southernness" and yet returned inescapably to that question. For the panel of French scholars he responds, "Yes, of course I am a southern writer." But he is so "in the sense that I depend on my southern background for the decor, the setting, the sense of place which any novelist must have." And, given his audience perhaps, he adds at once: "I owe less to Faulkner and southern writers and indeed American writers than to certain French writers: to be specific, Jean-Paul Sartre, Albert Camus, Gabriel Marcel, and to go back a way, Blaise Pascal."

In matters intellectual it is of course, as Percy well knew, most difficult to sort out one's influences. Nor does it help much to give an accounting of one's debt to particular thinkers, since such an attention to one's relation to other minds in the intellectual community, whose life is continuous in time and beyond discrete place through the mystery of sign itself, violates the reality necessary to that community. One is not so much indebted to a particular mind in imitation of that mind as he is an inheritor of truth about reality insofar as that mind has cogently expressed it and turned one to desire the truth of things. There is surely, between Percy and Faulkner, a shared climate of thought about time and place as manifested in their fictions, and there is certainly a common concern for southern stoicism between them. There is as well a recognition of that climate as encountered in Faulkner on the part of Jean-Paul Sartre. Sartre reveals this recognition in his essays on Faulkner. This climate of intellectual concern with time and place, for instance, which dominates discussions of "southern" literature at a largely superficial level, is inescapable to human experience of existence itself, whatever one's "South." It is crucial, at last, to any person's understanding of his own nature and is not reserved as what "any novelist must have."

Percy recognizes this mystery of our immaterial (intellectual) nature as involved in our material (incarnate) nature as the combining of person through the soul, which St. Thomas defines as the substantial form of the body. *Person* is thus necessarily situated circumstantially in a time and a place, a mystery Percy explores in his concern for the word, the sign. It is the concern that led him along the way to accept the Word made flesh. In his colloquy with the French professors, then, he must have anticipated their next question, as often asked as the one about his being a southern writer: are you a Catholic writer? And to this he gives an answer analogous to his first. His being Catholic as a writer has to do "not so much with explicit faith or transmitting an explicit faith in my writings as it has to do with what I would call an anthropology." He is not speaking of anthropology in the American sense, the sense that spawns much of the American discussion about his southernness, but rather of that intellectual concern — more typically European — for "a view of man, of a theory of man, man as more than an organism, as more than consumer, man as Gabriel Marcel describes him, a 'homo viator,' man the wayfarer, man the pilgrim, man in transit, on a journey."

It is no accident that Percy summons Flannery O'Connor to such questions as well; but unlike her, he does not anchor his response in St. Augustine and St. Paul (we have here no abiding place) nor in St. Thomas, whose argument is insistent that the poet's, the artist's, responsibility is to the good of the thing being made, not with the correction of appetites in his audience. What lies behind Percy's limitation of his answer, one suspects, is his sense of membership in that recent intellectual community concerned with man the wayfarer, a community descended most directly from Kierkegaard to that French intellectual who has been much celebrated in the academy as Existentialist. Flannery O'Connor, too, is sometimes concerned with that particular community of thought, and rather devastating in her satirical treatment of it. Her Bible salesman, for instance, in "Good Country People" may be said to make the point that one need not have a doctoral degree from the Sorbonne to believe in nothing. He "was born believing in nothing." Such a recognition allowed Miss O'Connor a somewhat more immediate access to "place" than Percy at first enjoyed. His is a journey from which he comes home at last by way of European thought of a recent vintage.

What began to be more and more certain for him was that the wayfarer is precisely that because of the circumstances of time and place, the wayfarer being one who wanders from place to place. But he seems increasingly to have realized that the wandering was primarily a journey of the mind. To have settled in Feliciana in Louisiana and lived there so many years, only reluctantly leaving that temporary home to go to Washington, D.C., or Notre Dame, or even abroad, allowed him a more manageable journey as a wayfarer within the immediate, the local, the concrete. For such is the great scandal to man, as he said in the Washington interview, of an "emphasis on individual life" (and here he means that Christian sense of personhood). There is the added scandal: that such an individual life can exist only in some place. Every thing has to be some *place*, and a person does not escape place by moving, as so many of the early American expatriates though possible in moving to France.

Such was Percy's recognition as he talked to the panel of French scholars about himself as a southern, Catholic writer, and he used his first protagonist, Binx Bolling of *The Moviegoer*, to talk about his own "identity." His concern is at a level deeper than the American anthropological concern with "religion" and "race" and "local history," the usual limits of his interlocutor's interest. Binx is a figure of modern man as wanderer. That is, Binx is deracinated, though he cannot escape his history and he is rather restricted geographically. The local signifies to him, but only when it is a part of that strange abstractionism practiced upon the local by the movie. He is fascinated by the movie's accommodation to place whereby place seems at last made real. It is made real not in itself, but through the images projected on a screen. One cannot escape a metaphorical analogue to Binx: the parable of Plato's cave. And to be reminded of that parable is to recognize Binx as a wanderer within a limited local compass: a small geography that provides all the complexity of place as one might discover that complexity the world over, insofar as man is wayfarer, that is, insofar as man is a soul seeking its cause as a "self." What is missing is a recognition of the full sun upon reality, to be encountered only if one abandons the tunnel vision of the self trapped in the cave of self-awareness, the Cartesian curse.

It is clear that Percy feels toward Binx as a father to a son, seeing more of himself in Binx than he might admit under direct questioning, though that kinship emerges in his own self-questioning interview. Here to the French scholars he says, for instance, that out of Binx's sense of dislocation he is searching for some way (in Binx's words) to "stick" himself "into the world." In his later interview on the occasion of the Jefferson Lecture, he speaks of modern man as *deranged*, the literal sense of that term most appropriate to the Cartesian dislocation of intellect that has effected our displacement from the proper range of our being in the world. What, he asks, "are the options for characters living in a deranged world in which the Church is no longer regnant, no longer terribly important in many places?" That is the question initiating his several protagonists' quests as wayfarers, whether Will Barrett's journey to New York City and points North and his return to his baffling South, or Binx Bolling's wanderings about New Orleans.

Binx, Percy tells his French admirers in his trans–Atlantic interview, is playing a certain game, though he "doesn't know it." He is "doing what

Kierkegaard would call exercises in repetition and rotation.... He is a victim of your great René Descartes, to whom I attribute many of the troubles of the modern world." But what is significant to Binx's journeying is his quest for signification: he "looks for signs." And, with a foreshadowing of the same concern for sign that Percy pursues in *Thanatos Syndrome*, Binx finds one particular sign to be his "particular way of thinking of the Jews." Try as he may, he cannot subsume them by sign. They escape "the theories of the books," being always something more than can be said of them by words. Binx recognizes a kinship here that escapes his understanding of himself as dislocated in time and place in relation to the Wandering Jew, who is not a literary shibboleth but a reality eluding his grasp. He feels a kinship that evades him. As for this dislocation in Binx, Percy says, "I balance the question very delicately between the hero or the protagonists of most of my novels." The question is the meaning of dislocation itself.

As for Binx specifically, his "real dislocation" is "from the ordinary modes of existence in America; existence as consumer, as recipient of all the goods and services of technology." But it is more complex, this dislocation, since Binx is "an exile from his own traditions. I placed him very consciously as a certain consciousness placed between two traditions in the South. One is from his father's side ... a very strong ethical stoic tradition which owes less to Christianity than it does to the Emperor Marcus Aurelius, and the stoic philosophers... The other tradition is his mother's family which is middle-class bourgeois New Orleans Catholic." In dramatizing Binx as dislocated intellectual, Percy raises the delicate question: "Who is dislocated — are the consumers, the businessmen, the professional men, the happy scientists who are busy; busy with their various works?" The answer to that question for Percy is that *all* are dislocated. All are dislocated by the very nature of human existence which necessitates one's being a wayfarer. He adds, "Maybe the philosophical progenitor is Pascal who said 'To be born and to live is to be dislocated.'"

The agony in wayfaring is the difficulty of orientation, which Binx solves inadequately by his obsession with moviegoing, his Kierkegaardian repetition and rotation. Percy implies its inadequacy in calling our attention to the time-span of his novel, "the two or three days at the end of the Mardi Gras season." And the last scene on the last day is an occasion of an epiphany, not only in the Joycean sense, but in the O'Connor sense as well. On Ash Wednesday, Binx, whose talent as observer of other people's wanderings is (as he says) "to see the way people stick themselves into the world," observes a black man leaving a church, a smudge on his forehead. It is a moment revealing Binx's displaced Cartesian awareness, in which he observes others and sees with a detachment that excludes him from the world into which those others insert themselves. It is Kate, practiced in observing Binx at his own detached observation, who most nearly draws him into the world, by recognizing the nature of the "game" Binx is playing in his Kierkegaardian exercises of repetition and rotation. The two moments: first, Binx's seeing the black man leaving the church after Ash Wednesday ritual, with an acceptance of the necessity, as Binx would have it, of "inserting himself into the world"; second, Binx's own ceremony of moviegoing whereby he seems to come to terms with place but in actuality does not. It is this latter moment that Kate explores. Binx's fascination with movies, she tells him, lies in their certifying place as a reality. *Place*, the old problem of "southernness" which is independent as a problem to any wayfaring man of any specific geography, as it is independent of any specific time in the history of place.

What Binx thinks to have accomplished experientially through his moviegoing is a rescue of place from its encumbrance by consciousness itself. It is a way of dissolving, as it were, the detachment from place, a moment of rest from wayfaring in which, as Kate says, place reveals its "peculiar reality." What his experience of place through the movies seems to overcome is that burden upon place which, as Percy remarks, is the Heideggerian "everydayness." Place seems in its reality transformed, and by the mystery of the movie as an art form. It is in this context of Binx's wonder that the momentary encounter with the sojourner on the church steps reveals both Binx's hunger and the inadequacy of the food his hunger finds. For truth is the proper food of intellect, and the existential food proves ersatz, as Percy suspects, though he is never quite able himself to escape its attraction. He is drawn to it always, as some of us are to McDonald burgers. Binx's "theory of certification," as Percy calls it, implies a search under way — very much Percy's own — whose object seems now near, now impossibly far away. But that sense of nearness or farness is teasing always, insofar as it always appears in our experience of time and place.

Let us say that the search, which is common to us all by our very given natures as created intellect, is for a valid self-forgetting in which place and time are real beyond geography and history. The adjacent world in this moment seems always inadequate to the desire, but only inasmuch as the wayfarer cannot escape the ambiance that his own consciousness imposes upon place in relation to his own awareness, that Heideggerian "everydayness." That is the obstacle to visionary encounter with place, a conspicuous manifestation of which is Descartes' legacy to Western though. What is desired, and made possible to *homo viator* through this moment in this place, is a visionary encounter, first with being and, necessarily consequential to that encounter, with the Cause of being. That is why the moment's encounter with the worshiper on the church steps is profoundly important, though but a moment's encounter to Binx. The deep is not necessarily the long or the large. Magnitude is, at last, not dependent on time-space, though Binx stops shy of that recognition and not many readers will themselves appreciate the dramatic burden carried by that brief encounter in the action of Percy's first novel.

The significant analogue to Binx's fascination with the movie is the Mass. The movie is the Cartesian reductionist version of reality, a substitute for the Mass, though which Binx attempts to certify his own validity as person. In the end, we might say, the rival philosophers are more ancient than those Percy cites in discussing his work in this interview. Rather than Descartes, Pascal, Kierkegaard, the French Existentialists, they are Plato and Aquinas, for the polarity in Binx's tensional quest is that between Idealism and Realism. The problem is older than Descartes and Pascal, as it is older than Aquinas and Plato as well, the wanderer's seeking an encounter of the timeless under the burden of time, the abiding under the burden of fading place.

This issue, and the inadequacy of Binx's solution at this point of his journey, is spoken to with subtle irony in relation to the movie "hero," with implications beyond Binx's understanding. Percy says to the French scholars: "Living in an ordinary neighborhood ... one is uncertified: one goes about one's business; one sees the same people who are, more or less, alive — maybe more dead than alive; victim to what Heidegger would call 'everydayness.' And yet when this very same, ordinary scene is represented in the movies, it all of a sudden becomes alive; it becomes certified." Percy is speaking of Binx's "theory of certification," but there is at least a degree of consent to that theory in his own speaking. We have seen Binx encounter the Ash Wednesday worshiper. We see him also observing people observe William Holden, on movie location in New Orleans. Binx is interested, says Percy, in "this extraordinary phenomenon — which I am, too — the aura of reality around movie stars who are perhaps the most unreal of all people, in truth."

One regrets that in the interview Percy did not underline more firmly the relation of this fascination with the unreal as if real, this malaise of the modern mind, by turning to that other hero, who once for all rescued sign in relation to place, the Christ on the altar, in Whom the Word is a presence orienting time and place, the abiding Signpost in the desert. He might well have pointed more sharply to his own wily juxtaposition of signs in the novel, that of the movie's illusion of reality and the moment's encounter of the black man on the church steps, the sign of the cross smudged on his forehead with the ashes of the inescapable exile in the wandering season of Lent that is man's lot as *homo viator*. But the pointing in an interview, not in the novel itself of course, is the place for remarking the juxtaposition explicitly. In the novel he is attempting the task proper to the poet, the recovery of signifying sign to his reader. In our age, in which we have lost the significance of the mystery in sign, let alone the limited signification of truth in any particular sign, it is not amiss in the poet, when he is confronted by inquisitive theorists and urged to pronounce upon the nature of his peculiar calling — the rescue of sign — to speak directly for that labor Eliot calls the purification of the dialect of the tribe.

That is the task Percy recognized, of course, out of his faith, his orientation through sign to the Word. But in his intellectual exploration as *homo viator*, he does not always seem to recognize the extent of his own accomplishment in justifying the profound "southernness" which is always at issue. In this "southernness" lies an anthropology beyond both the American and, at least since Descartes, the European species of anthropology — a recognition of the wayfarer as created intellect lost and wandering in the desert until he becomes oriented to reality through such signs as may rest their limited significance in specific time and place, as that complex is governed by the Word. The "everydayness" of the elements of the Mass mediate the reality of time and place to intellect, justifying existential reality at last as rescued. The ersatz food of art divorced from its relation to the creating Signifier though being, God, the Cause of moments of time and points of place, at this juncture of my next step on the journey, is poor food indeed. It is in turning from false to true that the soul finds the desert abloom. Recovered now "the salt savour of the sandy earth" as "the lost heart stiffens and rejoices" in hope of rescue, as Eliot discovered. That is a considerable step on the way to recognition that "all manner of thing shall be well." And that is the recognition that Percy, like Eliot before him, comes to in his journeying within the confines of time and place. That is the recognition Percy hints at, in remarking the background of that painted portrait of himself in his self-interview, "Questions They Never Asked Me So He Asked Them Himself": "The no-man's land barbed wire is not really wire but a briar and it is blooming! A rose!"

Part V

On Books and Schooling

15

Books, Books, Books: Difficulty Choices in Times of Intellectual Stress

Asked by the editors of The Southern Partisan *to submit a list of important books that should be read by the rising generation (general books in the Western tradition and books especially pertinent to southern readers), Montgomery submitted the two lists that follow this introductory essay. Montgomery's concern in the essay is to provide orientation to young readers living in a confusing, chaotic intellectual climate dominated by intellectual provincials in the academy and elsewhere. As always in his writing, Montgomery emphasizes the reader's responsibility both to his inherited tradition and to his community. The serious reader is a steward, and as Montgomery puts it toward the close of the essay, he is "obligated to pursue a rescue of tradition in the light of the truth of things."**

November 1999

Recently I was requested by the editor of *The Southern Partisan* to contribute to a special issue, its theme a recommendation by various contributors of those works a young scholar setting off for the academy ought to read. What was solicited was a listing of twenty titles in each of two categories: general works and works oriented to the American South. Not a promising invitation to me, since to give a list to any young waking intellect, without any accompanying orientation that might allow that young person some purchase on the "sage" providing him an intellectual roadmap, is problematic at best. How uncomfortable to him, to be confronted by a list of *oughts* at the outset of his journey. For that reason, I was myself somewhat uncomfortable when my list, along with those of others,

---

*These lists, along with lists submitted by other southern scholars, appeared in *The Southern Partisan* 19.2 (Spring 1999). The essay was not published.

appeared in cold print, and I was made the more concerned by an extrapolation from those lists of those works considered by survey as the "greatest of all time."

My own concern had been quite other: I intended rather to enable the serious young student a beginning, whereby he might discover first of all just where he now stands at the ending of our millennium. My list is concerned to alert him to recent travelers within his own most immediate country of the mind, considering that he (within the terms of the invitation) is most likely a young southern intellectual. My list suggests messages from significant travelers just ahead of him, located at disparate points of the current intellectual compass. My concern was that he might from these discover with more assurance just where he now stands as he is about to set out. By reasoned triangulation, he might with more confidence begin his own journey into what is in our moment a confusing intellectual desert.

Given, then, this difficult charge, and suspicious of lists as such, I accompanied my record of those messages with a brief introduction. But since that preface did not accompany my lists, I venture some rescue of it here. Concerning the question of "southern" books, I recall Stark Young's contribution to *I'll Take My Stand* (1930), that yet famous symposium by "Twelve Southerners": "[W]e defend certain qualities not because they belong to the South, but because the South belongs to them. The intelligent course sees first our southern Culture in relation to other cultures, and then in the light of its own sun." In the light of its own sun, as the intellectual sojourner may rescue that light from distorting and conflicted shadows which, by their local proximity to his seemingly lonesome trail, tend to distort those "qualities" properly sought as the permanent things. By those shadows he may be threatened to an arrested provincialism, a suspension of the journeying, or to an endless circling in shadows. Either way, that is to consent to a distortion of the viable, especially of the local in which one always begins to learn to read signposts. It is to betray one's inheritance of the immediate present and thus to betray the tradition inherited to this moment by grasping at shadows of the permanent things as if shadow rather than substance were desirable.

These signs—my listed works—are given as cautionary in the light of present intellectual crisis, the effect of which is a rapid degeneration of the academy itself, to which the young journeyman is presumed bound. And these initiating words may serve him in judging both me and my list. Such is the beginning of his responsibility to tradition. It is a responsibility which properly requires that he neither reject his inherited present tradition nor embrace it unexamined. He must instead sort it, since it is not *a* tradition but an amalgam of traditions impinging upon his waking reason. Thus, in the light of Young's rubric, I am at once suspicious of the awkward disjunction of *general* works from *southern* ones. I caution as well that my list is heavily exclusive, assuming for instance a commitment already made to that rich inheritance of literature and philosophy reaching back to the Greeks.

And so, because of the responsibilities of intellectual judgment in such undertakings as this, I should prefer (given happier circumstances) a personal tutorial conversation "about" these concerns, though circumstance dictates this elliptic approach by introduction and listing. Not easy, this attempt to encourage any young waking mind setting out to recover the rich intellectual history he has inherited. Certainly not easy, a colloquy denied, to sufficiently emphasize the paradox: his is an inheritance left him at no initial cost to him, though it is *dear* in an old sense of that word, its very richness progressively waking in him, one prays, that sense of responsibility to the inheritance—first to his own benefit and collaterally to the benefit of intellectual and social and political community itself.

And so I must especially remind him that he is responsible to and for that inheritance, which is already bequeathed to his sons and daughters before he has even come into his own inheritance. Through his responsibility as waking steward to that inheritance, he may increasingly gather from it a continuing viability to himself and thereby to his present family and community in this moment. For he will discover himself sustained by a mystery of recovery: he will discover himself member in a community beyond moments, becoming citizen among the living and the dead. He will discover a community transcending history itself, transcending even his locally inherited tradition confounded so often by history—tradition constricted by intellectual error to the confines of a merely immanent world by our century's dominant Modernist tradition.

In such a sorting of his own inherited moment, he will also discover that my numbered list proves to be works individually relative in their virtues to his particular pursuit of the permanent things: his pursuit of those "qualities" to which he both personally and communally most properly belongs. But may he discover as well that his first responsibility to his inheritance is the perfection of his own intellectual gifts. That is the first and always his central responsibility as steward: a perfection of his nature as *this person*. His integrity as person, his integral perfection as intellectual soul incarnate, is the end toward which he journeys beyond where he stands at any moment. (For this high journey he must first secure his own oxygen mask before attempting to help others in distress—as intellectual soul, that is.) As for my list, I repeat that I assume as implied but not set down many important works within the Western tradition, works he must engage in relation to what Young speaks of as "other cultures," cautioning the journeyman that in our present climate of intellectual corruption, advanced under the shibboleth of "multiculturalism," that false sign as usually explicated is a clear and present danger to intellect itself.

One must read such works as the Bible, then, and those "monuments of unaging intellect" as William Butler Yeats calls them — that literature through which any journeyman may begin to justify his entitlement: literature from the Greeks down to recent "southern" writers. There is rich sustenance as well as danger in old philosophy winnowed, and in poetry and drama: from Homer and Virgil and Dante, from Chaucer and Shakespeare and Milton: from many other feeding stations of the word along his way, in which word he will find stored sustenance. Perhaps more immediate to him (assuming him southern), those actual southern writers who prove larger than merely "southern": William Faulkner, Allen Tate, John Crowe Ransom, Donald Davidson, Robert Penn Warren, Flannery O'Connor, Walker Percy. As always more and more join him in his passage into high country. And so one is obligated to read a great range of present witnesses, as well as some long dead to the world but present nevertheless to his journeying. Not directly listed here, once recognized as belonging to the "Western canon" in the American academy up until World War II. There began at that time an intellectual provincialism, not only in our social and political institutions but, more destructively, in the academy. The effect is now evident in academic curricula, but evidenced increasingly in the general collapse of present community itself. Indeed, it was the editor's own sense of our loss of a community of the living with the dead that prompted him to solicit listings.

My choices are works of varying complexity, so that it would be reckless to attempt them too ravenously. As caution then, I list them alphabetically by author, a sign of the responsibility to a sorting. To start with the first and attempt them as a list would be like attempting to read the Bible through from "the front." One founders in the "begats" if not careful. Common sense must discriminate, then, but over a period of time. The task is now gradual: an awakening of common sense in response to evident truths. And perhaps with some help in the ordering and winnowing aided by a proximate mentor. For, as chaotic as is the present academy, persons yet survive there — a few heroic witnesses who are devoted to a pursuit of the truth of things. These persons will know as well how formidable those proximate antagonists to a concern for the truth of things, antagonists whose name is legion always, but seldom so concentrated one suspects as in this moment in the academy.

Such a mentor will know that, as Richard Weaver reminded us, ideas have consequences. He will know especially that bad ideas have bad consequences. Not only in present manifestations of untenable ideas, but in many ideas inherited as tradition, ideas always corroding present community. For ideas—both good and bad—as ideas have a property of vaporousness, to speak metaphorically. They affect particular intellects, and through them the present community, by a sort of osmosis. Or perhaps, by a trickle-down effect from established, inherited authority, whether legitimate authority or not.

But then bad ideas are, like the poor, always with us, making the journey dangerous but certainly not boring. Bad ideas—as ancient as the garden of Eden, made endless in variation by the oldest of all bad ideas: that by intellectual autonomy "I" am not simply equal to but the superior of all ideas and thus superior to the Cause of ideas as well. How endless those variations, and how seductive. Always as if new—as if resolving and simplifying the journey by an intentionality supreme. But it is out of this complex of ancient and recent ideas that we discover ourselves obligated to purifying them as it were, in an attempt to recover and sustain viable tradition, as tribute to the present community through our peculiar gifts as person. That is why the sound traditionalist knows himself obligated to the sorting of his inheritance, becoming thereby a responsible steward to complex tradition. For *tradition* proves always a complex of good and bad ideas. Ambiguous tradition is ours both in the brain and in the blood. That is, it affects our intellectual gift, which (more formally) is that gift of both *intuitive* and *rational* knowing, a mystery we must engage along our way as intellectual creatures.

With an obligation to pursue and recover Stark Young's "qualities" to which we properly belong, a suggestion of one foray into our list: consider St. Augustine's *Confessions,* and in its light a northern and a southern work: Henry Adams's *Education* and William Alexander Percy's *Lanterns on the Levee*. Adams quite deliberately writes his intellectual history in imitation of St. Augustine, whom I have sometimes suggested our first "Modern" novelist in his *Confessions*. That is, St. Augustine is concerned to witness by his art the progress of a soul (his own) from being lost in the always present desert of the world, only at last in turning from the Modernist presumption of autonomy to discover the desert as lying in himself. Increasingly, especially under the influence of Dante's *Divine Comedy,* this journey has become the poet's theme in Western literature, the poet himself becoming the protagonist, whether presented as hero or antihero. And increasingly, the necessities to art's transforming autobiography—what Aristotle would call history—into poetry have led to aesthetic sophistications effecting a severing of the poet from his art, lest he be too personally — too historically involved. Out of that severance, an action not reserved to the poet, we discover ourselves the "Age of Alienation," haunted by Y2K as Modernism's reminder of original sin.

Now St. Augustine is a soul most exceptionally gifted intellectually, a recognition which at first delights him in a self-love willfully pursued, the parabola of that action ordering his personal "novel." (It is a parabola of fictional action faintly echoed by James Joyce in his own *Portrait of the Artist as a Young Man.*) St. Augustine was at first possessed by self-love, until that turning in which he rejects his Manichaean autonomy. Henry Adams, like Augustine, is as well a gifted intellectual soul, and in that same tradition of the soul on pilgrimage, though by the eve of World War I he would not speak with a term like the "soul." He is also, at first intuitively and then quite self-consciously and rationally, aware of himself as at the lag-end of the Puritan "tradition." That is a tradition which, in its "northern" as opposed to "southern" manifestation, had become transformed out of an intellectual "Transcendentalism," more properly called *angelism,* through Pragmatism and Positivism, leaving Adams with his intuitive desire for an integrity beyond any conscious confessional recognition available to him. He continues alienated in the world. Forlorn, he deports himself as Stoic, a deportment which at last cannot redeem the time. Hence there is a climate of pathos to that marvelous attempt at self-rescue, *The Education of Henry Adams,* which is significantly cast in a third-person reflective detachment from himself.

And so Adams's attempt of self-rescue, of survival as intellectual creature through Stoicism, is made evident in a tonal unity of his episodic "confession." But that tonal quality yields a sense of pathos quite other than the triumphant confidence — out of faith and hope and love — which we find in St. Augustine, who in his own person ("I") is thankful for rescue through grace. Such the points and counterpoints of witness in these signs to our young journeyman as he reads this ancient and this modern message in relation to his own obligation to the journey. And should he be a southern journeyman, there is the interestingly parallel work of "Uncle Will" Percy's *Lanterns on the Levee,* a "confession" of a southern Stoic to be read along with the "Yankee" Stoic, Adams, as both may be enlightened by St. Augustine's *Confessions.* William Alexander Percy ("Uncle Will") is recognized as such a Stoic by his nephew Walker Percy, the novelist. ("Uncle Will" was a poet, as was St. Augustine at his outset.) Walker reflects on this species of tradition as he discovers himself a "southern" version of *homo viator,* discovering as well an inadequacy in Stoicism — Yankee or southern — to any safe passage for him. Thus it is that he will recognize closer kinship with St. Augustine. He comes to a rational appreciation of that lineage by discovering his intuitive affinity to St. Augustine as running deeper than that to his "natural" Uncle Will, to speak perhaps cryptically as we must.

Only after *The Moviegoer* is published does Walker recognize that his novel lands "squarely in the oldest tradition of Western letters: the pilgrim's search outside himself, rather than the guru's search within. All this happened to the novelist and his character without the slightest consciousness of a debt to St. Augustine or Dante." (Here, a playful detachment through third-person perspective, like that taken by Adams as a literary device, quite different from St Augustine's passionate first person monologue to God by that wayward pilgrim come home at last.) Walker Percy, in his essays and in interviews, comments on the inadequacy of southern Stoicism to a recovery of his own southerness as valid against the Modernist "angelized" world. He had been uncomfortable all along with a Stoic "southerness," inherited from Uncle Will most proximately, though through that inheritance sorted he will nevertheless begin to recognize certain "qualities" belonging not to the South, but through which qualities the South belongs to something extra-temporal and extra-geographical.

In another juxtaposition of works from our list: consider Gilson's rather fierce rejection of Cartesian Idealism on philosophical grounds in *Methodical Idealism*, along with Maritain's *Moral Philosophy*, in which Kantian "universalism" is rejected on rational grounds as well. For both Gilson and Maritain are concerned through philosophical analysis with causes whose effects will concern Walker Percy in what he rejects as the "Los Angelism" of community, a pseudo- culture he engages as satiric "poet"—as novelist. Both these French philosophers, both Thomists, are concerned to reveal the intellectually destructive (and so culturally destructive) effects of untenable ideas descended into the popular spirit through an osmosis—bad ideas inherited from the late Middle Ages. Through increasingly unsophisticated misunderstandings of tolerance, those bad ideas (Gilson and Maritain would contend) erode community and family. And to these add Gabriel Marcel, whose *Homo Viator* engages that erosion as it bears directly upon the family, more fundamentally destructive of community than the spectacle of World War II all about him as he writes.

Such works help us recover a position necessary if we are to take a stand in our present Modernist desert, for they recover to us those questions which must be asked in this crisis of dissolving intellectual responsibilities. One may well in this perspective also consider Fischer's *Albion's*

Seed as recovering at a social level of our recent history something of the complex cultural grounds feeding the nematodes of bad ideas that by now infect the soil of viable tradition. Fischer gives account of the imported cultural and religious tradition of the Puritan New Englander, of the southern Cavalier, of the Appalachian and Deep South Scotch-Irish-English borderers: invasions settling into our landscape and establishing tensional provinces on this continent, out of which an emerging confluence of cultures. Cultures further complicated by that Quaker Province in the Delaware River Basin, on the border of the "North" and the "South." Fischer's work not only helps reveal origins of some present consequences settled into our culture, but may reveal as well continuing dispositions out of those cultures that make us the more vulnerable to Cartesian and Kantian dissociation of intellect from reality itself, counter to our pursuit of a unity beyond provincialism, through the angelism of autonomous intellect.

The work throws historical light as well on residual northern-southern antipathies still with us, such misunderstandings as those which Donald Davidson engages in his *Attack on Leviathan*. For in such works, the tensional relation of regional and provincial forces in their historical aspects emerge, complicating (for instance) our understanding of the old and continuing relation between Tidewater Cavalier and Mountain clansman, or either of these in opposition to a Puritan residual inheritance. One discovers that more than geography is involved in the relation of Cavalier Planter and Mountain Yeoman, theirs a complex relation made emblematic in southern history in the figures of Robert E. Lee and Stonewall Jackson. That in itself is a complex juxtaposition of symbolic figures further unfolded by Frank Owsley in his two works, *King Cotton Diplomacy* and *Plain Folks of the Old South*. It may even lead one to such a recognition as expressed by a friend of mine who remarked, after reading into Fischer — my friend a North Carolinian: "Now I know why the _____ boys [from a local Scotch-Irish clan] threw rocks at me when we were children." Fischer's book, then, reveals something of the tensional relation between the Cavalier's social and religious mentality and that dogmatically inclined independent mentality still evident in our southern uplands and in parts of the Deep South, reaching even unto southern California, where it may become metamorphosed into Percy's "Los Angelism." There were differences affecting the uneasy alliance of Cavalier and Yeoman in defending the "southern Cause" against Yankee Puritan-Quaker intentionalities, those provincials themselves already metamorphosing to political and cultural Pragmatism and moving toward the triumph of Positivism at our own century's end.

And so such reflection gains a richer dimension to much of this century's literature, especially that associated with the "southern Literary Renaissance." It is a richness caught in Faulkner's postage stamp world in Mississippi and in Flannery O'Connor's recognitions of man as *homo viator* revealed in seemingly backwoods Georgians, her "Christ-haunted" protagonists. Light shed as well on that enigmatic iconography to things "southern" in the figure of the Cavalier Stoic Lee, with his "right arm" Presbyterian fatalist Stonewall Jackson. That is a recognition Walker Percy comes to, expressed in his "Why Are You a Catholic": "If one wished to depict the beau ideal of the South, it would not be the crucified Christ but rather the stoic knight — at parade rest, both hands folded on the hilt of his broadsword, his face as grave as the Emperor's [Marcus Aurelius']. In the South, of course, he came to be, not the Emperor or [King Richard of *Ivanhoe*], but R.E. Lee, the two in one."

In the light of our rubric from Stark Young, it becomes difficult to separate "general" from "southern" works, then. I have for many years written on this difficulty. My Lamar Lectures, *Possum and Other Receipts for the Recovery of "Southern" Being*, quite deliberately puts "southern" in quotes for reasons implicit in our rubric. I have written on Solzhenitsyn as "southerner," and on many others in this vein, including Homer, Dante, Eliot, Hawthorne, Dostoevsky. For to be a "southerner" in my sense — to belong to abiding principles as opposed to declaring that those principles belong to me as southerner — is determined neither by geography nor by history, as important as history and geography are. Instead, I believe myself a *person*, an intellectual soul incarnate, who by the *gift* of my being am required to address history and nature, and the accidents of my time and place, as steward to the inherent goodness of creation itself. Included most proximately is my responsible stewardship to myself as person, in which proper office (when properly pursued) I may benefit my local community.

What we discover in journeying creation is that willy nilly we are traditionalists. But once more we inherit a *mixed* tradition, to which we are responsible as stewards through our specific gifts as *this* person — each witnessing according to his gifts. That is a recognition which T.S. Eliot comes to, relatively late in his life, in recovering his own "southerness." In his Virginia lectures, *After Strange Gods: A Primer of Modern Heresy*, he begins with a tribute to those Twelve Southerners who had recently published *I'll Take My Stand*. Eliot goes on to explore the idea of *tradition*, suggesting it "a byproduct of right living, not to be aimed at directly." It is of the blood, so to speak, rather than of the brain. For that reason there rises in the person blessed by that inheritance the necessity to his "brain," to his intellect, to sort his blood inheritance: to separate and purify bad and good ideas in the blood. Thus T.S. Eliot will at last declare that, as poet, his responsibility is to "purify the dialect of the tribe."

This is a recognition of responsibility he comes to after considerable struggle with his own inheritance which is largely Puritan. How poignant, his remarks to Sir Herbert Read at the time of "Ash-Wednesday," a letter dated St. George's Day in 1928:

> I want to write an essay about the point of view of an American who wasn't an American, because he was born in the South [St. Louis] and went to school in New England as a small boy with a nigger drawl, but who wasn't a southerner in the South because his people were northerners in a border state and looked down on all southerners and Virginians [for which read our *yeoman* and *cavalier*], and who so was never anything anywhere and who therefore felt himself to be more a Frenchman than an American and more an Englishman than a Frenchman and yet felt that the U.S.A. up to a hundred years ago was a family extension [read Fischer's *Albion's Seed*], It is almost too difficult even for H.J. [Henry James] who for that matter wasn't an American at all, in that sense.

The essay, one might venture out of all this reading of our selected list, is to be Eliot's *Four Quartets*.

It is both a necessity and an obligation attendant upon our inescapable journeying of this world, this sorting of tradition. That is the consequent office of stewardship, benefiting community according to perfected gifts, whether by "purifying the dialect of the tribe" as poet or by serving in other offices made kindred and complementary by the obligation to community through our sojourning as person in that community. In Eliot's terms, from his *After Strange Gods,* homo viator discovers the important complementary relation of *orthodoxy* to *tradition:* orthodoxy oriented to the truth of things independent of what man may make of known truth. For through orthodoxy, one regains a devotion to community, maintaining as steward "a consensus of the living and the dead," that consensus discovered as his already by inheritance in this present moment to the journeyman, especially made evident through his sorting of the tradition in his blood.

It is through knowing himself thus obligated to pursue a rescue of tradition in the light of the truth of things, his labor of intellectual journeying, that the person may stand witness to community of the abiding "qualities" to which he properly belongs. But even if community refuse that witness, he must continue resolute, knowing (in Eliot's words) that old truth to our proper sojourning: "orthodoxy may be upheld by one man against the world," as was true in the ancient world in the resolute stand taken by St. Athanasius—as Eliot suggests. On another occasion

Eliot remarks that in our sojourning as intellectual soul incarnate, we must not be tempted to despair, for there is no such thing as a Lost Cause in this world. All causes prove subject to worldly decay, and so there is no gained cause that is absolute in this world.

In this recognition lies the spiritual burden to *homo viator,* in relation to intellectual causes that are always more or less lost, leaving the sojourner his spiritual burden as fundamental. What is constant to the community of the living and the dead is the obligation of the person as journeyman to a restoration, under the constancy of grace. The *person's* responsibility to himself and to community is that of steward to tradition, whereby he may contribute the vital necessities to any present community — according to his own gifts as spent in this continuous task. Thus with piety and humility, he must sort his inheritance toward recovering the goodness possible to any *person* (for community exists to this end). Always in a strangely shifting desert of this moment in this place. A simple truth to be recovered — but to be recovered by responsible labor among the monuments to our intellectual and spiritual responsibilities as persons, such as witnessed most variously in my recommended works. And may you as journeyman have safe arrival in that country which lies beyond the necessity of any lists.

Works Southern

Bradford, M.E., *Against the Barbarians, and Other Reflections on Familiar Themes*
____, *Remembering Who We Are: Observations of a Southern Conservative*
Davidson, Donald, *The Attack on Leviathan: Regionalism and Nationalism in the United States*
____, *Still Rebels, Still Yankees and Other Essays*
Foote, Shelby, *The Civil War: A Narrative*
Letters:
    Cleanth Brooks and Allen Tate: Collected Letters, 1933–1976
    The Literary Correspondence of Donald Davidson and Allen Tate
    The Correspondence of Shelby Foote and Walker Percy
    The Habit of Being: Letters of Flannery O'Connor
Lytle, Andrew, *A Wake for the Living*
O'Connor, Flannery, *Mystery and Manners: Occasional Papers*
Owsley, Frank L., *King Cotton Diplomacy*
____, *Plain Folk of the Old South*
Percy, Walker, *Lost in the Cosmos: The Last Self-Help Book*
Percy, William Alexander, *Lanterns on the Levee*
Twelve Southerners, *I'll Take My Stand*
Weaver, Richard, *Ideas Have Consequences*
____, *The Southern Tradition at Bay: A History of Postbellum Thought*
Winchell, Mark Royden, *Cleanth Brooks and the Rise of Modern Criticism*

    And on and on and on....

V. On Books and Schooling

Works General

Adams, Henry, *The Education of Henry Adams*
Augustine, *The Confessions*
Chesterton, G.K., *The Everlasting Man*
de Jouvenel, Bertrand, *On Power: The Natural History of Its Growth*
Eliot, T.S., *After Strange Gods: A Primer of Modern Heresy*
Federalist Papers
Fischer, David, *Albion's Seed: Four British Folkways in America*
Gilson, Etienne, *Methodical Realism*
Johnson, Paul, *Modern Times: The World from the Twenties to the Eighties*
Lewis, C.S., *The Abolition of Man*
_____, *The Discarded Image: An Introduction to Medieval and Renaissance Literature*
Marcel, Gabriel, *Homo Viator: Introduction to a Metaphysics of Hope*
_____, *Man Against Mass Society*
Maritain, Jacques, *An Introduction to the Basic Problems of Moral Philosophy*
_____, *The Person and the Common Good*
Niemeyer, Gerhart, *Between Nothingness and Paradise*
Pieper, Josef, *In Tune with the World: A Theory of Festivity*
_____, *Leisure: The Basis of Culture*
Rommen, Heinrich A., *The Natural Law: A Study in Legal and Social History and Philosophy*
Strauss, Leo, *Natural Right and History*
de Tocqueville, Alexis, *Democracy in America*
Voegelin, Eric, *From Enlightenment to Revolution*
_____, *Science, Politics & Gnosticism*

And on and on and on....

16

To My Son, Going Away to School

Writing to his son, who had just begun his last year of high school as an exchange student in Berlin, Germany, Montgomery uses agrarian metaphors to emphasize the necessity of proper cultivation in higher education and in our use of the primary instrument of education, language. Humanistic education (or the liberal arts education) is distinguished from vocational and professional training and is linked to "the company of faithful minds" and to the community — that is, to great thinkers in the Western tradition and to the local scene. These themes and others pertinent to higher education are examined more extensively in Montgomery's Liberal Arts and Community: The Feeding of the Larger Body *(Louisiana Statue University Press, 1990) and* The Truth of Things: Liberal Arts and the Recovery of Reality *(Spence Publishing, 1999).*

Crawford, Georgia
July 31, 1975

Dear Marion:

Is it possible? A week ago we sat on the tailgate of our truck, eating the first cantaloupe from the garden. Now we are separated by an ocean and several countries, and you are struggling with what must seem a barbarous language. A long way from crab grass and coffee weed and bull nettle in Oglethorpe County. And so I encourage you to believe that your wide change will be worth the shock. And I suggest that our summer garden work is closer to you still than you suppose and will hold us together. We know that a seventy-cent cantaloupe from A&P is not the same creature we enjoyed.

---

*"To My Son, Going Away to School" was originally published in the *Red and Black*, a student newspaper at the University of Georgia.

You will be returning sooner than you think for college and a new shock. Very quickly you will find yourself moved out of our high school climate, which a British critic describes as "organized amnesia," into one where mind is widely assumed an instrument to be calibrated for its technical service to a machine called society. I put it starkly, but only to assure you that, given its worst, you will survive the educational factory our age has devised. *If* you learn to discriminate, to distinguish. Hence an advantage of this radical experience abroad.

I don't think you'll hear as many of your classmates there ask, "What use is history, philosophy, algebra, literature?" It is a common question here, as you know. For how does one explain the "use" of a cantaloupe to those who have been given a stone for bread? The question of the "use" of humanistic studies is asked most destructively, not by the questioning student in whom it is proper, but by our political and intellectual leaders, who assume the question rhetorical, its answer *none*. Unless, of course, those ripening disciplines called the humanities may be convincingly shown to keep us ahead of the Russians in some technological way, or help multiply gross national product. A punctuation error in a legislative bill on "no fault insurance" may yet justify continuing English Departments, as Shakespeare cannot.

It was difficult enough to distinguish pea vine and coffee weed without getting some distance, remember. We leaned back a little to look at leaves and blossom. And it is no doubt early for you to worry about fighting back rank jungle growth that closes upon the campus. But you ought to be aware of it. What I mean is that I hope you will resist the predominant assumption in American higher education that the primary justification for training the young mind (i.e., spending tax money on education) is that it assures a supply of better air conditioners or cheaper cantaloupe, or more intricately engineered social and political structures to impose upon that beast "society."

There is a distinction to be made between social and economic mechanics and community life. Hence the necessity of my answer to that indiscriminating rhetorical question, which intends to negate the human dimension whatever pretty words deny the intent. *Because man is what he is, it is better to know than not to know.* There are many lifetimes of thought in those words. One's particular life, even its "useful" dimension, flows best from this educational principle and bears with it all manner of healthful, helpful, and pleasing things, visible and invisible. Let the "uses" of knowledge wait then, at least the duration of your educational retreat. When you are a "rising junior" (which locally means when you pass sixth grade grammar), we will talk of uses.

Such then my answer to false leaders, not original with me. You will find it in Plato, find it ratified by any number of minds in that sweep of civilization we call history. Not "What use is history?" but "What *is* history?" That question first. Thoughtful, you will find history an active part of your continuing present. As one knowingly participates in it, he bears lively witness to the best of the past, as aid to the present and hope for the future. That is to say, one becomes a patron of civilization. Your mind informed by active discrimination, you become a substantial support of a community larger than that touched by the present date on your calendar or on my letter.

History is not simply an aggregate of the past, anymore than philosophy is a catalogue of ideas. To become educated through the humanities is to enjoy the company of faithful minds. And it is to bring to that company your own private times and places and things, into that timeless place, your mind, wherethrough you are sustained in the world and the world through you. Let me give example of what I mean. You will hear Shakespeare's Hotspur say in a heated moment, in *Henry IV*, "out of this nettle danger we pluck this flower safety." Now last week we weeded butterbeans by hand, you and I, and you learned first hand, you might say, what bull nettle is. Action and knowledge seemingly far removed from any attempt to overthrow a king. Still, you know the shock of encounter with the prickly, poisonous weed. How quickly you learned caution, digging down a bit to grasp a smooth root.

Remembering all this, you will know Hotspur alive in his bravado and compare him to his cautious, wily Uncle Worcester. You will value a difference between Hotspur's *pluck* and its distortion of the heroic and your first innocent grabbing of a Georgia weed. You will no doubt conclude that Hotspur's character leaves something to be desired, even as you learn that words reveal not only actions in nature, but the character of the mind that acts in nature.

You will begin to discover that all labors go together where there is a discriminating mind to govern them. Any practical use of such knowledge is implicit, the largesse of knowing. As for instance when you listen next year to political rhetoric your first voting year, or when you encounter patent medicine or deodorant ads on television.

I have much more to say, but naming "labor" reminds me that those potatoes down by the lake are now ready to dig, before Dog Day rain rots them. You are not here to help — and yet you are. Next letter I'll say something about a phrase out of St. Paul — "each in his nature." So then you will have: *it is better to know than not to know, each in his own nature.* Through which guide we become members one of another, parts of body, not of a machine.

I remind you once more to remember that, whether the word be German, English, algebraic, "To use the wrong word is to bear false witness." Distinguish. Discriminate. You recall the newspaper story we read, the murdered man called an "alleged victim" by a cautious reporter? Last night's paper bore a headline, "Zoning Loopholes Glare." Enough to put even surrealist poets out of business. One might smile at such, if "higher education" were less the source of such contamination of the instrument of education, language. Here, from an official publication of your state university, very seriously put: "It is true that, in general, air space is coming to a screeching halt in this country." You must remember that such home-grown and disseminated weed is the great enemy of the mind's garden, out of heads gone to seed. They're blown constantly into our minds and take root when we don't think.

Welcome, then, to the labor of weeding the mind. But be careful not to mistake pea vine for coffee weed and pull it. You know the difference between the coffee weed quoted above and the careful garden we talked about last week, eating our cantaloupe at dusk. We were dirty, hot, tired of fighting the army of encroaching weeds. Looking over the garden, trying words in tribute to the bounty we shared, even before full harvest — shared not only with each other, but with the soil and seed and, as always, the weeds. The beginning of Dog Days, between old and new seasons for you and me. Autumn in July, the end of your summer. (We test our calendars against the world, remember, as we tested our watches against the whippoorwill's first call all summer. It came, we learned, not at the same point on our dial, but always at the same balance of light and dark in the world around us.)

So we talked the garden's promise. The watermelon vines had grown so fast they'd dragged most of the little melons off, and the corn ears were threatening to run out the shuck ends. But the potatoes! They'd have to be toted out of the field one at a time, like watermelons. We knew what we were saying. If you must sometime speak of space coming to a screeching halt, know what you are saying in the light of Ptolemy, Newton, Einstein; of Dante, Shakespeare, Milton. Not just in the light of Walt Disney. Words defend themselves; a man's metaphors are a judgment upon him, whether he knows or cares or not. Don't put your foot in your mouth without good cause. And above all, remember that I and a host of those you know and do not as yet know send you and yours our love and encouragement. That is to say, our words respectfully offered.
Dad

Books by Marion Montgomery

Darrell (Doubleday, 1964)
Dry Lightning (University of Nebraska Press, 1960)
Eliot's Reflective Journey to the Garden (Whitston, 1979)
Eudora Welty and Walker Percy: The Concept of Home in Their Lives and Literature (McFarland, 2004)
Ezra Pound: A Critical Essay (Eerdmans, 1970)
Fugitive (Harper and Row, 1974)
The Gull and Other Georgia Scenes (University of Georgia Press, 1969)
Intellectual Philandering: Poets and Philosophers, Priests and Politicians (Rowman and Littlefield, 1998)
John Crowe Ransom and Allen Tate: At Odds about the Ends of History and the Mystery of Nature (McFarland, 2003)
Liberal Arts and Community: The Feeding of the Larger Body (Louisiana State University Press, 1990)
Making: The Proper Habit of Our Being (St. Augustine's Press, 2000)
The Men I Have Chosen for Fathers: Literary and Philosophical Passages (University of Missouri Press, 1990)
Possum, and Other Receipts for the Recovery of "Southern" Being (University of Georgia Press, 1987)
The Prophetic Poet and the Spirit of the Age (Sherwood Sugden). Vol. I: *Why Flannery O'Connor Stayed Home* (1981). Vol. II: *Why Poe Drank Liquor* (1983). Vol. III: *Why Hawthorne Was Melancholy* (1984)
The Reflective Journey Toward Order: Essays on Dante, Wordsworth, Eliot, and Others (University of Georgia Press, 1973)
Romancing Reality: Homo Viator and the Scandal Called Beauty (St. Augustine's Press, 2002)
Romantic Confusions of the Good: Beauty as Truth, Truth as Beauty (Rowman & Littlefield, 1997)
Stones from the Rubble (Argos Books, 1965)
The Trouble with You Innerleckchuls (Christendom College Press, 1988)
The Truth of Things: Liberal Arts and the Recovery of Reality (Spence, 1999)
T.S. Eliot: An Essay on the American Magus (University of Georgia Press, 1970)
Virtue and Modern Shadows of Turning (University Press of America and the Intercollegiate Studies Institute, 1990)
The Wandering of Desire (Harper & Brothers, 1962)
Ye Olde Bluebird (New College Press, 1967)

Index

Acton, Lord: "The Civil War in America" 104
Adams, Henry 187; *The Education of Henry Adams* 187–188, 194
Aeschylus 37, 47, 49, 50, 51, 56
Agar, Herbert 98
Agrarian correspondence: *Cleanth Brooks and Allen Tate: Collected Letters* 13, 195; *Cleanth Brooks and Robert Penn Warren: A Literary Correspondence* 13; *Exiles and Fugitives* 13; *The Literary Correspondence of Donald Davidson and Allen Tate* 13, 195; *The Lytle-Tate Letters* 13
Agrarians 1, 2, 3, 6, 11, 12, 13, 14, 79–113, 114–119, 129, 142, 164
Aiken, Conrad 33
Angelou, Maya 155
Arendt, Hannah 4, 70–71, 99; *The Human Condition* 99; *The Life of the Mind* 71
Ariosto 6
Aristotle 2, 60, 66, 100, 101, 106–108, 111, 133, 141, 144, 146, 150, 155, 160, 162, 165, 166, 186; *Poetics* 107, 166
Armstrong, George 7
Athenasius, St. 192
Augustine, St. 8, 15, 19, 23, 155, 174, 187–189, 194; *Confessions* 187, 194

Barr, Stringfellow 97
Beard, Charles 83, 98
Bennett, Arnold 134
Berns, Walter 4, 73
Berryman, John 122, 123, 125
Bloom, Allan: *The Closing of the American Mind* 140, 159, 170
Boethius: *Consolation of Philosophy* 6
Bradbury, John M. 79, 83, 97, 99
Bradford, M.E. 1, 3, 7, 9, 10, 11, 12, 15, 142–166; *Against the Barbarians and Other Reflections on Familiar Themes* 193; "Not in Memoriam, But in Affirmation" 143; *Remembering Who We Are: Observations of a Southern Conservative* 142, 193
Brookes, Iveson 7
Brooks, Cleanth 13, 14, 69, 120–125, 152, 153, 154, 193; *Toward Yoknapatawpha and Beyond* 120; *Understanding Fiction* 125; *Understanding Poetry* 121, 123–124, 152; *William Faulkner: First Encounters* 120–122; *The Yoknapatawpha Country* 120
Brown, Harrison 94; *The Challenge of Man's Future* 94, 101–102
Browning, Robert 107, 146–147, 166; "The Bishop Orders His Tomb" 107
Bryan, William Jennings 103
Byrd, William 5, 90

Caldwell, Erskine: *Tobacco Road* 33
Camoes 6
Campbell, Donald 76
Camus, Albert 173
Capote, Truman 47, 54, 55, 63
Carson, Rachel: *Silent Spring* 99
Cartesian 139, 140, 160, 169, 175, 176–177, 178, 189, 190
Cazamian, Louis 124
Cervantes 6
Chaucer 42, 63, 65, 133, 141, 165, 186
Chesnut, Mary 6
Chesterton, G.K. 65; *The Everlasting Man* 194
Cicero 98
Cobb, Joseph B. 6
Comte, Auguste 64
Conant, James E: *Education of American Teachers* 159
Confucius 44
Conrad, Joseph 97
Corleone, Don Vito 9
Coulter, E. Merton: *College Life in the Old South* 89

201

Cowan, Louise 13, 82, 96; *The Fugitive Group: A Literary History* 82, 96; *The Southern Critics* 13
Crane, Stephen: "The Open Boat" 47–49
Crawford, William H. 21

Dabney, Robert Lewis 6, 7, 10
Daniel, Frank 31
Dante 6, 37, 42, 66, 101, 109, 113, 133, 135, 136, 137, 139, 141, 156, 160, 165, 186, 189, 191, 198; *Divine Comedy* 6, 38, 136, 156, 187
Darrow, Clarence 103
Davidson, Donald 13–14, 33, 79, 82–88, 90, 93–99, 102, 105, 108, 112, 113, 140, 146, 153, 158, 160, 162, 186, 190, 193; *American Composition and Rhetoric* 158; *The Attack on Leviathan* 112, 190, 193; "Conversations in a Bedroom" 85; "Lee in the Mountains" 124; *The Long Street* 98, 113; "A Mirror for Artists" 112; "On a Replica of the Parthenon" 93, 153–154; "Sanctuary" 96; *Southern Writers in the Modern World* 93; *Still Rebels, Still Yankees* 193; *The Tall Men* 83–87, 88; "The Thankless Muse and Her Fugitive Poets" 93, 97, 108
Davis, Maggie 33
Defense of the Destruction of Life Without Value 169
de Jouvenel, Bertrand: *On Power: The Natural History of Its Growth* 194
Descartes 155, 176, 177, 178, 179
Dew, Thomas Roderick 6
Dewey, John 101
Disney, Walt 198
Donne, John 66, 172
Dostoevsky, Fyodor 191
Dreiser, Theodore 47, 48, 50, 54; *An American Tragedy* 47, 50
D'Souza, Dinesh: *Illiberal Education* 159

Edmonston, Catherine 6
Edwards, Jonathan 90
Eichmann, Adolph 4, 69–74, 119
Einstein, Albert 150, 198
Eliade, Mircea 66
Eliot, T.S. 12, 19, 20, 23, 44, 46, 60, 74, 82–87, 91, 93–95, 97, 102, 104, 107, 108, 112, 137, 140, 141, 145, 148, 156, 163, 167, 179, 191–193, 194; *After Strange Gods* 191, 192, 194; "Ash-Wednesday" 84, 192; *The Cocktail Party* 84; *For Lancelot Andrews* 84; *Four Quartets* 83, 85, 192; "Gerontion" 83; "Little Gidding" 83; "Love Song of J. Alfred Prufrock" 94, 107, 110, 111; *Murder in the Cathedral*

85, 168; "Portrait of a Lady" 107; *The Rock* 102; "Sweeney Among the Nightingales" 107, 109, 111; *The Waste Land* 74, 82–86, 93, 96
Elliott, William Y. 97
Euripides 48; *Medea* 100, 102
Evans, Jane 6

Faulkner, William 12, 15, 39, 47, 48, 53–55, 56, 57, 58–59, 62–63, 64, 65, 66–67, 70, 90, 118, 119, 120, 121, 141, 145, 163, 173, 186; *Absalom, Absalom!* 47, 50, 66–67; "The Bear" 53; "Delta Autumn" 67; *Go Down, Moses* 53, 67; *The Hamlet* 50, 121; "Spotted Horses" 59; "Was" 53
Federalist Papers 194
Fischer, David Hackett: *Albion's Seed: Four British Folkways in America* 189–190, 194
Fish, Stanley 152
Fitzgerald, F. Scott 63, 95
Flaubert, Gustave 63
Fletcher, John Gould 13
Ford, Henry 90
Frazer, Sir James: *The Golden Bough* 83
Freud, Sigmund 124
From Under the Rubble 68
Frost, Robert: "Birches" 155
The Fugitive 148
Fugitives 6, 11, 12, 13, 14, 15, 44, 79–113, 142, 148
Fugitives' Reunion 86, 89, 95, 97, 106, 113
Furman, Richard 6

Galileo 150
Gentile, Giovanni 3
Gilson, Etienne 122, 125; *Methodical Realism* 189, 194
Ginsberg, Allen 43
Girardeau, John 10
Goldsmith, Oliver 172
Gordon, Caroline 13; *How to Read a Novel* 122, 125
Gordon, John B. 52–53, 54
Grady, Henry 54, 90, 91, 100–101, 112
Graff, Gerald 63, 75, 153; *Literature Against Itself* 75
Grau, Shirley Ann 63
Graves, Robert 99
Green, Julian 122

The Habit of Being: Letters of Flannery O'Connor 193
Hammett, Dashiell 172
Hampton, Wade 52–53
Hardy, Thomas 32
Havard, William 115

Hawthorne, Nathaniel 63, 75, 90, 104, 139–140, 191
Hegel: *The Philosophy of Right* 4
Hemingway, Ernest 5, 48, 54, 63, 79, 82, 95, 96, 97
Heraclitus 74, 95
Hitler 70, 113
Hobbes, Thomas 98
Holcombe, William 6
Holmes, George Frederick 7
Homer 2, 15, 37, 43, 45, 47–50, 53, 66, 98, 111, 116, 132, 133, 141, 146, 160, 165, 186, 191; *Iliad* 37, 107; *Odyssey* 37, 107
Hopkins, Gerard Manley 34
Howe, George 6
Huxley, Aldous 97, 99; *Brave New World Revisited* 99

I'll Take My Stand 2, 66, 68, 97–98, 112, 113, 114, 116, 119, 129, 152, 154, 184, 191, 193

Jackson, Stonewall 190, 191
James, Henry 63, 93, 104, 140
James, William 101
Jefferson, Thomas 5, 90, 91
Job, book of 32
John the Baptist 51
Johnson, Lyndon B. 104
Johnson, Paul: *Modern Times: The World from the Twenties to the Eighties* 194
Jones, David 117–118; *Anathemata* 117
Jones, Jim 4, 69–74, 119
Jones, Leroi 99
Jones, Madison 63, 133–141
Jonson, Ben 38, 42
Joyce, James 37, 38, 39–40, 48, 54, 55, 58–59, 108, 140, 172, 188; *Dubliners* 40; *Finnegans Wake* 40; *Portrait of the Artist as a Young Man* 40, 188; *Ulysses* 40, 108

Kazin, Alfred 48
Kempis, Thomas: *Imitation of Christ* 6
Kennedy, John F.: "New England and the South: The Struggle for Industry" 91
Kerouac, Jack 92
Kierkegaard 174, 176, 177, 178
Kilmer, Joyce: "Trees" 155
Kirkland, James K. 93, 95, 99

Lanier, Lyle 98
Lanier, Sidney 33, 52, 90, 91
Lee, Robert E. 52, 190, 191
Legare, Hugh 6
Lenin 9
Lewis, C.S.: *The Abolition of Man* 194
Lewis, Howard R.: *With Every Breath You Take* 99

Lincoln, Abraham 7, 145, 149
Longstreet, Augustus Baldwin 33
Lowell, Robert 122, 123, 125
Lytle, Andrew 3, 11, 12, 14, 63, 98, 99, 129–132, 140, 142, 146, 193; "The Habitable Garden" 129, 131; *The Hero with the Private Parts* 130; *The Velvet Horn* 130; *A Wake for the Living* 130–131, 193

Macaulay, Lord 104
Machiavelli 65, 72
Manly, Basil 7
Manson, Charles 70, 72, 74, 119
Marcel, Gabriel 167, 173, 174, 189, 194; *Homo Viator* 189, 194; *Man Against Mass Society* 194
Maritain, Jacques 13, 122, 125, 189, 194; *Art and Scholasticism* 125, 122; *An Introduction to the Basic Problems of Moral Philosophy* 189, 194; *The Person and the Common Good* 194
Maritain, Raissa 13
Marx, Karl 4, 5, 9; *The Enlightenment of Brumaire of Louis Bonaparte* 4–5
McConnell, James 113
McCullers, Carson 5, 33, 47, 48, 54–55, 63; *Clock Without Hands* 33, 47, 48
McGill, Ralph 79, 83, 97–98, 99, 112; *The South and the Southerner* 97
McLuhan, Marshall 10
Mencken, H. L. 51–52, 103
Miles, James Warley 10
Milton, John 86, 115, 119, 186, 198; *Paradise Lost* 115
Mims, Edwin 93
Mitchell, Margaret 59; *Gone with the Wind* 92
Mitchem, Gary 13
Mother Teresa 169
Moynihan Report 98, 99, 104, 113
Mussolini 3

National Review 9
Nero 46
New Critics (and New Criticism) 12, 13, 14, 15, 120–125, 142, 146, 148, 150–161, 164, 165
New World Writing 51
Newton, Sir Isaac 198
Niemeyer, Gerhart 66, 76, 118; *Between Nothingness and Paradise* 194

O'Connor, Flannery 4, 12, 14, 15, 33, 39, 47–48, 50–51, 57, 60, 62–63, 64, 65, 72–75, 76, 90, 116, 120–125, 132, 137, 140, 141, 149, 167, 168, 169, 174, 186, 191; "Good Country People" 63, 75, 174; "A

Good Man Is Hard to Find" 54, 72, 73; *The Habit of Being* 4, 193; *A Memoir of Mary Ann* 169; *Mystery and Manners* 193; *The Presence of Grace and Other Book Reviews* 120, 122–125; *The Violent Bear It Away* 50, 51, 55, 62, 72, 123; "You Can't Be Any Poorer Than Dead" 51

Original Sin 4, 44, 57, 70, 73, 76, 188

Owsley, Frank Lawrence 98, 99, 112, 190, 193; *King Cotton Diplomacy* 190, 193; *Plain Folk of the Old South* 190, 193

Page, Thomas Nelson 52, 53, 96
Page, Walter Hines 96
Palmer, Benjamin Morgan 10
Pascal, Blaise 173, 176, 178
Passos, John Dos 5, 47, 48, 50, 54; *U.S.A.* 47, 50
Paul, St. 8, 19, 23, 44, 46, 114, 136, 197
Peck, T.E. 10
Percy, Walker 8, 10, 14, 31, 38–40, 141, 163, 167–179, 186, 188–189, 191; "The Fateful Rift: The San Andreas Fault in the Modern Mind" 168; *Lost in the Cosmos* 193; *The Moviegoer* 167, 172, 175–178, 189; "Questions They Never Asked Me So He Asked Them Himself" 179; *Thanatos Syndrome* 168, 176; "Why Are You a Catholic" 191
Percy, William Alexander 188; *Lanterns on the Levee* 187, 188, 193
Perloff, Marjorie 123
Petronius 46, 105; *Satyricon* 46
Pieper, Josef: *In Tune with the World: A Theory of Festivity* 194; *Leisure: The Basis of Culture* 194
Pierce, George Foster 7
Piety (also discriminating reverence) 2, 3, 16, 41, 43, 46, 123, 142, 143–144, 193
Pisistratus 42
Plato 103, 111, 140, 155, 160, 167, 177, 178, 197; *The Apology* 103; *Crito* 103; *Phaedo* 111
Plutarch 38, 42, 105
Poe, Edgar Allan 6, 52, 96, 109, 111; "Philosophy of Composition" 111
Poetry: A Magazine of Verse 87–88, 93
Pound, Ezra 12, 20, 38, 41–42, 44, 82, 93–94, 97, 112, 113, 116, 133–134, 147, 156; *Cantos* 94; *Hugh Selwyn Mauberley* 84, 94; *Impact: Essays on Ignorance and the Decline of American Civilization* 112; "Possibilities of Civilization: What the Small Town Can Do" 112
Preston, Margaret Junkin 6
Ptolemy 150, 198

Randolph, John 5, 10, 90, 91
Range, Willard: *Rise and Progress of Negro Colleges in Georgia* 89
Ransom, John Crowe 14, 79, 80, 82, 87–88, 92–94, 97–100, 102, 105–107, 111, 113, 120, 123, 142, 152, 160, 186; "Bells for John Whiteside's Daughter" 79, 105–111; "Captain Carpenter" 94; "The Concrete Universal" 98; "Conrad at Twilight" 106; "Dead Boy" 109; "Janet Waking" 107; "The Most Southern Poet" 113; "Necrological" 106; *The New Criticism* 152; "Old Mansion" 92; *Poems about God* 106; "The South Is a Bulwark" 98; "Statement of Principles" 97
Reagan, Ronald 7
Reece, Byron Herbert 32, 33
Reed, Herbert 86
Regionalism 2, 8, 19, 22–23, 37–40, 41–46, 75, 80, 82
Rerum Novarum 8
Rivers, R.H. 7
Robinson, E.A. 38, 42
Rommen, Heinrich A.: *The Natural Law* 194
Roosevelt, Franklin Delano 104

Sartre, Jean-Paul 173
Sayers, Dorothy 9, 133, 134, 135–136; "Why Work" 133, 134
Schall, Father James 170
Schoolcraft, Henry Rowe 6
Scopes Trial 102–104, 105
Shakespeare, William 37, 38, 42, 133, 141, 172, 186, 196, 197, 198; *Henry IV* 197
Simms, William Gilmore 7
Simpkins, Francis B.: *The Everlasting South* 112; *The South Old and New* 112
Smith, William 7
Snow, C.P.: *Two Cultures* 99
Socrates 103, 133, 135, 141
Solzhenitsyn, Alexander 9, 14, 38, 39, 57, 68, 114, 115, 118–119, 191; "The Smatterers" 68
Sophocles 42, 54, 107, 111, 133, 141; *Oedipus the King* 42, 111, 166
South, the 1, 2, 3, 5, 6–7, 8, 11, 31, 35, 48, 51–56, 58–59, 68, 72, 81–82, 86, 87–92, 97–98, 100, 105, 108, 112–113, 120, 134, 145–146, 172, 176, 184, 189–191, 192
South, the New 90–92, 93, 96, 99, 100–101, 102, 112
South, the Old 5, 6, 10, 11, 38, 49, 53, 88–90, 148
Southern Literary Renaissance 58, 64, 81, 139–140, 156, 191
Stalin 42, 70

Stein, Gertrude 95
Stephens, Alexander 21
Stewart, John 5, 79–113: *The Burden of Time* 79–113; *John Crowe Ransom* 106
Stow, Harriett Beecher: *Uncle Tom's Cabin* 49
Strauss, Leo: *Natural Right and History* 194
Stringfellow, Thornton 7
Suetonius 105

Tasso 6
Tate, Allen 2, 6, 7, 13, 14, 37, 38–39, 41–42, 66, 75, 79–80, 81, 82–83, 87–88, 90–91, 92, 93, 95–96, 98, 99, 101, 102, 105, 106–107, 108, 113, 120, 123, 133, 140, 142, 145, 146, 147, 148, 157, 160, 186, 193; "Aeneas at Washington" 145; "The Angelic Imagination" 148; "Horatian Epode to the Duchess of Malfi" 108; *The Man of Letters in the Modern World* 160; "The New Provincialism" 38, 42, 75, 80, 82, 123, 147; "Ode to the Confederate Dead" 124; "The Profession of Letters in the South" 90, 112
Tennyson, Alfred Lord 172
Thomas Aquinas 15, 62, 66, 74, 120, 124, 133, 136, 150, 155, 173, 174
Thornwell, James Henley 7, 10
Thucydides 44, 45, 100, 105: *Peloponnesian Wars* 44
Tillman, Ben 52
Time magazine 47, 48, 53, 54, 55, 70
Timrod, Henry 6, 52; *Ethnogenesis* 6
Tocqueville, Alexis de: *Democracy in America* 194
Tolstoy, Leo: *What Is Art?* 9
Twain, Mark 49, 90; *Adventures of Huckleberry Finn* 49, 50, 89; *Life on the Mississippi* 89

Virgil 6, 37–38, 89, 102, 113, 116, 133, 139, 141, 145, 186; *Aeneid* 37–38; *Georgics* 38
Vitz, Paul C. 76; "Psychology: Advocate of the New Narcissism" 76; *Psychology as Religion* 76; "Psychology: Enemy of the Family" 76

Vivas, Eliseo: *Things and Persons* 92
Voegelin, Eric 9, 38, 39, 66, 69, 73, 75–76, 118, 122, 125, 139, 152–153; *From Enlightenment to Revolution* 76, 194; *The New Science of Politics* 140; *Science, Politics, Gnosticism* 139, 140, 194

Waddel, Moses 5
Wade, John Donald 98, 112
Warren, Robert Penn 13, 14, 53, 69, 79, 80, 82, 87–88, 93, 96, 97, 98, 99, 102, 108, 109, 113, 119, 120, 121, 123, 142, 152, 160, 186; *Brother to Dragons* 53; *The Legacy of the Civil War* 53; *Promises* 113; "Pure and Impure Poetry" 96, 106, 107; "Tracts Against Communism" 97, 119; *Understanding Fiction* 125; *Understanding Poetry* 121, 152; *Who Speaks for the Negro* 113; *You Emperor and Others* 113
Weaver, Richard 1, 9, 10, 12, 14, 15, 38, 66, 69, 72, 96, 103, 187; "Agrarianism in Exile" 96; *The Ethics of Rhetoric* 103; *Ideas Have Consequences* 69 193; *The Southern Tradition at Bay* 69, 193
Welty, Eudora 14, 15, 31, 33, 54, 167
Wesley, John 90
Whitney, Eli 90
Who Owns America? A New Declaration of Independence 98
Wiener, Norbert: *Cybernetics* 99
William of Occam 10, 69
Williams, Tennessee 47, 54
Williams, William Carlos 82, 96
Wilson, Edmund 7
Winchell, Mark Royden 13; *Cleanth Brooks and the Rise of Modern Criticism* 193; *Where No Flag Flies: Donald Davidson and the Southern Resistance* 13
Winkler, Reverend E.T. 6
Wordsworth, William: "Intimations Ode" 107

Yeats, William Butler 43, 44, 59, 97, 151, 186; "The Second Coming" 43
Yerby, Frank 59
Young, Stark 66, 184, 184, 186, 187, 191

www.ingramcontent.com/pod-product-compliance
Lightning Source LLC
Chambersburg PA
CBHW032058300426
44116CB00007B/794